DATE DUE

NO 8 '96	NO 27 '99		
MY 23 97			
JY 7 97			
30 97			
UE 8 97			
MR 11 98			
NO 7 98			
OC 19 99			
NO 1 '99			
DE 18 99			
DE 2 00			
NO 13 01			
OC 25 02			
NO			
DE 21 02			

BLACK YOUTHS, DELINQUENCY, AND JUVENILE JUSTICE

Janice Joseph

Westport, Connecticut
London

Library of Congress Cataloging-in-Publication Data

Joseph, Janice.
    Black youths, delinquency, and juvenile justice / Janice Joseph.
        p.   cm.
    Includes bibliographical references (p.   ) and index.
    ISBN 0-275-94909-5 (alk. paper)
        1. Juvenile delinquents—United States.   2. Afro-American youth.
    3. Discrimination in criminal justice administration—United States.
    I. Title.
    HV9104.J67   1995
    364.3′6′08996073—dc20   95-7987

British Library Cataloguing in Publication Data is available.

Library of Congress Catalog Card Number: 95-7987
ISBN: 0-275-94909-5

First published in 1995

Praeger Publishers, 88 Post Road West, Westport, CT 06881
An imprint of Greenwood Publishing Group, Inc.

Printed in the United States of America

The paper used in this book complies with the
Permanent Paper Standard issued by the National
Information Standards Organization (Z39.48–1984).

10 9 8 7 6 5 4 3 2 1

Contents

Preface

A report issued by the National Coalition of State Juvenile Justice Advisory Groups in 1989 indicated that blacks are overrepresented at various stages of the juvenile justice system. The National Coalition suggests two possible explanations for the differential rates between blacks and whites in arrest, conviction, and incarceration: (1) a racist system, or (2) greater involvement by blacks in delinquency. In either case, it seems that the racist society is responsible. The coalition also suggests that there is an urgent need to change the social structure of society, and accordingly proposes improving the educational system, creating job opportunities, and providing more services to black families. Finally the coalition recommends that the Office of Juvenile Justice and Delinquency Prevention examine police procedures and apprehension methods to determine why minorities, especially blacks, are at a greater risk of being handled differently from whites and to reduce or eliminate any subtle discrimination against minority youths.

Federal Bureau of Investigation data show that, while blacks make up 12% of the population, black juveniles accounted for 27% of all juvenile arrests, 49% of all juvenile violent offenses, and 26% of all juvenile property crimes in 1992 (Maguire & Pastore, 1994). To many delinquency experts, this pattern merely reflects racism and discrimination in the juvenile justice system. One way to examine this issue is to compare the racial differences in self-reported data with those of official delinquency. The results from the self-reported studies have been inconsistent, though generally nonsupportive of official findings. The overall indication from these studies is that the delinquent behavior rates of black and whites are generally similar and that the differences in arrest statistics may indicate a differential selection policy by police. Some criminologists indicate that the differences in delinquent behavior are insignificant and that therefore, the official differences are the result of bias in the juvenile justice system (Elliot et al., 1983; Hindelang, Hirschi & Weis, 1981; Huizinga & Elliot, 1987; Williams & Gold, 1972).

Some data also that suggest that black youths have a greater chance of being tried in juvenile court and, if found guilty, are 9% more likely to be institutionalized or transferred to adult court (Bishop & Frazier, 1989).

Although many books have been written in the field of criminology, criminal justice, sociology, and victimology, none has comprehensively addressed the relationship between black youth, delinquency, and the juvenile justice system. Existing research on the subject consists mainly of journal articles and chapters in books. There are three reasons for this neglect: (1) the politically sensitive nature of the race issue in the United States; (2) the belief that racial differences in official statistics reflect not real differences, but rather the result of the juvenile justice system bias, and (3) the difficulties in measuring racial differences with self-reported studies. Regardless of the motivation, this particular area remains one of the most neglected areas of research. Hence this book seeks to bridge the gap in this particular area of research and to provide the framework for more comprehensive research into the matter of blacks and juvenile justice.

Black Youths, Delinquency, and Juvenile Justice explores key issues as they relate to black youths in the United States and reflects an increasing need for greater understanding of the black youth and juvenile justice. The book consists of eleven chapters. Chapter 1 introduces the concept of delinquency and the difficulties in defining and measuring delinquency. This chapter also a discusses the extent of delinquency by critically examining three sources of data, namely police statistics, victimization surveys, and self-reported studies. Finally, the correlates of delinquency are discussed: gender, age, race, social class, family, and school.

Any examination of this subject must consider the significance of historical and present-day treatment of blacks who violate law. Chapter 2, therefore, discusses the experiences of black youth in a negative environment, beginning with a brief history of blacks in United States from slavery to the civil rights movement. This chapter also addresses specific social indicators such as education, employment, poverty, politics, and life expectancy and how these indicators affect black youths. Finally the chapter focuses on explanations for the present status of blacks in the United States.

Chapter 3 examines the nature and extent of delinquency among black youths. This involves a critical analysis of existing data and a discussion of specific types of delinquency such as homicides, drugs, and gangs. Chapter 4 provides a brief overview of traditional theoretical approaches of delinquency followed by explanations that have been utilized to understand delinquency among black youths.

Chapter 5 focuses on the differential treatment of black youths by law enforcement officers. Special emphasis is placed on arrests, police harassment, and police violence. Chapter 6 addresses the issues of detention, intake, and adjudication, with special attention given to disparity in sentencing.

Chapter 7 discusses the treatment of black youths in adult courts, including transfer to adult court and incarceration in adult prison. The chapter also examines the death penalty and black youths.

Chapter 8 analyzes the institutionalization of black youths, while Chapter 9 critically evaluates community-based corrections as an alternative to institutionalization. Chapter 10 reviews prevention programs: predelinquency and postdelinquency prevention programs at the individual and the group levels, and their relevance and success in preventing delinquency among black youths. Finally, Chapter 11 explores present and future attempts to deal with delinquency among black youths.

Acknowledgments

I am indebted to Professors Jacqueline Pope, Alan Arcuri and David Lester of Richard Stockton College and Dr. Zelma Henriques of John Jay College of New York for their encouragement and inspiration. My appreciation also goes to the Research and Professional Development Committee at Richard Stockton College for its support. I am also very appreciative to Dr. David Carr, Dean of Behavioral Sciences, Richard Stockton College for his invaluable support. Thanks to Juvenile Division of the Atlantic County Prosecutor Office in New Jersey, Southern Residential Center, Females in Transition, and high schools in Atlantic City and Pleasantville. Gratitude is extended to my former student, Dania Daniels, who assisted me with the research. Finally, I am very grateful to my relatives for their love and support.

1

Definition, Nature, and Extent
of Delinquency

Juveniles who engage in illegal behaviors and come to the attention of the authorities are considered delinquents. In 1992, more than 1.7 million juveniles were arrested for behaviors ranging from murder to loitering (Federal Bureau of Investigation, 1993).

Juvenile delinquency is a complex problem, and any study of delinquency necessitates a scientific analysis of this problem. This chapter focuses on the definition, nature, and extent of delinquency in the United States. Before any meaningful analysis of juvenile delinquency can be attempted, however, it is necessary to understand how the concept evolved.

HISTORY OF JUVENILE JUSTICE

In colonial America, children who were convicted of crimes were treated as adults; there was no separate system of justice for juveniles. Youths who committed minor offenses, such as stealing, gambling, or vandalism, were placed in community asylums, whereas those involved in serious offenses were given the adult punishments of imprisonment, whipping, or death.

In 1823, the Society for the Prevention of Pauperism of New York City called for the development of "houses of refuge" to save children from crime and poverty. The first House of Refuge established in 1825 was the first attempt to provide a separate "correctional" facility for juveniles. It was intended to house young thieves, vagrants, runaways, and neglected children. When the House of Refuge was criticized for its initial harsh approach, it was forced to become more lenient. The concept quickly expanded, and in 1826 the Boston City Council formed the House of Reformation for juvenile offenders. Houses of Refuge became popular in New York, and they quickly spread to other states.

Around the middle of the 1800s, the child savers movement, consisting of prominent Americans, began to fight for the establishment of a separate juvenile justice system that would try to rehabilitate young offenders rather than punish them. The movement focused on the issues of child labor, treatment of orphans, imprisonment of young offenders in adult jails, workhouses, and penitentiaries. The supporters of this movement believed that young offenders could escape a life of crime if they were guided and protected. In Massachusetts the recognition of the needs of juveniles in 1870 led to legislation requiring separate hearings for juveniles. New York followed with a similar law in 1877. Rhode Island enacted juvenile court legislation in 1898, and in 1899 the Colorado School Law was the first comprehensive legislation designed to adjudicate problem children. However, it was the 1899 Illinois juvenile law which created the first comprehensive juvenile court.

The first juvenile court was an independent court designed primarily to deal with predelinquent and delinquent youths between the ages of 7 and 14 years. The establishment of this court was based on the English common law known as parens patriae. This concept, when applied to juveniles, gave the court the right to become the legal guardian of all juveniles in its jurisdiction and to limit or terminate the rights of the parents. This doctrine viewed juvenile law violators as not legally culpable, and instead, in need of protection and guidance from the juvenile court. Consequently, to this day, juveniles who violate the penal code are placed under the jurisdiction of the juvenile court.

DEFINITION

A major problem associated with any study of delinquency is defining the phenomenon. Only a clear definition and accurate measurements can promote understanding of delinquency.

Two definitions of delinquency have become current. The first, the legal definition, holds the view that delinquents are youths who have been labeled as such by the juvenile justice system. The second, the nonlegal or behavioral definition, views delinquents as youths who violate the penal code whether or not they are officially labeled as such.

Legal Definition

Legally, a delinquent is a juvenile under the age of 18 who violates a criminal law or commits a status offense. A status offense is an act that is declared to be an offense only when it is committed by a juvenile, for example, running away, using alcohol, and immoral conduct. The legislation that defines and creates the status of being a delinquent is a state law. This definition refers to numerous types of behaviors and includes the violation of a law by young people under a certain age. A number of problems are connected with this definition.

One difficulty is that the various states arbitrarily determine by the upper legal age for juveniles. All juvenile codes observe two chronological age references: the maximum and the minimum of jurisdiction. The minimum age of jurisdiction refers to the earliest age at which a juvenile is held responsible for his or her actions. Under English common law, children under the age of 7 were thought to be incapable of forming criminal intent. Some of the states' juvenile statutes have, therefore, incorporated this lower age of 7, while other states do not specify a lower age limit for the delinquent jurisdiction. Most states, however, define an upper age limit as juvenile as age 16 or 18. The question that arises is: Why is a child under the age of 18 in New Jersey or Ohio incapable of making mature decisions when violating the law, but a child at that same age in New York (where a juvenile is a child under the age of 16) can make such mature decisions and is legally culpable for his or her actions? Since there are no apparent guidelines for determining the upper or limit ages of delinquency, the states are free to choose any age.

Another difficulty with this legal definition is the broad range of behaviors it encompasses. Some states include noncriminal acts such as disobedience, incorrigibility, disrespect for authority and dishonesty as forms of delinquency. Many states, however, have created a special category called status offenses for noncriminal behavior, and status offenders are processed differently from juveniles. In addition, some states label as juvenile delinquents, adolescents who are neglected, abused, or victims of family situations and in need of protection from the court as delinquents.

The legal definition of delinquency focuses on the legally prohibited and prescribed acts for juveniles, branding as delinquent any juvenile who has been processed through the juvenile justice system. This definition is limited in the sense that it cannot account for behavior that violates the law but is never brought to the attention of the juvenile justice system. The nonlegal or behavioral definition deals with this kind of behavior.

Nonlegal or Behavioral Definition

The behavioral or nonlegal definition focuses on juveniles whose behavior violates the law whether or not they are officially labeled delinquents. This behavioral definition is much broader than the legal definition, and the estimates of delinquency based on this term are much higher than those based on the legal term. This nonlegal term, therefore, can provide a more accurate picture of the extent of delinquency than the legal term. It emphasizes that a "hidden" delinquency exists which may never come to the attention of the juvenile justice system.

Whichever of the two definitions one uses depends on the purpose of the research. On one hand, when police, courts, and correctional procedures are the focus of attention, the legal definition is pertinent, for the legal definition answers the question: Who is eligible for the official label? On the other hand, when the emphasis is on the development of misbehavior in terms of deviation from accepted norms, the behavioral definition is more appropriate, The non-legal definition tries to explore the question; What causes a person to become delinquent? The behavioral definition is preferable because, by viewing delinquency from a broad perspective, realistic programs to control and prevent delinquency can be implemented.

EXTENT OF DELINQUENCY

How much delinquency is there? Who are the delinquents? What are the patterns and trends in delinquency? To answer these questions, we have to examine the three sources of information on delinquency: official statistics, self-report studies, and victimization surveys.

Official statistics are collected by law enforcement officials, the courts, and corrections. The most commonly used official statistics on delinquency are those collected annually by the Federal Bureau of Investigation in the form of the Uniform Crime Reports. The major unit of analysis is Index crimes, known as Part I, consisting of homicide, nonnegligent manslaughter, aggravated assault, burglary, larceny, arson, and motor vehicle theft. Part I also contains information regarding age, gender, race and, region and the offenses are used to calculate the crime rate. Part II includes all other types of crimes, and only arrest data are reported.

The data presented in the Uniform Crime Reports are presented in three ways. First, data are collected on "crimes known to the police." The FBI believes that the number of crimes known to the police is the best indicator of criminal behavior, and this is represented by the eight Part I or Crime Index Offenses. Second, the Uniform Crime Reports present information not only on crimes cleared by arrest, but also on those cases cleared by exceptional means, as when a known offender commits suicide. Third, the Uniform Crime Reports present information on the number of persons arrested for both Part 1 and Part II offenses. Information about the number of crimes known to the police and the percentage cleared by arrests are not provided for Part II offenses. Arrest statistics are the only data that are reported on for Part II offenses. The arrest figures consist of (1) the number of crimes reported and arrests made; (2) the percentage changes of crimes within a specific period of time; and 3) the number of crimes per 100,000 people.

In 1992, youths under the age of 18 made up 17% of all arrests in the United States. In addition, 17% of those arrested in 1992 for violent crimes and 33% of those arrested for property offenses were under the age of 18. Youths under the age of 18 accounted for 29% of all Index Crimes in 1992. Between 1983 and 1992, juvenile violent crimes increased 57%, and the increase for property offense was 11% (Federal Bureau of Investigation, 1993). The violent trend among juveniles reached its highest peak in 1990. Three of every four states experienced significant increases in juvenile arrests for violent offenses between 1980 and 1990, indicating that juvenile violence is a general problem and should be a national concern for everyone (Federal Bureau of Investigation, 1991).

CRITICISMS OF OFFICIAL STATISTICS

Despite their importance, official police data have several limitations as accurate indicators of the level and trend of delinquency in the United States.

Police statistics suffer from definitional idiosyncrasies. First, attempted offenses are included in the same category as completed offenses, with attempted murder as the only exception. Second, the counting procedure varies with the type of offense. For example, for offenses against person, some states count only one offense for each victim, while for offenses against property, one offense is counted for every operation, regardless of how many persons were victims. Third, a delinquent act in which several delinquents were involved is considered a single incident. Fourth, in the case of multiple offenses committed by a person in one incident, only the most serious offense is recorded in the police statistics. Finally, police statistics report the number of arrests rather than the number of different persons arrested, and one person can be arrested several times on several charges. Consequently, a person simultaneously charged with more than one offense is recorded only once. This particular procedure of scoring makes it difficult to equate delinquent acts with delinquents, since one delinquent may be responsible for several acts. Because of the above procedures followed when compiling police statistics, a great deal of information is inaccurate, thereby making police statistics inaccurate.

The police statistics also suffer from problems of representativeness. Arrest patterns are influenced by discretion, type of jurisdiction, and other law enforcement practices. A significant number of juveniles are screened out at the point of entry into the juvenile justice system and so are never included in the official statistics. Moreover, a large, unknown quantity of delinquent acts are never brought to the attention of the police and are, therefore, not recorded in the official statistics. One study estimates that only 2 to 3% of crimes are detected by police (Harlow, 1985). The police statistics provide data on law enforcement activities rather than criminal activity in general.

Crime and delinquency data manipulation is another major problem with police statistics. The statistics can be presented to convey the impression that crime and delinquency are under control or that crime and delinquency are increasing in an effort to prevent cutbacks or initiate spending. Data manipulation can occur through a technique called "clearing the books" (Selke & Pepinsky, 1982).

Despite the shortcomings of the official statistics, one cannot and should not discount the official statistics because they are still the best source of information on crime and delinquency. However, caution is necessary when using such information.

VICTIMIZATION SURVEYS

While official statistics focus on the perpetrator of delinquency, victimization studies focus on the victims. The National Crime Victimization Survey conducts yearly surveys of victims of crime and delinquency. These surveys which began in 1973, collect detailed information on the frequency and nature of rape, personal robbery, aggravated and simple assaults, household burglary, and personal and household theft.

The National Crime Victimization Survey retains the households in the sample for three years and conducts interviews at six-month intervals. Even if the family moves, the household remains in the survey. The Survey includes approximately 60,000 households, and about 50,000 complete the survey. Each household is surveyed a total of seven times: upon entering the study and then at six-month intervals over the next three years. The crimes surveyed by the National Crime Victimization Survey were developed to parallel those of the Uniform Crime Reports. Crime victimization is assessed through a two-step process: through a series of screening questions and then a series of questions about each incident. Finally, the Survey reports two kinds of data: personal victimization and household victimization.

The Survey includes both reported and unreported crimes, but excludes homicides, arson, commercial crimes, and crimes against children under 12 years of age, all of which are included in the Uniform Crime Reports. In addition, the National Crime Victimization Survey rates are calculated per household.

The Survey gives information about the characteristics of the criminal events, such as the time of day, relationship between victim and assailant, weapons used, economic loss, and physical injuries for crimes of violence.

The National Crime Victimization Survey data for 1992 indicated that males, younger persons, blacks, Hispanics and the poor residents of cities had higher rates of victimization than whites living in suburban areas. Moreover, Survey data showed that young males were two and half times as likely as females to be victimized. This is particularly true of young black males. The National Crime Victimization Survey data also revealed a pattern of victimization, indicating homogeneity in the backgrounds of the victims and offenders, especially of juveniles. In general, youths victimize youths, blacks victimize blacks, whites victimize whites, and males victimize males (U.S. Department of Justice, 1993a). Persons from households with low income experienced higher violent criminal victimization than wealthy households. Black households had the highest victimization, especially of serious crimes. Urban households were more likely than rural households to be victimized (U.S. Department of Justice, 1993b).

Victimization surveys pose several problems. There is the problem of memory lapses whereby the respondents forget personal and familial victimization. Respondents also exaggerate or underreport their victimization (Levine, 1976). Some telescope the events by reporting that the victimization took place within the time period being studied. Moreover, people may report that they were victimized when in fact they were not.

Bias also results from deception on the part of respondents who want to appear helpful; they may report incidents they would otherwise not have considered important. Coding and mechanical errors from humans or machines can also affect the results.

Yet other problems are associated with the National Crime Victimization Survey. For each type of crime examined, the household is counted once, regardless of how many times the victimization took place. For example, if a household was burglarized twice and one of its members was robbed, it is counted once, even though it was burglarized twice. This type of counting procedure somewhat distorts the volume of victimization.

SELF-REPORT STUDIES

An alternative to official statistics and victimization studies is self-report studies. These studies make it possible to identify not only those who were legally processed as delinquents, but also those who have been able to evade the juvenile justice system. These studies, therefore, provide a broader and more comprehensive picture of the distribution of delinquency. These studies are designed to obtain knowledge about delinquency from the "delinquents" themselves. Information is obtained by means of questionnaires or interviews with juveniles that request them to report on the types and frequency of offenses they have engaged in during a specific time period. In addition, information about the youth's background characteristics are collected as well.

Self-report studies ask respondents to indicate not only if they have engaged in delinquent behavior, but also how frequently they committed each type of offense listed on the self-report scale. Asking these two questions is critical because they provide information on the prevalence and incidence of illegal acts. Prevalence refers to the number of persons who committed the act once, and incidence refers to the number of times the incident occurred. In addition, the respondents are requested to report their illegal activities for a specific period of time.

Self-report studies present several problems. Juveniles interviewed by means of these studies tend to underreport or overreport their delinquent activities (Hindelang et al., 1981; Huizinga & Elliot, 1987; Lab & Allen, 1984). Juveniles may also lie about their activities. In general, self-report studies tend to measure nonserious delinquent acts while ignoring serious violent acts (Hindelang, 1981; Tracy, 1987).

Data from self-report studies indicate that a substantial amount of delinquency goes unreported (Bachman et al., 1988; Elliot et al., 1985; Erickson & Empey, 1963; Gold, 1966).

SOCIAL CORRELATES OF DELINQUENCY

To understand the meaning of delinquency requires knowledge not only of the definition and extent of delinquent behavior, but also the social context in which delinquency occurs. Research has shown that delinquency occurs within various social contexts, namely, age, gender, race, social class, family, school and peers.

Age and Delinquency

In 1992, 6% of those arrested for crimes were under the age of 15 and 16% were under 18. Of those arrested under the age of 18 that year, 35% were under the age of 15 and 65% were between 16 and 18. Furthermore, 30% of all juveniles arrested for violent crimes were under the age of 15, while 70% of those arrested for similar offenses were between 16 and 18. Forty-three percent of all juvenile arrests were arrests of youths under the age of 15, and 57% arrests were of juveniles between 16 and 18 (Federal Bureau of Investigation, 1993).

Based on the official data, the older juveniles were arrested more often than the younger juveniles in 1992 (Federal Bureau of Investigation, 1993). Participation in delinquency declines with age, since juveniles become less involved in delinquency as they mature. This is referred to as the aging-out, desistance, or spontaneous remission phenomenon (Siegel & Senna, 1993). Some criminologists argue that age is not a very important determinant of delinquency (Gottfredson & Hirschi, 1983), while others maintain that age is a very important factor in delinquency (Farrington, 1986; Greenberg, 1985).

There are several explanations for the aging-out or desistance phenomenon. One argument is that delinquency is fun for juveniles, and as they mature, it is no longer hedonistic (Trasler, 1987). Another argument is that many delinquents eventually develop long-term goals and resist the need for immediate gratification (Mulrey & LaRosa, 1986). A third suggestion is that the aging-out process is the natural course of the life cycle (Wilson & Herrnstein, 1985).

Gender and Delinquency

All three sources of data on delinquency generally agree that males are more delinquent than females. The Uniform Crime Reports typically show that the male/female ratio for violent crimes is 8 to 1 and for property crimes, it is 4 to 1 in favor of males. The overall arrest ratio is usually about four males to one female. Studies have found that gender differences for serious offenses are similar to those reported by the Uniform Crime Reports (Hindelang et al., 1981; Sarri, 1983; William & Gold, 1972).

Statistics for 1992 indicate that 77% of the juveniles arrested were males and 23% females (Federal Bureau of Investigation, 1991). The data showed that male arrests exceeded that of female arrests in all offenses except running away. The statistics also showed that 483,205 male juveniles compared with 131,852 female juveniles were arrested for Index crimes in 1992: a ratio of 4 to 1 in favor of males (Federal Bureau of Investigation, 1992). The arrest data for 1991 versus 1992 indicate that female delinquent behavior increased by 5% while the male increase was 2%. From 1988 to 1992, juvenile male arrests increased 10% and female arrests increased 17% (Federal Bureau of Investigation, 1993).

The data in Table 1.1 indicate that the male and female ratios between 1960 and 1992 decreased for all offenses except murder. The largest decreases were for burglary, motor vehicle theft, and robbery.

Self-report studies have also indicated that male delinquency exceeds that of females delinquency (Chesney-Lind & Shelden, 1992; Hindelang et al., 1981; Sarri, 1983). However, a few of these studies show that female delinquency is much higher than is projected in the official statistics. The reasons are that most female delinquency is hidden, and the police are less likely to arrest a female than a male (Hindelang, 1973; Jensen & Eve, 1976; Short & Nye, 1958; White & LaGrange, 1987).

Since the 1960s, the number of offenses committed by female delinquents has increased at a much higher rate than that of males. Some self-report studies indicate that the sex ratio is lower than the official statistics indicate, with a ratio of 2 to 1 (Canter, 1982; Cernkovich, 1979; White & LaGrange, 1987). The differences in the Uniform Crime Reports and self-report studies occur because self-report studies measure relatively minor offenses and the Uniform Crime Report measure serious offenses (Hindelang et al., 1981).

Explaining Gender Differences

Why are women less involved in delinquency? The early criminologists answered this question by suggesting that female delinquency was related to biological characteristics. For example, Lombroso (1911) argued that women were lower on the evolutionary scale, but they were restrained from committing delinquent acts because they were biologically less aggressive than men. Pollack (1950) suggested that females were inherently more deceitful than males and that much of their delinquency went undetected because they three distinct stages, which were influenced by the biological changes of menstruation, pregnancy, and menopause.

Other criminologists believe that the gender gap can be explained by gender-role socialization (Weisheit & Mahan, 1988; Wilson & Herrnstein, 1985). Mothers tend to supervise their daughters more closely than their sons. Research also suggests that boys are socialized to acquire certain attitudes such

Table 1.1
Male and Female Ratios for Persons under 18 Years, 1960 to 1992, Selected Years

	1960	1970	1980	1992
Murder	13.5:1	13.1:1	11.3:1	16.1:1
Robbery	19.9:1	12.6:1	12.6:1	10.1:1
Aggravated Assault	8.5:1	5.7:1	5.6:1	5.1:1
Burglary	31.7:1	12.0:1	13.6:1	9.8:1
Larceny	5.7:1	2.7:1	2.6:1	2.4:1
Motor Vehicle Theft	24.6:1	17.5:1	8.3:1	6.8:1

Source: Federal Bureau of Investigation, 1960, 1970, 1980, and 1993. *Uniform Crime Reports*, (Washington, D.C.: Government Printing Office).

as aggressiveness and impulsiveness, which predispose them to delinquent behavior (Hagan et al., 1985; Horwitz & White, 1987; Loy & Norland, 1981).

Structural barriers also limit the involvement of females in delinquent behavior; female involvement in gangs, for example, is limited. Giordano and associates (1986) argued that peer groups seem to amplify delinquency in boys but tend to inhibit such behavior in girls.

Race and Delinquency

Official data consistently find that blacks are more delinquent than whites. Black youths are overrepresented in the arrest statistics. While blacks make up 12% of the general population, they constituted 27% of all juvenile arrests, and whites 70% in 1992. Black youths accounted for 49% of all juvenile arrests for violent crimes and 26% of all property crimes in 1992. Overall, blacks constituted 29% of all juveniles arrested for Index crimes in 1992 (Federal Bureau of Investigation, 1993).

Arrest rates for 1991 showed that 1.2% of juveniles arrested for violent crimes and 1.7% arrested for property crimes were Asians or Pacific Islanders. The rates for American Indians or Alaskan natives were 0.6% of all juvenile arrests for violent crimes and 1.1% of all arrests for property offenses (Federal Bureau of Investigation, 1993).

Self-report studies are an alternative to official data; most of these studies focus on the racial differences between black and white youths. Many of these studies find smaller differences between black and white youths with regard to delinquency. For the most part, self-reported studies fail to show higher rates of delinquency for blacks when compared with whites. Several studies (Elliott & Voss, 1974; Gold, 1970) found no difference in delinquency between black and white youths. Hirschi (1969) found slight differences by race, with the rates for blacks higher than those of whites. In addition, some researchers found that blacks tend to commit more serious offenses (Elliot et al., 1980; Hindelang et al., 1981; Huizinga & Elliott, 1987; William & Gold, 1972).

As noted earlier, there are two major explanations for the racial disparity in delinquency between blacks and whites. One school of thought is that the overrepresentation of black youths in the juvenile justice system results from discrimination and bias from the system itself. The other school of thought is that black youths really do commit a higher proportion of delinquent acts than white youths. These issues are discussed in more detail in the following chapters.

Very few studies have examined the delinquency of racial groups other than blacks. One survey in Seattle reported that 36% of Japanese youths compared with 52% of whites and 53% of blacks admitted to some delinquent activity (Chambliss & Nagasawa, 1969). Gould (1969) also reported lower rates for Asian Americans than for black or white youths. Jensen and associates (1977) found that American Indian youths attending public high school had higher rates than white or black youths.

Social Class and Delinquency

Official statistics indicate that delinquency rates are generally higher in inner-city, high-crime, and poverty-stricken areas than in suburban and wealthier areas. The Uniform Crime Reports and the National Crime Victimization Survey provide information on gender and age but no information on socioeconomic status. Sociologists and criminologists disagree as to what constitutes socioeconomic status.

In the 1950s and 1960s, a number of sociologists who used official data in their research postulated that socioeconomic status was a major factor contributing to delinquency (Cloward & Ohlin 1960; Cohen, 1955; Merton, 1938; Miller, 1958). However, later research suggested that socioeconomic status was a determining factor in whether a juvenile becomes part of the official statistics rather than in whether a particular juvenile will become delinquent (Jensen & Rojek, 1992). Police may devote more resources and time to lower socioeconomic areas, such as the inner city, and consequently, the apprehension and arrest rates may be higher in these areas. This relationship may also be explained by police discrimination whereby police may be more likely to arrest and apprehend lower-class juveniles more often than those from the middle and upper classes.

Several self-report studies have provided support for the postulated inverse relationship between socioeconomic status and delinquent behavior (Boggs, 1965; Hamparian et al., 1978; Singh et al., 1980; Wolfgang et al., 1972). On the other hand, a number of self-report studies have failed to find any relationship between socioeconomic status and criminal behavior (Kelly & Pink, 1973; Nye, et al. 1958; Weis, 1973; William & Gold, 1972).

Explaining Class Differences

Class-delinquency relationship remains one of the most controversial issue in criminology. There are several reasons for this. First some of the strongest evidence for a relationship comes from ecological studies in which samples come from poor neighborhoods. Such samples amplify the relationship between social class because persons from a low socioeconomic status are generally more vulnerable to arrest, prosecution and conviction than those from a upper socioeconomic status because of selective law enforcement. Second, several self-report studies found that delinquency was found in all classes with the same frequencies (Hindelang et al., 1981; Hirschi, 1969; Tittle, 1983). Third, social class has been measured differently by various researchers. Social class is often based on the juveniles' background such as parental income, education and occupation, even though the juvenile may have a job which may be different from the parents. Other measures of social class include prestige, unemployment, welfare status, and place of residence.

Family and Delinquency

Many researchers contend that delinquency is related to family situations. The broken home in particular is said to be a strong determinant of delinquency. For example, Chilton and Markle (1972), using official data, found that children living in a home other than one with two parents were disproportionately represented in juvenile court statistics. Many self-report studies, however, have found that the differences in delinquency between children from intact and broken homes were small (Gove & Crutchfield, 1982; Rosen & Neilson, 1982). The broken home factor may be related only to official delinquency, because youths from broken homes may get arrested, charged, and convicted more often than youths from two-parent families (Rankin, 1979). So the findings on broken homes and delinquency are inconclusive.

Research has consistently shown that family relationships, either the child-parent or the parental relationship can affect delinquency. Some researchers have found that children who feel unloved, unwanted or rejected by their parents are more likely to be delinquent than those who feel warmth and love (Hirschi, 1969; Loeber & Stouthamer-Loeber, 1986; Pulkkinen, 1982). Other researchers have found that family conflict and hostility between child and parents affect delinquency (Hanson, 1984; Jaffe et al., 1986; Nye, 1958, 1957; Rosenbaum, 1989). Some research focuses on the effect of parental relationships on delinquency. Nye (1958) found a strong association between reported marital happiness of parents and delinquent behavior, and his findings have been supported by other researchers. Most have found that children from families where there is marital discord and conflict exhibit more delinquent behavior than those from happy families (Rosenbaum, 1989; Stouthamer-Loeber & Loeber, 1986).

Parental methods of discipline, control, and punishment can also have an impact on delinquency. Studies using official and self-report data show that extreme or lenient discipline has been associated with delinquency (Nye, 1958; Patterson, 1982). There is also evidence that families that use inconsistent or erratic forms of discipline experience delinquency as well (Agnew, 1983; Laub & Sampson, 1988; McCord, McCord & Zola, 1959).

A number of studies have found that children from deviant or criminal families are the most likely to engage in delinquency (Laub & Sampson, 1988; West, 1982; West & Farrington, 1977). One type of criminality that greatly affects delinquency is child abuse. Some researchers believe that abused children have a greater probability of growing up to be delinquents than children who were not abused (Brown, 1984; Conger, 1980; Gelles & Cornell, 1985; Lynch, 1978; Schmitt & Kempe, 1975).

School and Delinquency

Numerous research studies have confirmed that schools and delinquency are related. For example, Elliot and Voss (1974) found that school-related variables are more important contributors to delinquent behavior than are the effects of either family and friends. In addition, the school itself has been the scene of a significant amount of violence. For example, the National Crime Victimization Surveys indicate that about 2 million students (age 12 to 19) are victimized in school every year. In 1993, 25% of students reported having their property deliberately damaged in school; 5% were injured with a weapon; 13% were injured without a weapon; and 16% were threatened with a weapon. Moreover, victimization surveys showed that, in 1993, 16% of students reported getting into serious fights in school; 15% damaged school property on purpose; and 4% hit an instructor or supervisor (Maguire & Pastore, 1994). In addition, most researchers agree that the educational system contributes to the high delinquency rate in this society.

Studies indicate that delinquency correlates with school failure in some American research as highly as .70 (Empey & Lubeck, 1971; Polk & Schafer, 1972). Although these studies do agree that school failure is related to delinquency, there is conflict as to the direction of this relationship. One view is that there is a common cause for both failure in school and delinquency. Hirschi and Hindelang (1977), for example, found a significant relationship between IQ scores and delinquency; this relationship accounted for more variance than social class.   School performance in school may be related to delinquency. Youths who are doing poorly may become frustrated and angry, have few future goals, and may consider themselves "failures" within the system. One result of academic failure is the loss of self-esteem (Empey & Lubeck, 1971; Quicker, 1974) and delinquency (Gold, 1978; Hirschi, 1969). Social researchers maintain that the school is actually responsible for the high failure of students, especially members of the lower socioeconomic status. This in turn leads to delinquency (Gold, 1978; Greenberg, 1985; Toby, 1983). The relationship between academic performance and delinquency is very significant with regard to chronic delinquents (Shannon, 1982; West & Farrington, 1977; Wolfgang, Figlio & Sellin, 1972).

Many researchers have examined tracking or streaming and delinquency. Tracking is the practice of assigning students to groups based on the school's assessment of the child's ability and potential for the future. The major breakdowns are generally college and noncollege tracks. One outcome of nonacademic and noncollege tracking is that the students are often stigmatized as being academically inferior to the rest of the students. Such labels could result in delinquent behavior. Researchers have found that lower track students experience greater failure and do not participate much in extracurricular activities, have an increased tendency to drop out of school, engage in frequent misbehavior and commit a greater number of more delinquent acts than higher track students (Kelly & Pink, 1973; Polk & Schafer, 1972; Schafer & Schafer, 1972).

Delinquent behavior has been linked to the irrelevance of the curriculum to the students' needs (Polk & Schafer, 1972; West, 1981). Rebellion has been linked to the students' perception that the curriculum is irrelevant to future job prospects, especially for students who have no intention of attending college. These youths are likely to engage in delinquent behavior (Hirschi, 1969). This issue of relevancy is particularly important to minority and lower class youths. American schools are middle-class institutions. Methods of instructions as well as content of the curriculum reflect middle class values, mores, and customs, which have very little meaning or relevance to the lower class or minority student (Polk & Schafer, 1972). This can lead to frustration, which in turn can lead to delinquency.

Negative experiences in school can create alienation. When students experience alienation in school, school then becomes a place where the child may feel unwelcome. Disruptive behavior in class, vandalism, and violence are often indicators of alienation. There is evidence to suggest that alienated youths form delinquent subcultures in school (Polk & Schafer, 1972).

Peers and Delinquency

The pioneer study on gangs in the United States was done by Frederick Thrasher in 1927. According to Thrasher, gangs are formed to fulfill the need for adventure, which sometimes leads to delinquency (Thrasher, 1927). Delinquent gangs have existed since the 1950s, but by the end of the 1960s, gangs seemed to have disappeared, possibly, because the juvenile justice system was effective in controlling them. After 1970, however, gangs reappeared and continued to grow, some becoming national organizations. In 1990, a survey identified sixty-six gangs in New York, eighty in Dade County, Florida, and thirty-five in San Diego (Spergel, 1990). Gangs in Los Angeles County have an estimated 70,000 members. Los Angeles is considered the gang capital of the nation, with the Bloods and the Crips having an estimated total membership of 35,000 members. (Ruester, 1989). Many of these gangs have long lives and highly structured organizations, claim geographical areas, and engage in a range of illegal activities.

The age of the gang member ranges from as low as 8 to as high as 55, but the average age has been estimated to be between 17 and 18 years (National School Safety Center, 1990). Many juveniles join gangs in order to gain status and prestige and to be part of a family.

Most gangs are racially exclusive, and the racial composition of these gangs corresponds with particular geographical areas. For example, in the cities that have large black populations, black gangs dominate, but on the West Coast, Asians gangs are more evident. In New York and certain parts of California,

Hispanic gangs outnumber other gangs, while white gangs are found elsewhere, such as New York and Philadelphia.

Delinquent gangs seem to be motivated by violence, extortion, intimidation, and illegal trafficking in drugs and weapons. Members of these gangs commit a disproportionate number of illegal acts as compared to their nondelinquent counterparts (Burt, 1987). The fight to control the drug trade has led to the escalation of violence against rival gangs, but recently their "drive-by" shootings have led to the deaths of innocent individuals. In such cities as New York, Chicago, Los Angeles, Miami, and Washington, D.C., gang-related homicides number several hundreds annually. Gang violence is exhibited not only on the streets but also in the schools, where students are routinely shot to death. About half of teenage violent crimes occur in school buildings, on school property, or on nearby streets. Every day 135,000 guns are brought to school, and much of this violence in school is gang related (Reynolds, 1993). Gangs are also involved in vandalism, harassment, and intimidation, armed robbery, extortion of businesses, and drug dealing. Illegal gang activities are beginning to become a problem in suburban and rural areas, too.

Juvenile gangs and their illegal activities create a complex problem for society. However, some efforts, though superficial, have been made by state, federal, and local authorities. Many states have established special units to deal with gang activities. Such units include youth service programs, which focus on gang control as part of youth illegal activities. The gang detail consists of one or two officers who focus exclusively on gangs, and the gang-crime unit is a division established exclusively to work on gangs. Programs have been implemented in many schools across the country to alert students to the dangers of drugs and the gangs. Neighborhood groups have also mobilized in various cities to combat the influence of gangs on the youth. The federal government has attempted to administer severe penalties to gang leaders, so that such punishment would act as a deterrent for other members of the gangs.

SUMMARY

Both the legal and nonlegal definitions of delinquency present problems. The legal definition focuses on juveniles who have been processed through the juvenile justice system. However, the use of this definition is misleading because not all delinquent acts come to the attention of the authorities. The nonlegal definition includes not only those who have been processed through the juvenile justice system, but also all the unofficial delinquency. Like the legal definition, it, too, presents problems.

The three sources for rates of delinquency are official statistics, victimization surveys, and self-report studies. Each source of information has its limitations. Official data reflect only a small proportion of all delinquent behavior and are subject to compilation errors. Victimization surveys and self-report studies are subject to underreporting or overreporting, deception by respondents, and interviewer bias.

The data discussed in this chapter indicate that delinquents are overrepresented in official statistics for illegal behavior. There is also evidence of gender and racial disparities. Males commit more delinquent acts than females, and blacks are arrested significantly more than any other racial group.

Criminologists argue that family, school, and peers are crucial for the understanding of delinquency. Research on these factors, however, varies in assigning importance to each factor and the specific ways these factors influence delinquency.

2

Black Youths and American Society

In order to provide some insights into the background of black youths, in delinquency, Chapter 2 focuses on their status in U.S. society.

HISTORICAL EXPERIENCE

Blacks in the United States have a long history of racial oppression and discrimination. They were involuntarily brought to this country as slaves to labor on the plantations and as such, they were considered property and were frequently subjected to inhumane treatment. From its inception, the institution of slavery was based on a dual legal system: one for blacks and one for whites. For example, marriages between slaves were not recognized by the masters, and it was illegal for slaves to learn to read. Their lack of legal rights was also evident in laws prohibiting them from voting, owning property, and signing contracts. The enforcement of these laws was left to the slave masters rather than the courts. "Justice" for slaves who violated these laws included such brutal forms of punishment as castration, flogging, mutilation and executions. The abused slaves had no legal redress against this kind of cruelty.

White ethnocentrism formed the basis of the institution of slavery. The difference in cultural and physical traits between blacks and whites resulted in racism based on pseudoscientific evidence, indicating that blacks were biologically inferior to whites and were even subhuman. Racist notions of physiological differences between the two races explained differences in behavior, and it was on this basis that slavery was justified. During the 1830s, the institution of slavery came under attack by abolitionists, and slavery was finally abolished throughout the nation in 1865 by the Thirteenth Amendment. Nevertheless, it left a legacy of racism and discrimination that has persisted to this day.

The end of slavery led to Reconstruction, which lasted from 1865 to 1877 and ended the paternalistic relationship between blacks and whites. During these years, blacks exercised the right to vote and were even elected to political office in state and federal governments. This competitive spirit, however, led to the disenfranchisement of blacks and the implementation of a system of segregation.

When whites realized that they might have to share power with blacks, they implemented laws and policies that disenfranchised blacks. Many of these legal obstacles including literacy tests, the poll tax, white primary elections, and the "grandfather clause," that automatically disqualified blacks from the voting process. The literacy tests, which required voters to be able to read or write, excluded many blacks because they could not read or write. The poll tax stipulation of a $1 payment and the grandfather clause exempting persons who were registered voters in any state prior to or on January 1, 1867, the sons and grandsons of such persons, and male persons of foreign birth naturalized before January 1, 1898, from the literacy tests, prevented blacks from voting and thereby served to maintain white domination (Key, 1949). In addition to the legal restrictions, intimidation was employed to prevent blacks from voting. Many were beaten and lynched, or their property destroyed.

Disenfranchisement was followed by the Jim Crow laws, which resulted in racial segregation. These laws mandated the use of separate facilities, such as schools, transportation, neighborhoods, and drinking fountains, for blacks and for whites. Under this system of segregation, two castelike systems that were separate and unequal were established, and racial exogamy was strongly prohibited, as was evident in the enactment of measures against intermarriage.

Jim Crow laws also created psychological separation, based on a system of racial etiquette. Whites were encouraged not to shake hands with blacks. Blacks were expected to address whites as "Sir" or "Mister" whereas whites would refer to blacks as "Boy" or by the black person's first name. Blacks were also expected to show respect to whites and to address them in terms of honor and prestige.

Segregation was maintained both by a racist ideology and by coercion. When legal measures failed to keep blacks "in their places," extralegal tactics were permitted. Racist groups, such as the Ku Klux Klan, used physical intimidation or violence to maintain black subservience. This system of segregation, which was designed to ensure the blacks' cooperation and loyalty, was well established in all the states by 1860. Jim Crow laws remained in effect for more than a century, until 1965.

When labor shortages developed in the North, many blacks in the South moved North, especially during World Wars I and II. This influx of blacks resulted in discrimination since the presence of so many lacks threatened the economic stability of whites and increased the competition for jobs and housing. As the competition grew intense, violence and intimidation against blacks became prevalent. Consequently, hostilities between blacks and whites resulted in several race riots in numerous cities during the first two decades of the century (Rudwick, 1964; Rudwick and Meier, 1969; Tuttle, 1970).

Between 1945 and 1965, the National Association for the Advancement of Colored People (NAACP) fought for the repeal of racist laws. In 1954, the association won a major victory in its long struggle for civil rights when the Supreme Court ruled in the case of *Brown v. the Board of Education* that racially segregated schools were unconstitutional.

The 1960s became known as the "golden years" for blacks because at last they had achieved some genuine economic, social and political progress. Two of the most significant gains of that decade were the 1964 Civil Rights Act, which prohibited racial discrimination in employment, and the 1965 Voting Rights Act, which removed the legal obstacles to black voting, resulting in en-franchisement of thousands of blacks.   In addition, a series of federally and state-funded initiatives were established such as Head Start, Job Corps, and busing.

Despite the gains of the 1960s, blacks today still lag behind whites in the areas of education, economics, and politics. More than thirty-seven years after the *Brown* decision, the economic and social status of blacks has not improved very much relative to that of whites.

THE STATE OF BLACK YOUTH

The African-American population is relatively young. More than one third are nineteen years and younger.[1] The median age in 1991 was 28 years. Seventeen % of the black population was between the ages of 15 and 24 years, and many of the hardships experienced by blacks today are faced primarily by youths.

Education

Although African Americans have made educational progress over the last several years, they still lag behind whites. For example, in 1970 the median years of schooling for African-American males 25 years old and over was 9.8 years compared to 12.3 for white American males. By 1991, the gap had almost closed, with the black male's median years rising to 12.5 compared with 12.9 for white American males. For African-American females in 1970, 25 years old and over, the median years of schooling was 10.3 versus 12.2 for their white counterparts. By 1991, the black/white female differential was only 0.3, with African-American females having a median number of years of 12.5 and white American females 12.8. In addition, the absolute gap between the proportion of African Americans and white Americans who had not completed high school was 18.8% in 1980, but by 1992 the gap had decreased to 13.% (U. S. Department of Commerce, 1993).

In 1991, only two-thirds (66.7%) of African Americans 15 years of age and over had completed high school compared with 87.5% of white Americans

(U.S. Department of Commerce, 1991). The data in Table 2.1 below show that the dropout rate for African-American youths was much higher than that for white American youths (13.6% versus 8.9%). There was little difference in the dropout rate between males and females.

African-American college-bound students typically do not do as well on the Scholastic Aptitude Test (SAT) as white Americans. In 1994 blacks scored 352 on the verbal portion of the SAT and 388 on the mathematical section for a combined score of 740. In contrast, white Americans scored 443 and 495, respectively, for a combined score of 938, or 198 points higher on the combined scores than African Americans (Chronicle of Higher Education Almanac, 1994). Although the disparity is narrowing, white Americans continue to score significantly higher than African Americans.

The data in Table 2.1 indicate that African Americans lag behind white Americans by 21% with regard to four years of high school, 17% for between one and four years of college, and 14% for more than four years of college education. Although African Americans have decreased the educational disparity at the college level over the past several years, they still lag behind white Americans. In 1991, only 29% of African Americans had attained one or more years of college education compared to 46% of white Americans. African Americans constituted 10% of all students enrolled in colleges in 1992 compared with 75% for whites. In the fall 1993, 10% of the freshmen in colleges were blacks and 80% were whites (Chronicle for Higher Education Almanac, 1994).

In 1982, only 7% of African-American males 20 years of age and over had four or more years of college education, compared with 19% for whites. By 1991, this figure had increased to 9% for African-American males and 22% for white American males. For African-American females, the rate was only 7% in 1982, and by 1991 it had increased to 10%. White American females had rates of 12% in 1982 and 17% in 1991 (U.S. Bureau of Census, 1992).

The proportion of African-American high school graduates enrolled in college, relative to the proportion of white Americans, however, has declined during the period 1982 and 1994. For example, in 1991, only 76% of African Americans were as likely as white Americans to attend college, compare with 87% in 1980 (U.S. Bureau of Census, 1992).

Reasons for the Educational Disparity

There are several possible reasons for the poor school performance and high dropout rate of blacks: academic difficulties, economic factors and pregnancy.

Nationally, over 80% of African Americans are educated in less than 4% of all school districts (Robinson, 1987; Yetman, 1985). Three-fourths of all African-American children attend schools that have 90% minority children, and this situation is acute in the nation's twenty-six largest cities (Yetman, 1985). These inner-city schools, which are often understaffed and under financed, have been facing increased hardship as a result of the federal govern-

Table 2.1
Education Rates by Race (Black and White), 1991

Schooling	Total	African	White
	All Races	Americans	Americans
High School Dropouts			
Both genders	12.5%	13.6%	8.9%
Male	13.0	13.5	8.9
Female	11.9	13.7	8.9
Years of schooling			
Completed 15 years and Over			
4 years high school	74.4	66.7	87.5
1-4 years college	37.2	29.0	46.3
4 or more years college	18.5	11.5	25.5

Source: National Center for Educational Statistics, *Digest of Education*, 1992; U. S. Bureau of Statistics Educational Attainment in U. S., March 1991.

ment's reduction in funds and programs to these schools. Despite the high enrollment of African-American students in major cities, African-American professionals are underrepresented in the schools; that is, it is white Americans who continue to operate the schools. Members of the school board, the school superintendent, many of the principals, teachers, and counselors are primarily white Americans. Eighty-nine percent of the elementary school teachers are white, and a miniscule 6% are black. By the time students reach the senior year in high school about 92% of the teachers are white (U.S. Department of Commerce, 1989).

For several decades now intelligence tests have been used to determine the students so-called ability. Although the use of these tests is very controversial in some quarters, many educators still believe that they are good measures of a child's ability to perform in school. However, these tests are racially and culturally biased against African Americans because the knowledge and thought processes are based on white American middle-class ideals. Despite this bias, many African-American students are placed into tracks on the basis of these tests.

Tracking is the practice of assigning students to a group based on the school's assessment of the student's ability. The major divisions of the tracking system are college and noncollege tracks, or academic and nonacademic tracks. A minority student is three times more likely than a white student to end up in the vocational tracks (*U. S. and World News Report*, 1987). As early as the preschool years, a large proportion of African-American children are placed in "low-ability or special education classes" (Mcbay, 1992:142). Edelman (1988) noted that black children are disproportionately routed into public school classes for the "educable mentally retarded" (EMR) (1988:154). Placing African-American students in these lower tracks puts them at risk of permanent low achievement. Schafer, Olexa and Polk (1972) found that students in college tracks achieve far better grades than those in noncollege tracks. In addition, students in noncollege tracks may be effectively locked out of a chance to achieve educational success. Moreover, low-track students achieve low academic success (a self-fulfilling prophecy), display antisocial behavior and become stigmatized (Dreeban & Garmoran, 1986; Eder, 1981; Rosanthal & Jacobsen, 1968). This kind of tracking represents a barrier to equal educational opportunity for African-American students, and, for many of these students, such inequality undoubted contributes to failure in the school system.

The curriculum in many of the schools is irrelevant to African Americans because it is designed primarily for middle class white Americans. There is a lack of congruity between the social and cultural background of the African-American child and the school curriculum; consequently, the curriculum is not germane to the life of the African-American child. Moreover, little effort has been made to incorporate the experiences, achievement and needs of the African-American child into the curriculum. The conspicuous absence of notable African Americans in public school textbooks sends a powerful and neg-

ative message that African Americans rarely make any contribution to this society. This, of course, is not true. Recently, educators in some schools have
attempted to present curricula that reflect the multicultural, multiracial, and
multiethnic student population in some schools. However, more needs to be
done in this area.

The typical teaching styles in the school are inappropriate for the African-
American student. Boykin (1978) in his study of the behavioral patterns of
black children at home and in school, found that in the home black children are
exposed to a "high activation level", characterized by noises from television,
stereos and a steady flow of people in and out of the home. Consequently,
they learn verbal concepts better through instructional movement than through
the passive learning that is typical of American schools (Guttentag & Ross,
1972). Shade (1982) reviewed research on the cognitive styles of black students and concluded that they have an African-American cognitive or percep-
tual style that emphasizes people rather than objects. Such an orientation creates or magnifies difficulties for the African-American student because schools
are usually object- oriented in their approach.

The result of the lag in educational attainment among African Americans
relative to whites is that they are more susceptible to change in labor market
conditions. They are unable to successfully compete with others for jobs, and
such educational disadvantages also impact on wages, unemployment, and
poverty.

Economic Factors

Economic disparity is the most glaring gulf separating between African
Americans and white Americans. Although the income gap between the two
groups narrowed in the 1960s, this phenomenon began to reverse itself starting
in the 1980s. In 1992, the median income for African Americans age 25 years
and over was $21,609 compared with $27,325 for white Americans--a deficit
of $5,716 for blacks. Therefore, in 1991, African Americans earned 79% of
what white Americans earned. (U.S. Department of Commerce, 1993).

In 1992, the median income was $22,942 for African-American male com-
pared to $31,737 for white Americans. The difference was $8,795, with
African American males earning 72 cents on the dollar earned by white American males. African-American females, on the other hand, earned a median income of $20,299 compared to $22,423 for white counterparts; they earned 90
cents on every dollar earned by white American females (U.S. Department of
Commerce, 1993).

In the first three quarters of 1992, the employment rate for African-American youths 16 to 19 years of age was 23% compared to 45% for White Americans. Similarly, in 1991, the rates were 23% for African-American youths and
47% for white Americans (Swinton, 1993). The data showed that African-
American youths were only about half as likely as white American youths to

be employed. Moreover, white American youths earn more than black youths. For example in 1991, African-American youths earned 43 cents on a dollar that white youths in the same category earned, with a median income of $8,603 compared with that of white American youths of $19,803 (U.S. Department of Commerce, 1992). Table 2.2 shows median income for several groups.

One major source of economic inequalities is occupational status. African Americans are overrepresented in unskilled and semiskilled jobs and underrepresented in professional and white-collar jobs. In 1991, for example, 5.7% of African Americans as compared with 27% of white Americans, were employed in managerial jobs, and 22% of African Americans compared to 12% of White Americans were employed in service jobs. African-American males were only 51% as likely as white American males to be employed in the three top positions--executive, administrative and managerial; professional; and sales. African-American females were 68% as likely as White-American females to employed those top professions (U.S. Department of Labor, 1992).

The unemployment rate reflects the labor force participation of black youths. In 1972, 35% of black youths 16 to 19 years of age were unemployed. In 1991, the official rate was 36%, but by the first three quarters of 1992, the official figure was 40%. In 1991, the black/white ratio was 2.4:1 and in the first three quarters of 1992, the index was 2.3:1. What these data reflect are the high unemployment rate of black youths relative to white youths; blacks are more than twice as likely to be unemployed (U.S. Department of Labor, 1991, 1992). With the present high unemployment rate nationally, black or minority youths are facing dismal employment prospects. In fact, the unofficial rate of unemployment among black youths is estimated to be 60% (Tidwell et al., 1993). Table 2.3 shows the unemployment rates for black and white youths. In all the years listed, the unemployment rate of black youths 16 to 19 years was twice that of white youths.

One major reason for the high unemployment of black youths is the shortage of jobs. Many of these youths live in highly populated cities where only a few jobs exist at the present time. Another major reason for the high unemployment is the lack of employable skills found among black youths relative to whites, especially among those who fail to complete high school or college. Moreover, racial discrimination has reduced the demand for black labor.

Poverty is another way to examine the economic status of blacks. In 1992, 33% of blacks compared with 12% of whites lived in poverty. The number of black men living in poverty in 1992 was 29% compared with 10% for whites. The number of black females living in poverty in 1992 was 37% compared with 13% for white females (U.S. Department of Commerce, 1993). For all persons, the black/white index of poverty was 2.8 in 1992, indicating that blacks were almost three times as likely as whites to live in poverty. Black children were almost three times as likely as white children to live in poverty in 1992: 45.6% and 16.1%, respectively (U.S. Department of Commerce, 1993). The poverty of black youths is intricately related to the "feminization of

Table 2.2
Median Income of Households by Selected Characteristics and Race, 1991

Characteristics	African Americans	White Americans	B/W Index
All Households	$18,838	$31,594	59.6
Persons 16-24	8,603	19,803	43.4
Single-female Household	12,196	21,213	57.5
Inside metro areas	20,211	33,988	59.5

Source: U. S. Department of Commerce, Bureau of Census, *Money Income of Households, Families and Persons in United States: 1991*, August 1992.

Table 2.3
Unemployment Rate of Black and White Youths, Selected Years

	Blacks	Whites	Ratio
Age 16 to 19			
1992[a]	39.8%	17.2%	2.3:1
1991	36.2	14.9	2.4:1
1981	41.5	17.3	2.4:1
1972	35.4	14.2	2.5:1
Teenaged Unemployment, 1991			
Official			
Both Genders	36.3	16.4	2.2:1
Male	36.5	17.5	2.1:1
Female	36.1	15.2	2.4:1
Hidden Unemployment			
Both Genders	57.0	29.0	1.96:1
Male	56.9	30.8	1.85:1
Female	56.9	29.0	1.96:1

[a]Data represent average of first three quarters
Source: U.S. Department of Commerce, *Money Income of Households, Families and Persons in United States,* August 1992.

poverty." In 1992, 46% of black households were headed by females compared with 13% for white females. More than half (54%) of all black children live in female-headed households, and of these, 68% are poor compared to 47% of white children in a similar situation (U.S. Department of Commerce, 1993). In 1991, the income for a black family headed by a female was less than that of a family headed by a white female. For example, black female-headed households had a median income of $12,196 in 1991, while the same type of household among whites had a median income of $21,213 (U.S. Department of Commerce, 1992). In addition, nearly half of all black families were headed by females in 1992: 46% of all black children compared with 14% of white children lived with only their mothers (U.S. Department of Commerce, 1991).

The distribution of persons in poverty is shown in Table 2.4. The table shows that, although the ratio of black children to white children living in poverty over the past twenty years has decreased, the ratio remains high.

The increasing number of unemployed and unemployable black youths in urban areas has created an underclass and an illegal economy dominated by drugs, gambling, violence and gangs. To put things in perspective, as of 1991, two out of three black children living in female-based households were poor, and the average black child could expect to remain poor for about twenty years (American Public Welfare Association, 1986). The chance that a black child will experience poverty increases 35% if he or she lives in a female-headed household.

The economic disparity between blacks and whites has persisted over the last several decades. Years of racism, Jim Crowism, and discrimination have resulted in economic inequality which still continues today. According to Duster (1987), blacks are three times more likely than whites to be poor; their median income is slightly over half that of whites, and black men are twice as likely to be jobless as white men.

Family Structure

Black families have been the focus of much attention over the last three decades. Black families, as discussed earlier in the chapter, are more likely than white families to be poor and headed by a female. About two-thirds of children born to black women are born out of wedlock. In 1992, nearly half of the black families were headed by a female (U.S. Department of Commerce, 1993).

The black family pattern is the result of slavery, migration to the North, declining economic prosperity, racism, and discrimination. The black family is in crisis at the moment, with large numbers of mothers and children living in poverty and a high birth rate for teenagers. This situation perpetuates the cycle of poverty.

Although the birth rate of black teenagers is declining, blacks still have a

Table 2.4
Poverty Rates of Selected Groups by Race, 1971, 1981, and 1991

Groups	Blacks	Whites	B/W Ratio
Persons in Poverty			
1991	32.7	11.3	3.6:1
1981	34.2	11.2	3.1:1
1971	33.5	9.9	3.4:1
Children in Poverty			
1991	45.6	16.1	2.8:1
1981	45.2	15.2	3.0:1
1971	41.5	10.5	4.0:1
In Female-headed Households			
1991	54.8	31.5	1.7:1
1981	56.7	29.8	1.9:1
1971	58.7	28.4	2.1:1

Source: U.S. Bureau of Census (1991) *Poverty in United States: 1990* (Washington, D.C.: U. S. Government Printing Office).

higher teenage birth rate than whites. In 1990, for example, the birth rate for black teenagers was 26 per 1,000 compared with 4 per 1,000 for white teenagers. In addition, 46% of children born to black teenagers in 1990 were out of wedlock in comparison to the 11% for their white counterparts (U.S. Department of Commerce, 1992). This high illegitimacy rate, especially among teenagers, is attributable to several factors. Marriage and employment are closely linked; unemployment means fewer marriages, but not necessarily fewer children in the black community. Moreover, there is a "male marriage-able pool index," which relates to the number of single men to single women. With the high number of black men incarcerated, unemployed, unemployable, and victims of drugs, homicide, and suicide, the ratio of young black females to males increases (Gibbs-Taylor, 1988). This imbalance and unavailability of adequate numbers of "marriageable" young black men result in high rates of illegitimate children and female-based households, many of whom are poor. In 1960, 60% of black women 15 years of age and over were married, but by 1991, the proportion had declined to 38%.

The number of female-headed households among blacks more than doubled from 1950 to 1991: from 18% in 1950 to 46% in 1991. In addition, the number of female householders who were never married more than quadrupled between 1950 (9%) and 1991 (41%). In 1991, only about one-third of black children under the age of 18 lived with both parents compared to 67% in 1960--a decline of 31%. White families experienced a 12% decline for that same period: 91% to 79% (U.S. Department of Commerce, 1991).

The proportion of black families with no income earners almost doubled between 1967 and 1990, from 10% to 19% of all black families. At the same time, the percentage of two-income earners in black families decreased from 46% in 1967 to 36% in 1990 (U.S. Department of Commerce, 1991). The number of these households increased from 3.4 million to 7.5 million between 1960 and 1991 (U.S. Department of Commerce, 1992).

Mortality and Life Expectancy

The average life expectancy of blacks is about six years less than that of whites; in fact the blacks" life expectancy is one of the lowest of all groups in the United States. In 1991, black males' life expectancy was 65.6 years while that for white males was 73 years. For black females, life expectancy was 74 years compared to 80 years for white females. Overall, life was 70 years for blacks and 76 years for whites (U.S. Department of Health and Human Services, 1992). Black males had a 33% higher death rate than black females; they also experienced a 4% higher rate than white males (National Center for Health Statistics, 1992). The death rate for blacks is also higher than whites among those who are between 20 and 24 years of age.

The infant mortality rate is higher among blacks than whites. Black infants were more than twice more likely than white infants to die before their first year of life in 1989: 18.6% for blacks and 8.1% for whites. The racial disparity was greatest among females. Moreover, black female infants were 2.5 times as likely as white female infants to die before their first birthday (National Center of Health Statistics, 1991; 1992).

The high infant mortality rate could be attributed to the rate of teen pregnancies, which are often complicated by several problems, such as premature birth and low weight. In 1989, 13.3% of all babies born to black teenagers had low birth rate compared to 6% for white teenagers (National Center of Health Statistics, 1991). Because of their social and economic status, many of these mothers may not receive the prenatal and postnatal care that they need.

The death rate for black children between 1 and 14 years of age is 1.5 times higher than that of whites (National Center for Health Statistics, 1991). One of the leading causes of high mortality among young blacks, especially black males, is homicide. It is the leading cause of death for black males 15 to 24 years. In 1960, the homicide rate among black males 15 to 24 was 46.4 per 100,000; by 1989 the rate was 61.1 per 100,000 compared to 5.4 per 100,000 for whites. In 1989, a young black male had a 1 in 21 chance of being murdered before he reached his twenty-fifth birthday. Black males are seven times more likely than white males, and black females are five times as likely than their white counterparts to become victims of homicide or legal intervention (National Center of Health Statistics, 1992). The homicide risk for black youths increases if they reside in the inner cities and are involved in gangs. The increased use of drugs, accessibility of firearms and sociodemographic factors place young black males at risk.

Blacks are three times as likely as whites to die from diseases. Even black youths have higher disease rates: those between the ages of 15 and 24 years are four times as likely as white youths to die from disease. In 1989, the death rate for cancer among black males was higher than that of any other race-by-gender group. Their death rate was 230.6 per 100,000 persons, 47% higher than that for white males (157.2 deaths per 100,000), 76% higher than that for black females (130.9 deaths per 100,000) and more than twice that for white females (110.7 deaths per 100,000) (National Center for Health Statistics, 1991). In 1989, black males were about one and one-third more likely than white males to die from heart disease, with a rate of 272.6 per 100,000 persons compared with a death rate of 205.9 for white males; black females were about 60% more likely to die from heart diseases than white females, with a death rate of 172.9 per 100,000 persons compared to 106.6 for white females (National Center for Health Statistics, 1991). In addition, black males have the highest rate of stroke among all race-by-gender groups. In 1989, their rate (54.1 per 100,000) was slightly over twice as great as the rate for white males (28.0 per 100,000). In addition, black males are about 20% more likely to die from stroke than black females (National Center for Health Statistics, 1991). In addition, blacks have a higher rate of diabetes than whites, with a rate of 179 per 100,000 persons for blacks and 90.8 per 100,000 for whites in 1989. The pattern is the same for hypertension: blacks had a rate of 101.4 per

100,000 and whites a rate of 76.5 in 1989 (National Center for Health Statistics, 1991).

The newest threat to the lives of young blacks is Acquired Immunodeficiency Syndrome (AIDS), whose incidence is increasing rapidly among intravenous drug users in the inner cities. Between 1981 and 1986, 25% of all reported cases of AIDS were among blacks, and black males accounted for 23% of all cases among males (Centers for Disease Control, 1986b). By 1991, the incidence of death from AIDS for blacks was three times that of whites with blacks having a rate of 30.4 per 100,000 versus 9.4 per 100,000 for whites. The racial differential was more pronounced among females; black females were eight times more likely than white females to die from the disease (12.2 and 1.5 per 100,000, respectively). However, black males are the most affected by this disease, with a death rate of over four times that of the national average. In 1991, 50% of the deaths of black males were AIDS related (National Center of Health Statistics, 1992).

The AIDS epidemic in the black community is frightening and has far-reaching effects. Some mothers are transmitting the disease to their unborn babies. If the present pattern of the disease continues, the black community will face a health disaster as the twenty-first century approaches.

Alcohol and drug addiction is a major problem in the black community. Young black males consume large quantities of alcohol, and by middle age, a high proportion of them are diagnosed with alcohol-related disorders. In addition, the incidence of deaths from drug overdoses has also increased among black youths (National Center For Health Statistics, 1986).

Higher diseases rates may be related to smoking, poor nutrition, substance abuse, and stress, but many young blacks have limited access to health care. Poverty prevents many of them from having comprehensive health-care insurance, and public health services are inadequate for the black neighborhoods. The high mortality rate of young blacks is also related to the self-destructive and life-threatening behaviors in which they engage. Gibbs-Taylor stated that "Young blacks are continuing to maim, narcotize themselves faster than they could be annihilated through wars and natural disasters" (1988b, p. 282).

Residential (The Formation of Ghettos)

Presently, many blacks reside in black enclaves in the cities. These black enclaves, commonly referred to as "ghettos," have remained entrenched and stable over a long period of time. Blacks in the inner cities have not experienced social mobility similar to that experienced by the immigrant groups who occupied these cities before them. In the past, other ethnic groups have been able to leave these neighborhoods behind, to be succeeded by another unfortunate group. This form of ethnic succession has not been replicated by blacks; instead, they have remained well established in these metropolitan areas.

These black enclaves are poverty stricken and economically deprived, with the median income for blacks living in the central cities being $20,559 in 1991 compared to $32,722 for those living in suburban areas (U.S. Department of Commerce, 1992). There is a perception among many whites that blacks prefer to live in these depressing and deteriorating neighborhoods because they prefer such conditions (Huttman, 1981). This perception is inaccurate; because of discrimination, they are sometimes forced to live in the inner cities. Using several techniques in the past, white real estate agents have steered blacks to black neighborhoods and whites to white neighborhoods. Some have engaged in "blockbusting," a tactic in which they warn of a black invasion, which then frightens whites into selling their houses cheaply. These houses are then sold to blacks at inflated prices. In addition, institutions, such as banks and other lending institutions, employ a tactic called "redlining," through which certain areas in these neighborhoods are ineligible for loans. Moreover, certain zoning regulations have been established, specifying that only certain types of housing can be erected, thereby excluding low-income persons. United States has "unofficial" dual housing markets: one for blacks and one for whites. These discriminatory patterns in housing have persisted over the past years because the federal government has failed to enforce the fair-housing laws (Marger, 1991).

Their increased isolation from the black middle class, together with alienation from white society, have caused hopelessness and frustration for black youths in these areas. It is this kind of frustration and alienation that exploded in the Los Angeles riots in 1992 and that has periodically erupted in urban violence, crimes, homicides, and a wave of terror and destruction in major cities and elsewhere. The Los Angeles riots of 1992 were a clear reminder of the level of frustration, anger, and disillusionment that exists among urban blacks.

Political Power

Blacks have gained considerable political power in the past three decades. There has been an increase in electoral participation of black voters, and the black vote has become a significant force in some jurisdictions. Black migration to the cities has resulted in a high concentration of blacks in several large cities. By 1990, half of America's ten largest cities had elected black mayors. In 1989, the first black governor was elected in the state of Virginia.

The increase in the number of black officials may signify increased political power for blacks, but a more critical examination of these political positions reveals that "real" political power continues to elude them. Despite the increase in their numbers, their proportion is not representative of the black population which constitutes 12% while the officials constitute only 1.3% of all elected officials (Joint Center for Political Studies, 1988). Although there is a visible black presence in the Clinton administration, many of the black politicians are elected locally. It is at the national level, however, that policy-making takes place, and blacks have been conspicuously absent at the highest ranks of the executive branch of government.

Many of the positions to which blacks have been elected may be symbolic only because the official's ability to bring about fundamental changes in these cities is very limited. Local conditions in many of these cities are deplorable, and federal and state funds are inadequate to improve conditions, thereby making significant changes difficult, especially for black youths.

Factors Contributing to the Status of Young Blacks

The present status of young blacks in the United States is related to economic, social and political factors.

Economic Factors

The plight of young blacks is considered to be related to the structural changes in the economy. Julius Wilson (1987) argued that the ghettos are outgrowths of fundamental changes in the economy, whereby jobs were shifted from the cities to the suburbs and from the Rustbelt to the Sunbelt. According to Wilson, this shift led to high unemployment, more poverty, more female-based households, and some forms of deviance among blacks. Wilson provided data to support his argument. For example, he found that higher income black men were more likely to be married than low-income black men.

Another economic factor is the status of occupations that blacks hold. Historically, blacks have held low-paying jobs. College-educated blacks not only received lower wages than their white counterparts, but they also faced difficulties in the job market.

Social Factors

Racial discrimination is a major factor in the plight of young blacks today. Although blatant racism and negative stereotypes of blacks to a large extent have diminished, subtle forms of discrimination persists. Discrimination still holds African Americans back in areas of employment, education, housing and health services. Hostility against blacks is evident in all aspects of life in the American culture. Moreover, blacks are facing a backlash from such policies as minority college grants and affirmative action. Affirmative action is presently under attack in all three branches of government over whether it discriminates against whites. Republican leaders in Congress are debating the elimination of most affirmative action programs, and President Clinton has asked for a review of over 100 federal programs involving affirmative action. On April 17, 1995, the Supreme Court left intact two court cases won by white men who said that they were victims of reverse discrimination (*The Star-Ledger Wire Services*, 1995).

Historical experience indicates that racial hostility increases in times of general economic decline. The country has been facing such a decline in the last twelve years, and this situation undoubtedly has had an impact on the increasing racial discrimination against blacks. It is quite clear that the abolition of slavery and the implementation of desegregation did not change the pattern of relations between blacks and whites for a very long time. The civil rights movement of the 1960s brought some changes, but racial stigma, discrimination, and racism, though subtle, have not been eradicated.

Some observers argue that class, not race is the main contributor to the plight of young blacks today. Julius Wilson (1980, 1981, 1987) argues that, although race was a factor in discrimination in earlier times, class factors are more important in explaining the status of blacks in the United States today. According to Wilson, despite slow gains made by blacks over the past several decades, a small group of blacks have experienced economic upward mobility. This middle class has moved away from the inner cities producing a social vacuum and depriving youths of real leadership or role models. This has created a black underclass with high rates of joblessness, school dropout, crime, teenage parenthood, and drugs. Wilson has predicted that the black underclass will continue for a long time because high unemployment and female-headed households threaten to continue the cycle of poverty. Wilson's main argument, then, is that the class structure rather than racial discrimination is responsible for sustaining the black underclass.

Hill (1981) counters Wilson's argument by pointing out that black college graduates have a much higher jobless rate than white college graduates and that white school dropouts have much lower jobless rates than their black counterparts. In addition, he criticized Wilson for not measuring the extent to which disparity in education, employment, and other factors are the result of racial discrimination.

Political Factors

The present situation of black youths can be attributed to the conservative political climate that existed in the country for the twelve-year period 1980-1992. The Reagan-Bush era resulted in extensive racial inequality for blacks, especially black youth. During that period, many social programs designed primarily to benefit disadvantaged youths were severely cut or eliminated. Such programs included job employment programs, loans for college, and affirmative action programs (Swinton, 1993). The social impact of such actions has resulted in fewer educational and occupational opportunities for young blacks.

Blacks have great optimism that the Clinton-Gore administration will focus on the economic and educational problems of blacks in America. The hope is that this administration will find viable solutions for the problems faced by blacks, especially young blacks. The administration's approach is to examine the underlying problems for the racial inequality and devise policies that will bring economic and social parity between blacks and whites. If these issues are not adequately addressed, then violence, gangs, drugs, and other types of delinquency (to be discussed in Chapter 3) will continue among young blacks.

SUMMARY

The experience of blacks in the United States is unlike that of any other racial group. They were subjected to all kinds of cruelty and human indignity under slavery, which lasted from the 1600s to 1865. After the Civil War, a brief period of Reconstruction was instituted, but it was followed by the Jim Crow laws which created racial segregation. The 1960s decade was considered the "golden years" because blacks experienced many significant gains. However, in the following decades, the rate of progress has slowed drastically, especially in the 1980s during the Reagan-Bush administration. Presently, blacks lag behind whites in income, employment, and education. They have a lower life expectancy rate than whites, a higher poverty rate, and higher rates of crime and delinquency. Black youths are the most disadvantaged of all groups, and their future looks very bleak.

NOTE

1. The sources used in this chapter use both the terms *blacks* and *African Americans*. These terms are used as presented in the sources. The term *blacks* refers to persons of African descent, which would include African Americans, persons from Africa, the Caribbean and elsewhere. However, African Americans make up the largest group.

3

Black Youths and Delinquency

Data have constantly shown that black youths are more overrepresented in delinquency statistics than any other racial group. The questions is: To what extent are they involved in delinquency? This chapter examines the nature and extent of delinquency among black youths as offenders and as victims. Specific types of delinquency are also discussed.

NATURE OF DELINQUENCY AMONG BLACK YOUTHS

Official data, victimization surveys, and self-report studies have been used to measure the nature and extent of delinquency. There is some disparity between these three methods as to the extent and nature of delinquency among blacks.

Official Data

The primary source of official data is Uniform Crime Reports which were discussed in Chapter 1. These reports indicate that black youths are disproportionately involved in delinquency for youths under the age of 18. Although blacks make up 12% of the general population, they constituted 27% of all juvenile arrests in 1992. They made up 29% of all arrests for Index crimes and 49% of all violent crimes in 1992. They were overrepresented in all juvenile arrests for violent crimes, with 57% of all murder/manslaughter arrests; 46% of rape arrests; 63% of robbery arrests; and 42% of aggravated assaults arrests. Although black youths; only made up 26% of all property crimes of persons under the age of 18, they were still overrepresented in property crime arrests with burglary (22%); larceny-theft (24%); motor vehicle theft (39%); and arson (15%). In 1992 for Part 11 of the Uniform Crime Reports, black youths were also overrepresented in all arrests, but some significant arrest rates that need noting include 74% of all gambling arrests, 47% of all drug violations arrests, 37% of stolen property arrests, and 37% for weapon violations (Federal Bureau of Investigation, 1993).

When trends are examined, the racial disparity is startling. Table 3.1 shows that between 1980 and 1990, the rate of arrests for violent crimes of blacks increased 19% compared with the increase for whites of 44%. Despite the higher increase for whites, the juvenile arrest rate for blacks for violent crimes is five times that of whites. Moreover, the data show that blacks had an arrest rate for murder three times that of whites. The drug arrest rate for whites decreased 48% between 1980 and 1990 but increased 159% for blacks. Similarly, the arrest rates for whites involved in weapons law violation increased only 58%, while that of blacks increased 103% (Federal Bureau of Investigation, 1992).

Victimization Surveys

The National Crime Victimization Survey showed that since 1981, the peak year for victimizations, crime levels have dropped overall. Blacks were more likely than whites in 1992 to be victims of crimes. Persons under the age of 25 years had a higher victimization rate than any other persons. In addition, those living in households in the lowest income category were more likely to be violent crime victims (U.S. Department of Justice, 1993a). Table 3.2 shows that, overall, young blacks living in the central cities are at risk of victimization.

The National Crime Victimization Survey data for 1992 show that blacks had a victimization rate of 110.8 per 1,000 persons age 12 and over compared with 88.7 per 1,000 for whites. The data also showed that black males between the ages of 16 and 19 years had personal victimization rates of 158.1 per 1,000 persons for violent crimes. White males of the same age group had a rate of 88.6 per 1,000 persons. Black females, between 16 and 19 years of age, also had a higher rate of victimization than white females, with 94.8 per 1,000 persons for black females and 51.9 per 1,000 persons for white females 5 (U.S. Department of Justice, 1993a). For the crime of theft, the pattern was exactly the same, with black males and black females having a higher victimization rate than their white counterparts.

Data from the National Crime Victimization Survey for the period between 1979 and 1986 show that black victims were more likely than white victims to be physically attacked during a violent crime (48% versus 41%); to be injured (34% versus 28%); and to sustain more serious injuries (25% versus 16%) (U.S. Department of Justice, 1992a).

Victimization data for 1992 reveal that black households were more likely than white households to be victimized. For example, the victimization for black households in 1992 was 199.1 per 1,000 households, and the rate for

Table 3.1
Percent Changes in Juvenile Arrest Rates for Crimes Related to Violence, United States, 1990 over 1980[a]

Offenses	All Races	White	Black	Other
Violent crime (Total)	27.3	43.8	19.2	53.4
Murder	87.3	47.5	145.0	-45.4
Forcible rape	36.7	85.9	8.5	-66.0
Robbery	-7.5	12.3	-15.6	-67.4
Aggravated assault	63.7	59.2	88.9	-38.8
Weapons Law Violations	62.6	57.6	102.9	-48.1
Drug Abuse (Total)	-20.1	-47.6	158.6	-77.0
Heroin/Cocaine	713.4	251.1	2,372.9	126.8
Marijuana	-66.0	-66.7	-47.5	-80.1
Synthetic	-26.5	-34.1	144.7	-77.4
Nonnarcotic	-5.5	-34.6	223.3	-87.5

[a] Arrest rate per 100,000 for the age group 10-17.
Source: Federal Bureau of Investigation, 1991, p. 289. *Uniform Crime Reports*, (Washington, D.C.: Government Printing Office).

Table 3.2
Victims of Crimes of Violence, 1992 (per 1,000 persons)

	Total	Robbery	Aggravated Assault	Simple Assault	Crime of Theft
Race					
White	88.7	4.7	7.8	16.8	58.8
Black	110.8	15.6	18.3	15.2	60.4
Other	88.3	23.7	18.6	5.3	64.6
Gender					
Male	101.4	8.1	12.0	18.1	62.6
Female	81.8	3.9	6.1	15.0	55.9
Age					
12-15	171.0	9.8	20.1	44.7	95.3
16-19	172.7	15.4	26.3	34.5	94.8
20-24	177.0	11.4	18.1	38.0	106.9
25-34	111.1	7.7	9.3	20.1	73.4
34-39	75.1	3.8	6.8	10.2	53.9
60-64	43.3	2.8	2.3	4.8	33.3
65+	21.1	1.5	1.3	1.8	16.3
Residence					
Central City	116.5	10.8	12.1	19.4	73.3
Suburban	84.4	4.4	7.3	15.3	56.5
Nonmetro Areas	72.4	2.7	7.8	14.3	47.2

Source: U. S. Department of Justice (1993a), *Criminal Victimization 1992* (Washington, D.C.: U. S. Department of Justice).

white households was 146.1 (U.S. Department of Justice, 1993b). Black households were also more likely than white households to fall victim of serious crimes. The rate of theft was about the same for both types of households. Households in the urban areas were more likely than those in the rural areas to experience victimizations (U.S. Department of Justice, 1993b).

Blacks are often victimized by other blacks. The data in Table 3.3 show that blacks were victimized by other blacks in all violent crimes for 1992. The pattern was the same for victimization where there were multiple offenders. In 1992, 90% of the black victims were victims of violent crimes in which all of the multiple offenders were black. Only 3.3% blacks were victims of violent crimes in which all the multiple offenders were white (U.S. Department of Justice, 1993c). One can assume that young blacks are victimizing young blacks, because victimization surveys have consistently indicated that persons of the same race, gender and age group victimize each other. This supports the proximity hypothesis that assumes that criminals and victims live in close proximity to each other, and that criminals tend to select victims who share similar characteristics, backgrounds, and circumstances (Fagan, Piper & Cheng, 1987).

The School Crime Survey is conducted as part of the National Crime Victimization Survey, and youths between the ages of 12 and 19 years, who are attending school at the time of the survey, are interviewed. The data for 1990 indicate that 67% of blacks reported that drugs were available in schools and 40% had attended drug education classes during the previous six months. In addition, 60% reported the availability of alcohol in school; 60% reported the presence of gangs; 22% said that they were fearful at school; and 21% avoided certain places in school for fear of victimization (U.S. Department of Justice, 1992b).

Black students were also victimized in school. Specifically 41% of black youths from the class of 1993 reported that they had something worth under $50 stolen from them at least once in the past twelve months; 27% had something worth over $50 stolen; 23% were threatened with a weapon; 11% were injured without a weapon; and 26% had their property damaged (Maguire & Pastore, 1994).

Self-report Studies

Official data constantly show that blacks have higher rates of arrests for delinquency than whites. Many self-report studies, however, question the findings of the official data.

The National Youth Survey was a longitudinal study involving a sample of 1,725 youths between the ages of 11 and 17 years who were interviewed for a five-year period from 1976 to 1980. Using the first wave of data in 1976, Elliot, Ageton & Canter, (1980) found that black youths had higher rates of predatory crimes (sexual assault, aggravated assault, simple assault, and

Table 3.3
Violent Victimization by Race and Age of Offender and Victim, 1992

	Percent of Single-Offender Victimizations			
	Perceived Race of Offender			
Type of Crime and Race of Victim	White	Black	Other	Not Known or available
Crimes of Violence				
White	73.0%	17.8%	7.6%	1.6%
Black	10.5	84.1	2.8[a]	2.5[a]
Robbery				
White	48.9	43.2	6.9[a]	0.9[a]
Black	2.7	88.2	5.7[a]	3.4[a]
Aggravated Assault				
White	74.0	14.3	9.1	2.6[a]
Black	16.2	82.1	1.7[a]	0.0[a]
Simple Assault				
White	76.7	14.9	7.0	1.4[a]
Black	10.7a	82.5	2.3[a]	4.5[a]
Rape				
White	72.7	11.7[a]	15.6[a]	0.0[a]
Black	0.0[a]	100.0	0.0a	0.0a

Total does not add up to 100% because of rounding.
[a]Estimate is based on about ten or fewer sample cases.
Source: U.S. Department of Justice, Bureau of Statistics (1993c), *Criminal Victimization in the United States, 1992.*

robbery) than white youths. However, the greater involvement of black youths in serious crimes against persons indicated by the 1976 data was not found in later years of the study (Elliot et al., 1983).

Two national studies examined the issue of race and delinquency and found little evidence of racial disparity in delinquency. One study conducted by the Institute of Social Research at the University of Michigan found that black youth reported less delinquency than white youth (Bachman, Johnson & O'Malley, 1991). Social scientists at the Behavioral Science Institute in Boulder, Colorado, reported that, although the delinquency rate of black and white youths was the same, black youths had a greater chance of being arrested and taken into custody (Huizinga & Elliot, 1987). Several other self-report studies found no difference between blacks and whites (Elliot & Voss, 1974; Epps, 1967; Gould, 1969) and William and Gold (1972) found no difference when social class was controlled.

More recent research (Elliot, Ageton & Canter, 1980; Hindelang, Hirschi & Weis, 1981) indicates that blacks are likely to commit more serious offenses than whites. Studies have also found that black youths were more likely to conceal their involvement in delinquency than white youths (Hindelang, Hirschi & Weis, 1981; Huizinga & Elliot, 1987).

The reports of high school seniors in the United States provide some insight into the extent of delinquency among black youths in school. Data for 1991 showed that 27% of black youths as compared with 17% of white youths reported carrying a weapon to school thirty days prior to the survey (Centers for Disease Control, 1991). Black youths may feel more compelled than white youths to arm themselves because of the high levels of violence in their inner-city schools. Black youths reported less use of alcohol than white youths thirty days before the survey (4% and 11%, respectively). The rate for selected self-report delinquent acts for black and white senior high school youths are shown in Table 3.4. The data indicate that only in the cases of serious fight, group fight, and assault were the rates higher for blacks than for whites, and the ratios are not as high as indicated by official statistics. What accounts for this discrepancy in official and self-report data?

There are several explanations for the racial disparity in delinquency between blacks and whites. One school of thought is that the overrepresentation of black youths in the juvenile justice system results from discrimination and bias from the system itself. According to this view, police and courts treat black youths harshly but deal with white youths leniently. There is support for differential treatment of black youths in the juvenile justice system. Bishop and Frazier (1989) found that blacks were more likely than whites to be recommended for formal processing, adjudicated as delinquents, and given harsher dispositions. Other studies have reported evidence of racial discrimination in the criminal and juvenile justice systems (Piliavin & Briar, 1964; Smith, Visher & Davidson, 1984; Thornberry, 1973).

Another explanation is that blacks do indeed commit a higher proportion of delinquent acts than white youths. One such advocate of this position is

Table 3.4
High School Seniors Reporting Involvement in Selected Delinquent Acts at Least Once in the Last Twelve Months by Race, 1980 and 1992

	Race of Respondent		
Delinquent Acts	White	Black	Ratio
Stole things from a store	31%	27%	1:.87
Got traffic ticket or warning	32	17	1:.53
Took car that didn't belong to you	5	7	1:1.40
Went into a building when you weren't supposed to be there	27	19	1:.70
Argued or had a fight with parents	92	74	1:.80
Got into a serious fight	19	17	1:.89
Took part in a group fight	21	25	1:1.19
Took something not belonging to you under $50	34	22	1:.65
Took something not belonging to you over $50	11	9	1:.82
Hurt someone badly enough to need bandages or doctor	12	14	1:1.16
Got into trouble with the police	24	20	1:.83
Did damage to school property on purpose	15	11	1:.73

Source: Maguire and Pastore (1994), *Sourcebook of Criminal Justice Statistics 1993*. Washington, D .C.: U.S. Government Printing Office.

William Wilbanks (1987), who states that the perception that the criminal or juvenile justice system is racist is a myth. He argues that the system actually discriminates in favor of blacks by giving them lenient sentences. He also contends that blacks are more "racially prejudiced" than whites and victimize whites more often than whites victimize blacks.

Georges-Abeyie (1989) criticized Wilbanks for ignoring the "petit apartheid realities" in law enforcement activities such as stop-and-question, stop-and-frisk practices, unnecessary searches, and harassment. He also pointed out that there were less rigorous standards of evidence in courts for blacks than for whites. Georges-Abeyie maintains that if the official statistics are indeed valid, then they reflect ecological differences between blacks and whites. Many blacks reside in urban areas characterized by deteriorating houses, high unemployment, poverty, high incidence of single-parent families, and limited wealth.

Duster (1987) argues that the lack of economic opportunities for blacks has an influence on the crime and delinquency rates. Duster found among blacks a permanent black teenage underclass whose membership lacks the basic job skills needed to be part of society. He found that blacks are over three times as likely to be poor as whites; their median income is only half that of whites, and their net worth is only one-twelfth that of whites. Furthermore, black males are twice as likely to be unemployed as whites. Duster viewed these circumstances as contributing factors of delinquency among blacks.

Overall, the evidence on racial differences in delinquency rates is very controversial one and remains inconclusive. Official data indicate an overrepresentation of black youths in serious offenses, but a number of self-report studies suggest that the racial differences either do not exist or are insignificant. Those who believe that there is no racial difference in the rate of delinquency between blacks and whites suggest that discrimination accounts for the racial disparity in official data. If the official data are valid, then there are those who view the high rate of delinquency among blacks as a function of their socioeconomic position in the American society.

SPECIFIC TYPES OF ILLEGAL ACTS

Homicide

The phenomenon of blacks killing blacks is astoundingly prevalent in the homicide statistics, especially in urban neighborhoods. Although blacks make up 12% of the population in the Unites States, they account for 55% of all murders and nonnegligent manslaughter arrests in 1992 (Federal Bureau of Investigation, 1993). Moreover, 93% of these black victims were killed by other blacks, and only 6% by whites and 1% by others (Maguire & Pastore, 1994).

In 1992, 49% of murder victims known to the police were black (Federal Bureau of Investigation, 1993). Blacks were seven times more likely to be victims of homicide than whites: 35 per 100,000 persons compared with 5 per 100,000 for whites. In addition, the rate of murder for black males between 10 and 13 years of age in 1992 was 4.8 per 100,000 persons compared with 0.8 per 100,000 for white males of the same age. The disparity is smaller for black and white females in the same age group, with a rate of 2.8 per 100,000 for black females and 0.7 per 100,000 for white females (Maguire & Pastore, 1994). The murder rate among blacks is so alarming that some health officials have suggested that it should be considered a public health issue (Minsky, 1984).

As note above, most blacks are murdered by other blacks. Between 1976 and 1992, 93% blacks were killed by blacks and 7% blacks were killed by whites. Similarly, 86% of black males were killed by other males and 69% of black females were killed by males. In addition, 31% of black female victims were killed by other females. Seventy-five percent of black males murdered blacks, and 90% of black females killed other blacks (Maguire & Pastore, 1994). Given these statistics, the tendency is for black males to kill black males and black females. It appears that black females tend to kill black males more often than black females. Mann (1986) found that, although black women made up 11% of the female population in United States, they committed three-fourths of all homicides.

Homicidal risks increase for those black youths who reside in urban areas, use drugs, and have access to weapons. Using alcohol on a regular basis to cope with stress is believed to be a common practice in poor neighborhoods. Rose (1990) in his study of black homicides in several cities found that 70% of the offenders used alcohol. He also found that 44% of victims and offenders used drugs on a regular basis, but drug use occurred more often with offenders than victims.

The availability of weapons increases the risk of homicides. In urban areas, where there are elevated levels of violence, people often arm themselves with weapons, primarily handguns, as a form of protection. Blacks use weapons more often than whites when committing violent crimes (U.S. Department of Justice, 1990). Rose (1990) found that many of the homicides in his study were committed with handguns: Atlanta 79%, St. Louis, 75% and Detroit 76%. The Centers for Disease Control reported that 78% of homicides of black males in 1987 were committed with handguns, an increase of 50% since 1984 (Centers for Disease Control, 1991).

Causes of Homicide among Young Blacks

One of the most common explanations for black-on-black violence is the subculture of violence theory. Wolfgang and Ferracuti (1967) proposed that black homicide is the product of the ghetto environment that advocates and sanctions violence. According to these researchers, young, lower class, black males possess a value system that deviates from that of the larger society in its emphasis on violence as an acceptable form of behavior. Membership in this subculture produces higher rates of violence, especially lethal violence, among young, lower class, black males.

Harvey (1986) argues that the subculture of exasperation relates to homicide in the black community. The conditions of poverty, unemployment, and poor housing create such a situation. Chilton (1987) suggests that conditions in black communities will get worse if these environments do not improve.

Some black psychiatrists (Grier and Cobbs, 1986; Pierce, 1986; Poussaint, 1983) have proposed that the frustrations experienced by black youths in this society create anger, but this anger becomes displaced onto convenient targets in their immediate environment. The high incidence of homicide reflects this anger displacement.

Others relate this violence to the black historical experiences of blacks. Comer (1985) argued that enslavement of black people has left them very angry. Such anger has intensified because of racism and discrimination. Conger (1968) explains that intraracial violence is the blacks' reaction to their inability to cope with the society at large. Silberman (1978) also views black violence within the context of their historical experiences.

Social ecologists postulate that the high level of violence found among blacks relates to the environment. Rose (1990), Farrington (1982), and Farley (1980) relate homicide to the social environment. These social scientists suggest that many aspects of the ghetto environment, such as poor housing, poverty, overcrowding, and social disorganization, are pathogenic for black youth. Such conditions produce high levels of stress, depression, despair, and social alienation, and these in turn create homicidal tendencies.

Gang Involvement

The first black teenage gangs were organized in the early 1920s. In the 1960s, it was estimated that 300 black youths belonged to gangs, but today, there are approximately 39,000 gang members in the two major black gangs: Bloods and Crips (Witkin, 1991). The average age of youth gang members continues to decline. Most experts believe the average age to be 15, but the members could be as young as 9 or 10. These young recruits are called "peewees" (slang for little members) or "wanabees" (slang for "want to be" gang members). These young members are involved in jobs such as delivering packages or serving as "lookouts" for the police (Rogers, 1991).

The Bloods and the Crips are the most common black gangs. Each gang consists of "sets," and the Crips are estimated to have 190 such "sets" whereas the Bloods have 65 "sets." It is estimated that the Bloods have a membership of about 9,000 and the Crips 30,000 (Witkin, 1991). These gangs also consist of "rollers" and "gang bangers" who are in their early 20s and 30s and supervise and control the activities of the younger teenaged members. The expansion of these gangs took off in late 1980s, and they have spread out of Los Angeles into 32 states and 113 major cities. Their reach also extends to the rural areas (Robbins, 1988; Witkin, 1991).

Another black gang gaining notoriety is the Jamaican Posses who are believed to be linked to the Jamaican "ganja" (marijuana) trafficking groups that flourished in the poverty-stricken areas of Jamaica. Members of these groups immigrated, many illegally, from Jamaica to the United States in the mid-1980s. They quickly formed gangs in an attempt to participate in the drug trade. There are about forty gangs with a total estimated membership of 22,000, and they dominate the crack market in New York, Boston, St. Louis, Philadelphia, and Washington, D.C. (Swanson, Chamelin & Territo, 1992; Witkin, 1991). The Posses are extremely violent, and it has been estimated that these gangs are associated with 3,000 homicides nationwide (Witkin, 1991). Intelligence Reports show that Jamaican Posses have established a national distribution network of narcotics, gun smuggling, firearms, and money laundering (Witkin, 1991).

In Chicago, the two major rival black gangs are the Black Gangster Disciples Nation and the Vice Lords. The Black Gangster Disciples Nation is the strongest gang on Chicago's South Side and is known for its turf wars with Blackstone Rangers in the late 1960s and early 1970s, The Vice Lords is the oldest street gang in Chicago, dating back to the 1950s. This gang operates throughout the city but is strongest in the poor West Side neighborhoods. Of the street gang-motivated offenses recorded during 1987 and 1990, 28% were committed by the Black Gangster Disciples Nation, 18% by the Vice Lords, and the remainder was committed by other types of gangs. Both the Black Gangster Disciples Nation and the Vice Lords are involved in drugs, primarily cocaine, and have reintroduced heroin, which has proven to be a disturbing development for the police. These gangs have also been involved in gang-motivated homicides and in acts of instrumental violence (such as the possession and sale of drugs), while other gangs in acts of expressive violence, such as turf defense (Block & Block, 1993). These two black gangs have established branches in Milwaukee, which has been estimated to have between 2,000 active members and 6,000 peripheral members (National School Safety Center, 1990).

Black gangs share certain characteristics. They use graffiti as a way to delineate gang turfs as well as a form of dispute. They also communicate by means of speech patterns, slang, and hand signs. Clothing is also symbolic for the gangs. For example, some black gangs in Boston wear sneakers or jackets with a particular logo in order to identify their members. In Los Angeles, Crips are identified by the color blue and Bloods by the color red, which can be worn on hats, belt, shirts, or jackets. Black gang members also display particular hairstyles, which include cornrows, braids, or shaven head. Moreover, they give each other nicknames (Siegel & Senna, 1993).

Black youth gang members are involved in a number of illegal activities, especially violence. Gang violence is becoming more intense and is spreading across the nation. In large cities such as New York, Chicago, Philadelphia, Miami and Los Angeles, gang-related homicides and other forms of violent incidents number in the hundreds, if not thousands, annually. Even the nation's capital is not immune from this gang violence. Much of this violence results from gang wars over turfs and retaliation.

Violence has become more lethal today because of the proliferation of automatic and semiautomatic guns found among gang members. Gangs no longer use knives, clubs, and sticks; instead, they use sophisticated weaponry--"AR-15s, M-16, grenades and plastic explosives that would do credit to a military assault troop" (Territo, Halstead & Bromley 1992, p. 564). Guns are easily accessible, and many are quite concealable. In Chicago, for example, where handguns have been banned since 1982, an inner city youth can get a gun within two hours. For $20 he or she can buy a .22 caliber pistol (Henkoff, 1992). Maxson and Klein (1990, p. 219) put it well:

The notion here is that more weapons yield more shootings; these in turn, lead to more "hits"; and these in turn, lead to more retaliations in a series of reciprocal actions defending honor and territory.

Another illegal act committed by black youth gangs is drug trafficking, which has become an important source of income. Competition for control of the drug trade often results in violence. Black gangs are often linked to the sale of cocaine and crack. The operation of "rock houses" or "stash houses" can yield thousands of dollars a week, and these "businesses" have the overseas connections and financial backing needed to wholesale drugs (Cox & Conrad, 1991). The gangs have also engaged in the purchase of legitimate businesses, such as car washes and liquor stores in order to "launder" drug money (Siegel, 1992). The Bloods and the Crips have infiltrated cities from Alaska to Washington, D.C., selling cocaine and crack (Robbins, 1988). Witkin (1991) suggests: "America is caught up in a pincer movement: Los Angeles street gangs moved east and Jamaican Posses moved west from the east coast and between them, they have introduced the rest of the country to crack" (p. 29).

The gangs also engage in other illegal activities, including arson, vandalism, and extortion, as well as prestige crimes, whereby members commit theft or assault to gain prestige in the gang (Siegel & Senna, 1993). They also engage in burglary, harassment, and intimidation (Cox & Conrad, 1991).

Reasons for Joining Gangs

Economic gain is one reason for joining gangs. Indeed, the major inducement for the increase in gang membership is the lure of financial rewards from drug trafficking. Many of the juveniles who join gangs come from the inner city where unemployment is high, crime is high, and legitimate opportunities are limited. The financial rewards of being a gang member are tremendous. For example, "weapons carriers" can earn from $200 a week to $100 a day. "Runners" can earn up to $300 a day, and street level drug dealers can earn between $400 and $1,000 a day (Rogers, 1991). The meager wages earned in unskilled jobs such as working in fast-food restaurants, are not as attractive to an inner-city youth who can make much more money from selling drugs. The crack-cocaine trade provides many inner-city youths with job opportunities.

Youths who are alienated from society and cannot achieve societal goals through legitimate means join gangs for a sense of belonging. The gang can provide a sense of identity and self-esteem for youths who experience a sense of failure and hopelessness in the larger society.

Gangs also provide a sense of family for many of their members. Many gang members come from broken homes or homes that have no strong male authority figure. The male figure may be a criminal or a drug addict. As a tightly knit group, the gang provides psychological and physical security for its members. For many young black males, the gang can provide the family unit they may not have.

Use of Illegal Drugs

Drug use has become a serious problem in the United States. Since 1975, University of Michigan researchers have annually interviewed about 16,000 students on about 125 high school campuses. In addition to the annual survey, there is a follow-up of ten years after high school to determine their continued use of drugs. Although the most recent data available, for 1993, indicate that marijuana use among youths in high school is declining (46% in 1981 compared to 26% in 1993), illegal drug use remains a serious problem (Maguire & Pastore, 1994).

Data on the extent of illegal drug use among black youth is very sparse. The arrest data for 1992 indicate that 47% of those arrested for drug violations under the age of 18 were blacks. Black youths under the age of 18 had an arrest rate for drug violation in 1992 of 483.9 per 100,000 persons compared with 88.5 per 100,00 for white youths (Federal Bureau of Investigation, 1993).

Over the past several years there has been an increase in illegal drug use by inner-city youths. The major drugs of choice are heroin, cocaine, and crack (*N.Y. Times, 1987*). The National Institute of Drug Abuse (1980) predicted an increase in drug abuse among Hispanic and black youths through 1995 because they constituted the fastest growing segment of drug users in the nation. In a high school survey (1992), 34% of blacks reported having used marijuana, 9% cocaine, 3% crack, and 2% inhalants (Maguire & Pastore, 1994).

The use of illegal drugs by black youths has serious consequences, for it is related to other types of crimes. Several studies (Anglin & Speckart, 1988;

Incardi, 1986) show that drug users are extensively involvement in crimes. Many of these users are addicts and commit crimes to support their habits. Such crimes include burglary, larceny-theft, fraud, arson, and stolen property (U.S. Department of Justice, 1993d). Another way to examine the relationship between drugs and crimes is to look at how many arrestees tested positive for drugs.

Data from twenty-four cities for a sample of males arrested in 1992 revealed that the percentage testing positive for any drug ranged from 47 in Phoenix to 78 in Philadelphia. Similarly, data on female arrestees for 1992 indicate that females testing positive for drugs ranged from 44% in San Antonio to 85% in Manhattan (U.S. Department of Justice, 1993d). Many homicides in the inner cities are related to drug use. Given what is known about drugs and crimes, the use of drugs by black youths should be considered a major concern for society.

The newest drug-related threat to black youths is Acquired Immunodeficiency Syndrome which can be spread by the sharing of needles among intravenous drug users. The health consequences of drug use are very frightening indeed. It has been estimated that by the year 2002, 42% of blacks between the ages of 15 and 50 compared to only 3% of whites may carry the disease (Findlay & Silberner, 1990).

Another serious problem resulting from drug use is the birth of many "crack babies." It was once thought that the placenta served as a barrier protecting the baby from toxic substances during pregnancy, but today doctors have come to realize that drugs such as cocaine, marijuana, and heroin invade the placenta and infect the fetus. No one knows the extent of the problem nationally, but the American Hospital Association has estimated that there might be between 50,000 and 100,000 drug-impaired babies in the United States (Burns, Chasnoff & Scholl, 1986; Rist, 1990). Many of these crack babies are black, born to unwed mothers, abandoned and addicted to drugs. The harm done to these babies includes mental retardation, deformities, hyperactivity and speech and language impairment. The cost to care for these babies is staggering with medical bills ranging from an average of $7,500 to $31,000. The explosion of drug-affected infants in the inner city will have a devastating effect on the black community.

Reasons for Using Drugs

One explanation of drug use is the subcultural approach which views drug taking as related to the social environment. Residing in deteriorating inner-city slums is often correlated with involvement in the drug subculture. Many of these young black drug users live in depressed neighborhoods with intolerable social conditions. They also face racism and discrimination from the white society and often lack economic opportunities. Many often feel a sense of hopelessness and alienation and have low self-esteem. Drugs provide an escape from such depressing circumstances. The unfortunate situation is that many of these youths become addicted, thereby intensifying their use of drugs.

According to social psychologists youths use drugs because they are taught to do so by significant others, such as family members, friends, and peers. Those who learn from others that drug is pleasurable are often the most likely to use drugs (Winfree, Griffiths & Sellers, 1989). It is also not uncommon for young drug users to come from families with histories of drug use and abuse.

SUMMARY

Official data have shown that black youths have higher rates of arrest and conviction than any other racial group. Some self-report studies, however, suggest that the rate of delinquency among black youth is no higher than that of white youths. There are two major explanations for the overrepresentation of blacks in official juvenile statistics: the juvenile justice system discriminates against blacks, or black youths are more delinquent than other youths.

With regard to the involvement of black youths in homicide, gangs and illegal drugs, research has shown that two in every three deaths of black youths between the ages of 15 and 24 years can be attributed to homicide; black gangs in major cities across the United States are a growing concern, primarily because of their level of violence; and drug use is quite common in the inner city. Not only are gangs involved in drug trafficking, but also illegal drug is an integral part of the ghetto environment.

4

Explanatory Approaches to Delinquency

The causes of delinquency have been debated for hundreds of years. Attempts to explain delinquency reflect many different disciplines, including history, biology, psychology, and sociology. The first part of this chapter provides a brief overview of some of the major theories of delinquency causation in biology, psychology, and sociology. The second part discusses explanations as they relate to the delinquency of black youths specifically.

BIOLOGICAL EXPLANATIONS

Biological theories focus on the individual as the unit of analysis. One group of such theories focuses on physical characteristics, such as physical traits and body type, as contributing factors, whereas another group explains crime and delinquency as resulting from genetic traits. Other areas of biological research concern the relationship between biochemical factors and delinquency.

Positivist Theory

One of the leading proponent in the positivistic school was Cesare Lombroso (1911) who depicted criminals as atavistic or "throwbacks" to primitive man. He believed that born criminals suffer from physical anomalies, such as enormous jaws, strong canine teeth, flattened noses, asymmetrical faces, strange nose shape, sloped forehead, and supernumerary teeth (double rows, as in snakes). Lombroso's theory created so much controversy that he was forced to revise it by replacing biological determinism by free will as the main principle for explaining crime and delinquency. His revision also included the suggestion that only about one-third of the criminal population was born atavistic.

His other categories were the epileptic criminal, the criminally insane, criminals of passion, and criminaloids.

Somatatype Theory

William Sheldon (1942) focused on the physique or body type as a predictor of crime and delinquency. He identified three body types, consisting of the endomorph, ectomorph and mesomorph. The endomorph has a soft, round and plump physique, and tends to be relaxed, easygoing, and extraverted. The ectomorph is a tall, lean, fragile, introverted, sensitive individual who is self-conscious and afraid of people. The mesomorph is well built, muscular, aggressive, extraverted, impulsive, and insensitive to pain. Sheldon, comparing samples of "problem" youths with college males, concluded that problem youths tended to be more mesomorphic than college males.

Inheritance/Genetic Theories

Another group of researchers focuses on genetic makeup as the source of crime and delinquency. Studies on twins show a much higher significant relationship between criminal activities among monozygotic (MZ) or identical twins than between dizygotic (DZ) or fraternal twins (Christiansen, 1968, 1977; Ellis, 1982; Mednick & Volavka, 1980; Rowe, 1986; Rowe & Osgood, 1984). These data suggest that monozygotic (MZ) twins have a similar genetic makeup that increases their risk of criminal or delinquency behavior (Shoemaker, 1990). Adoption studies have also shown that the criminal behavior of the *biological* parents of adopted children is more predictive of criminal or delinquent behavior in their children than that of the *adoptive* parents (Mednick, Gabrielli & Hutchings, 1984; Rowe, 1990).

Another genetic factor that has received a great deal of attention since 1965 is the XYY syndrome. The discovery that some violent offenders possess an extra Y chromosome has led some researchers to link crime and delinquency with the XYY genetic defect (Jacobs, Brunton & Melville, 1965). The XYY variation received a great deal of publicity when Richard Speck, who murdered eight nurses in Chicago in 1966, was reported to have this abnormality (though later this turned out to be false). There was so much public concern that XYY males were potential killers that the California Center for Study and Reduction of Violence set up a program in 1972 to screen junior high school boys for the XYY chromosome (Katz & Chambliss, 1991).

Biochemical Factors

One area of research interest concerns the relationship between antisocial behavior and biochemical factors. Researchers have argued that an overabundance of sugar, insufficient supply of vitamins such as Vitamin B_3, B_6, and C, as well as lack of minerals such as sodium, potassium, calcium, zinc, and copper are linked to antisocial behaviors (Krassner, 1986; Schauss, 1980; Schauss & Simonsen, 1979; Schoenthaler & Doraz, 1983). Hormones also are believed to influence antisocial behaviors. Evidence suggests that high levels of the male hormone, testosterone, in certain males can produce aggressive and violent behaviors (Baucom, Besch & Callahan, 1985; Ellis, 1982; Gove, 1985; Schiavi et al., 1984). On the other hand, imbalance in the female hormones that trigger the menstrual cycle can cause premenstrual syndrome (PMS), which is reported to cause antisocial behaviors in some people (Dalton, 1971; Ginsburg & Carter, 1987).

Neurological Studies

Another focus of biological research is the neurological system. Neurological studies suggest that criminals are more likely than noncriminals to exhibit abnormal electroencephalogram (EEG) patterns (Mednick et al., 1981; Shah & Roth, 1974; Williams, 1969). Studies of adults have associated slow and bilateral brain waves with hostile, hypocritical, nonconforming, impulsive, and insane behavior (Volavka, 1987; Zayed, Lewis & Britain, 1969).

PSYCHOLOGICAL EXPLANATIONS

Psychological theories assume that crime and delinquency result from underlying psychological problems. Four major categories are discussed here: psychoanalytic, behaviorist, personality-disorder, and developmental.

Psychoanalytic Theory

Psychoanalytic theory was pioneered by Sigmund Freud (1856-1939) who theorized that individuals progress through five stages of development: the oral, anal, phallic, latency, and genital stages. Freud also proposed that the personality consists of three parts: the id, ego, and superego. The id is the unrestrained, primitive, pleasure-seeking component; the ego develops through the reality of living in the world; and the superego represents the development of the conscience. Psychoanalytic theory asserts that some criminal and delinquent behaviors result from an overdeveloped superego which causes a feeling of guilt and a wish to be punished. Delinquents, on the other hand, are believed to be id-dominated individuals who cannot control their impulsive, pleasure-seeking drives (Abrahamsen, 1944; Halleck, 1977), which leaves the superego underdeveloped (Abrahamsen, 1944, 1960; Friedlander, 1947; Martin, Sechret & Redner, 1981).

Behaviorist/Social Learning Theories

The basic assumption of behaviorist/social learning theories is that criminal and delinquent behaviors are learned. These theories delineate three major types of learning: classical or Pavlovian conditioning; instrumental or operant conditioning; and social learning.

Classical conditioning (Pavlov, 1928) involves a process of learning to respond to a formerly neutral stimulus which has been paired with another stimulus that already elicits a response. Delinquency is a behavior that is learned in the same way.

Operant conditioning (Skinner, 1974) is instrumental learning because the learner must do something to the environment in order to obtain a reward, or in some cases avoid unpleasant situations. It is concerned with the effect that an individual's behavior has on his or her environment and, subsequently, the consequences of that effect for the individual. It involves the use of positive or negative reinforcements (rewards) to increase the probability or frequency of a given response. Youths engage in delinquent behavior because of the positive rewards such behavior can bring.

Social learning theory (Bandura, 1973) assumes that criminal and delinquent behaviors are learned through the same process as conforming behavior. According to Bandura, individuals learn to be delinquent or criminal through direct experience or the imitation of other people's behavior. Their models are the family, peers and the mass media and they also learn from direct experience.

Personality Disorder Theory

Personality disorder theory links criminal and delinquent behaviors to defective personalities. According to Yochelson and Samenow (1976), criminals and delinquents feel a sense of superiority and have inflated self-images. They also propose that criminals are not the victims of society, but rather the victimizers. Hans Eysenck (1964) identified two important dimensions of personality that are associated with criminal behavior: extraversion and neuroticism. Individuals who are extraverts are impulsive, sociable, outgoing while neurotic individuals are anxious, tense, and emotionally unstable. Eysenck and Eysenck (1976) identified a third dimension: psychoticism. A person who exhibits this personality trait is cold, impersonal, hostile, untruthful, strange and lacking sympathy. Another group of researchers view crime and delinquency as the result of an antisocial personality disorder or psychopathy or sociopathy (Abrahamsen, 1960; Cleckley, 1959). The sociopath displays a pattern of aggressive, irresponsible and antisocial behavior. Antisocial personalities are very skillful at manipulating others and usually appear to be charming and carefree when they are first encountered. They have underdeveloped consciences and experience little or no remorse and are incapable of experiencing any truly deep emotion.

Developmental Theory

Some researchers have suggested that early childhood development can lead to delinquency. Such experiences include poor parent-child relationships, parental rejection, irrational discipline, and child abuse (Fareta, 1981; Feldman, 1977; Pemberton & Benady, 1973; Rutter & Quinton, 1988). Children raised in dysfunctional families are at risk of developing some type of personality disorder. Other researchers believe that juveniles are suffering from childhood conduct disorders which produce revengeful, destructive, quarrelsome behaviors. These juveniles are usually hostile, disobedient, aggressive, and impulsive (Stewart et al., 1980).

SOCIOLOGICAL THEORIES

Sociological theories focus on the societal forces that predispose individuals to crime and delinquency. These theories also examine the effect of social change on human behavior and its relationship to delinquency and the interaction between the individual and social institutions. The major sociological perspectives are social structural, social process, and social conflict.

Social Structural Theories

Social structural theories suggest that some individuals are criminal or delinquent because of their lower class background. These theories state that forces such as poverty, slum neighborhoods and high rates of unemployment predispose some individuals to crime and delinquency. Theories with such an approach include strain, subcultural and cultural deviance.

According to *strain theories*, crime and delinquency are epidemic in the lower class because such individuals are economically excluded from society. In this view, crime and delinquency result from the inability of members of the lower class to achieve legitimate social acceptable goals (Blau & Blau 1982; Merton, 1938).

Subcultural theories argue that delinquent subcultures emerge in response to problems that members of the lower class encounter in American society. Marginalization and alienation from conventional society cause members of the lower class to form subcultures (Cloward & Ohlin, 1960; Cohen, 1955).

The *cultural deviance* approach suggests that delinquent behavior is the result of adherence to lower class cultural norms and values that run counter to those of the larger society. These cultural norms and values are passed from one generation to the next and such subcultures exist in specific ecological areas. Sellin (1938) in his culture conflict theory argues that culture conflict between ethnic groups and the larger society is mainly responsible for crime and delinquency. Miller (1958) suggests that delinquency is the product of a united, not a divided, lower class culture. He contends that lower class culture is organized around a female-based household and life patterns and experiences called "focal concerns," which include toughness, trouble, smartness, excitement, fate, and autonomy (Miller, 1958: 5). Those who respond to these "focal concerns," according to Miller, can violate the law through their behavior. Social disorganization theory (Shaw & McKay, 1942) links crime and delinquency to the disorganized urban neighborhood. In such neighborhoods, there are high levels of unemployment, single-parent families, transient residents, and loss of social control. Loss of control encourages the development of street gangs. "Membership in such groups is an important factor in delinquency" (p. 102).

Social Process Theories

Social process theories emphasize that criminality results from the interactions of individuals with organizations, institutions, and processes in society. They focus on the experiences of individuals in families, schools, peer groups and similar social institutions. Three types of social process theories are social control theories, differential association, and labeling theories.

Social control theory suggests that the impulse to be delinquent is present in everyone and that delinquent acts are made possible by the absence of effective beliefs forbidding them. Control theorists start with the question as to why people conform. The answer given is that conformity is the result of social controls placed on individuals by the society. When these controls become weakened or when they break down, deviant behavior may result (Hirschi, 1969; Reckless, 1961).

Sutherland (1939), the pioneer of *differential association theory*, maintains that people commit criminal and delinquent acts through association with significant others, such as peers, who teach them antisocial values, attitudes, definitions, and delinquent patterns. Individuals are more likely to commit criminal or delinquent acts if they are exposed to an excess of definitions favorable to the violation of the law. According to differential association theory, crime and delinquency are learned through a process of communication and in a manner similar to other forms of learning.

Labeling theory focuses on how and why some people come to be defined as deviant. According to this perspective, it is not the nature of the behavior that makes it deviant, but the label placed on that behavior. Labeling theorists argue, that rather than the actions of individuals, it is the reactions of others to those actions that place individuals in a deviant role (Becker, 1963; Lemert, 1951; Tannebaum, 1938).

Social Conflict Theories

Social conflict theories emphasize that criminal law and the criminal justice system are instruments which the wealthy use to control the poor. Proponents of this school of thought believe that the wealthy commit as many crimes as the poor, but use the law and the criminal justice system to punish the poor.

Social conflict theory (Chambliss, 1966; Turk, 1982) suggests that society is composed of different groups and is characterized by conflict among these various groups. The definition of crime arises out of the special interests of groups, such as the wealthy, the police, and religious groups. Laws are created by those in power to protect their rights and interests and to keep the powerless in their place.

Radical theory (Quinney, 1977; Young, 1988a) claims that capitalists create laws to protect their own interests but criminalize working-class behaviors. Radical theorists advocate the overthrow of capitalism, which they believe perpetuates criminal behavior by keeping the oppressed classes under the domination of the capitalist oppressors.

EXPLANATIONS OF DELINQUENCY OF BLACK YOUTHS

These mainstream theories were designed specifically to explain the delinquency of white males, and so, in many cases they may be inappropriate to understanding the delinquency of black youths. The second part of this chapter focuses on attempts to explain their delinquency and proposes a perspective that can be useful for understanding why some black youths resort to delinquent behavior.

Biological Explanations

Biological theories of crime have been used to explain the high rate of crime and delinquency among blacks. One such approach links genetics to black delinquency. Wilson and Herrnstein (1985) implicitly suggest that the higher incidence of crime and delinquency among blacks in the United States may be evidence of biologically inherited propensities. They argue that if one can show a correlation between physical or biological characteristics and crime, then one must assume a causal link. This kind of logic is astounding and thoroughly racist. The argument suggests that because persons with black skin make up a disproportionate number of persons involved in crime and delinquency, then it must be the black skin, which is genetically determined, that must be the cause of crime and delinquency. This argument is illogical.

Low intelligence has also been linked to black delinquency; it is an association that has been embroiled in controversy. Blacks, on an average, score fifteen points lower than whites on intelligence tests. Some scholars have used this difference in intelligence test scores to explain the difference in delinquency rates among black and white youths. Some researchers have contended that intelligence is inherited and, when blacks score lower than whites on intelligence tests, it is solely the result of genetic differences between the two races (Jensen, 1969; Shockley, 1967).

Gordon (1976), focusing on the association between delinquency and intelligence, also suggests that intelligence might account for the differences between black and white rates of delinquency. He points out a similarity between the distribution of intelligence test scores and the distribution of delinquency. Additional support for the association between intelligence and delinquency has been presented by Hirschi and Hindelang (1977), who have reviewed a number of studies on the subject. They assert that intelligence test scores are valid predictors of intelligence and that these predictors are more important than race or social class for predicting delinquency through the effect of school performance. They believe that differences in delinquency between blacks and whites are the result of genetic differences in intelligence or aptitude. Furthermore, Hirschi and Hindelang (1977) suggest that the intelligence tests are not class or racially biased.

Herrnstein and Murray (1994) recently reignited the debate regarding intelligence and race. They argue that the unequal endowment of intellectual ability has created a cognitive elite as well as an underclass. More importantly, they suggest that intelligence levels differ among ethnic groups and that a range of social problems, such as crime, unemployment, and poverty, is related to low intelligence. They state that blacks score lower than whites on every known standardized test of cognitive ability, but they dismiss cultural factors or socioeconomic status as contributing to these differences. Instead, they conclude that differences in test scores between blacks and whites are largely related to genetic differences in intelligence between the two groups, with blacks having lower intelligence.

These research inferences are deeply flawed. Intelligence test scores measure not innate ability, but qualities that are related to class, environment, and culture (Chambliss, 1988; Mercer, 1972; Simmons, 1978). White children in the upper classes are likely to have the academic background that increases their intelligence test scores. This does not prove that they are more intelligent than blacks from low socioeconomic background. Furthermore, intelligence scores may be affected by test-taking ability rather than by intelligence. These tests measure knowledge which is determined by environmental factors such as neighborhood, upbringing, economic conditions, family life and schools (Scarr & Weinberg, 1976; Simmons, 1978; Wilson & Herrnstein, 1985). Finally, contrary to Hirschi and Hindelang's arguments (1977), intelligence tests are culturally and racially biased (Hillard, 1984; Silberman & Yanowitch, 1974). These tests are designed primarily for white middle-class students, and scores on them do not reflect the intelligence or academic ability of black youths. In a dramatic demonstration, a black sociologist devised an intelligence test based on cultural concepts and language of the black ghetto. Black respondents did well on the test, whereas white middle-class students did poorly (Pfohl, 1985).

The use of intelligence tests to attempt to demonstrate the genetic inferiority of blacks is very dangerous. To link the delinquency of blacks with low intelligence can have serious ramifications for young blacks in the way the criminal justice system and society at large treat them.

The Colonial Model

One model that has been used to explain crime and delinquency among blacks is the colonial model. According to this model, blacks residing in urban areas are seen as subjected people, totally dependent on whites for their existence. Like most colonies, the institutions in their neighborhoods such as schools, businesses, and housing are owned, operated, and controlled by persons outside of those communities, thus placing blacks in a subjected position (Marger, 1991). According to this model, the colonized are often excluded from the decision-making process, which in turn can cause alienation and, ultimately, crime and delinquency.

Using this model, several analysts have examined the plight of blacks. Frantz Fanon (1965), a black psychoanalyst and author, posits that violence among blacks is a necessary prerequisite to their attaining independence from their colonial masters. Staples (1974, 1975, 1989) attributed black crime to the fact that the system in United States denies blacks their basic humanity which violates their constitutional rights to equal justice under the law.

Tatum (1994) argues that, although the colonial model is valuable in explaining crime and delinquency among blacks, it has several theoretical and empirical limitations. These limitations include lack of clarity, a failure to address the importance of experiencing one or more aspects of alienation and the class differences among the colonized, and a failure to account for variations in the experiences of other minorities.

Subculture of Violence Perspective

The subculture of violence theory was proposed by Wolfgang and Ferracuti (1967) who maintained that young, lower class black males possess a distinct subculture that emphasizes the use of violence, which accounts for their relatively high rates of violence. According to these researchers, although the members of this subculture share dominant values, they use violence to solve disputes and conflicts. Violence is condoned, legitimized, and considered appropriate for members of this subculture.

Curtis (1975), examining the high levels of violence among blacks, also used the subculture of violence approach. He claimed that the emphasis on manliness in the black community encourages the use of force and violence.

Instead of backing down and looking for alternatives solutions for problems, black males typically resort to force for settling disputes. Other research, however, questions the racially based subculture of violence. Sampson (1987) claims that the same socioeconomic processes explain both black and white violence, thus undermining the subculture of violence hypothesis.

Social Influences and Delinquency

A number of researchers have focused on structural factors as the units of analysis; these include the family, environment, social class and poverty, and racism.

Family

The black family has been considered a key determinant of delinquency. More than half of black youths under the age of 18 live with a single parent, primarily the mother. The family in the inner city tends to be dysfunctional and many researchers consider this kind of family structure to be a contributor to delinquency (Conger, 1976; Hindelang, 1973; Hirschi, 1969; Nye, 1956; Reiss, 1951).

According to Moynihan (1965), "at the heart of the deterioration of the fabric of negro society is the deterioration of the negro family" (p. 51). Implicit in his report is the view that the black family is the source of problems, including delinquency, in the black community. By asserting that the high rates of illegitimacy and female-based households were the major sources of social and economic problems of blacks, he suggested that the black family was pathological.

Sampson (1987) has found that black family disruption is common in the inner city and that the best predictor of homicides and robberies is the percentage of female-based households. Zinsmeister (1990) argues that the family is an important source of violence in the inner city. Dorsey (1991), in his analysis of the overrepresentation of black youths in the juvenile justice system in New Jersey, claims that female-based households have had a direct impact on the propensity of black youth to commit delinquent acts because the members of these families often live in poverty. Cullen (1984) points out that the nonconforming behavior among blacks can be traced to the breakdown in social control caused by the "disorganized" black family.

Gray-Ray and Ray (1990), using data from a study conducted by the Behavioral Research and Evaluation Corporation, address the issue of familial control over both minor and serious delinquency of lower and middle-class black males. They examined family structure, perceived parental rejection, and parental supervision and control, and their findings indicate that only "perceived parental rejection" has a significant effect on black youths' involvement in delinquency. These researchers believe that the lack of correlation between family structure and delinquency in their study was related to the role of the extended family in the black community. They argue that the extended family networks among many blacks act as a factor inhibiting delinquency among youths in female-based households. They also propose that the strong bond between some single mothers and their children should not be overlooked as another inhibiting factor.

Joseph (1995), in her study on African-American youth, has found that family structure is not related to delinquency. Furthermore, her results indicate that "attachment to parents," a variable based on Hirschi's bonding theory, does not correlate with the delinquency of these youths. She concludes that the role of the family structure in the etiology of delinquency among black youths is perhaps overestimated and that the measures used by Hirschi (1969) to determine parental attachments (1969) are of questionable validity in their applicability to black youths.

The issue of family and delinquency is a complex and disputed one. Further research is needed to explore the relationship between the nature of the black family and delinquency. If familial factors alone could explain delinquency among blacks, then one could argue that the delinquency rate should be higher given the fact that over 50% of black youth under the age of 18 live in female-headed households. Many researchers on this issue have ignored the relationship between poverty and female-based households in the black community, even though these two variables are interrelated. For many black families in the inner city, female-based households are indicative of poverty.

Environmental Factors

Urban ecologists (Shaw & McKay, 1942; Thrasher, 1927) maintain that the physical and social environments can promote deviant behavior, such as crime and delinquency.

Approximately 69% of the black population lives in metropolitan areas, with about 56% of that number living in the inner city (Pace, 1993). Such neighborhoods are socially toxic, characterized by high unemployment, poverty, overcrowding, public housing, and physical decay. Also prevalent in these neighborhoods are drug addiction, welfare dependency, single-parent families, and other pathologies. Residents in these neighborhoods are often excluded from the mainstream and are increasingly trapped in a culture of poverty from one generation to the other (Bartollas & Miller, 1994). Rose (1990) and Farley (1980) suggest that the ghetto environments in which many blacks reside are pathogenic for black youth. Overcrowding, social isolation, and social disorganization contribute to feelings of powerlessness, despair, social alienation, crime, and delinquency.

Social Class

In American society, there is a group of individuals, referred to as the underclass, consisting primarily of blacks and Hispanics (Dinitz, 1978). Members of the underclass suffer joblessness, economic deprivation, and poverty and they viewed as economic failures for generations (Lewis, 1966). The existence of this underclass is supported by Duster (1987) who has found among blacks a permanent black teenage underclass whose members lack the basic job skills needed to be part of society. He reports that blacks are over three times as likely to be poor as whites; their median income is only half that of whites, and their net worth is only one-twelfth that of whites. Furthermore, black males are twice as likely to be unemployed as white males. Duster argues that the lack of economic opportunities for blacks has had an influence on their crime and delinquency rates.

Blau and Blau (1982) maintain that lower class people who feel economically deprived because of their class position eventually become resentful and discontent. According to their model, youths growing up in an inner-city area such as New York, Chicago, and Los Angeles will experience status frustration since their neighborhoods are in close proximity to wealthy areas. Relative deprivation is experienced most acutely by black youths, since they suffer consistent racial and economic deprivations that give them lower status than the rest of society. Constant frustration produces pent-up aggression and eventually violence and crime.

Joe (1987) claims that minority black youths are overrepresented in the criminal justice system because they see little or no chance of economic success. Simons and Gray (1989) have found that a moderate relationship exists between perceived occupational opportunity and delinquency among lower class blacks.

When youths are denied legitimate opportunities, the gang and its illegal activities provide one means of achieving financial success for inner city youths who are denied legitimate opportunities. The drug trade has become a profitable economic enterprise for such youths (Brown, 1988; Voight et al., 1994).

Racism

Blacks experienced centuries of discrimination under the system of slavery. Although legal forms of racism have now been abolished, covert, subtle forms of discrimination still exist, and a "more sophisticated, less blatant form of racism accompanies these new forms of discrimination" (Marger, 1991: 257). Racist beliefs are still firmly rooted at the core of the American society.

Racism has no doubt contributed to many of the social ills of the black community, including crime and delinquency. Although other groups, such as Asians and Jews, have also experienced discrimination, it is possible that it has a more profound effect on blacks than on any other group for the simple reason that centuries of racism and discrimination have left a legacy that some blacks are unable to escape.

Williams (1989) contends that the racism faced by young black males sometimes generates rage, which is often unleashed on other blacks in the form of violence. These youths are ceremoniously displayed to the rest of society in the "halls of shame," police stations and the courts, where they are led away to jail, heads down, and arms shackled in full view of camera lights. Poussaint (1983) also posits that racism has created severe frustrations for black males, which engender feelings of aggression and rage. Black-on-black violence, according to Poussaint, reflects the displacement of this rage. Comer (1985) argues that the intraracial nature of black violence is in reaction to blacks' inability to cope with the larger society, and this anger is taken out on their own people.

Class Position versus Racism

One question that has been debated extensively is whether class position or racism contributes to the delinquency and plight of blacks in this country. Banfield (1974) maintains that most of the behaviors, such as crime and delinquency, of urban blacks that are considered racially determined are better explained by their class position.

Most delinquency studies examine class and race factors as independent variables. Elliot and Ageton (1980) found that class and race were unrelated to nonpredatory crimes but related to the more serious crimes against persons. Their data strongly indicated that race and class differences correlate with serious delinquency. However, their analysis failed to examine the combined effects of class and race on delinquency. Until there is some meaningful research on this issue, the debate will continue.

These unidimensional explanations are very limited in explaining delinquency among blacks. Each explanation ignores critical variables in the experiences of these youths. A multifactor explanation would have more heuristic power in helping to understand the delinquent behavior of blacks. The proposed perspective is outlined in the following sections.

Sociohistorical Perspective

The perspective proposed is new not in substance but in its application. The perspective to be utilized combines social control, structural, and historical processes that can explain involvement of black youths in delinquency. This approach provides a more holistic view than other explanations offer.

This sociohistorical perspective forces the analyst to examine society rather than the individual as the unit of analysis. For too long, many professionals have viewed crime and delinquency as a "black problem." Such an approach has resulted in failure to examine external factors that predispose black youths to delinquency. Black youths' historical background is essential to understanding their involvement in delinquency because present-day structural forces have been shaped by the historical past. Historical and structural factors operate jointly rather than independently in explaining the delinquency of black youths.

The freedom to engage in delinquency is the result of weakened bonds to society, and a segment of the black population does indeed have a fragile bond to society. However, these weakened bonds should be interpreted within the context of their historical and present-day experiences in American society.

Two centuries of slavery have had a profound effect on blacks to the point that they continue to be a special group in the socioeconomic hierarchy. The levels of prejudice and discrimination against blacks have been historically severe and persistent. Under slavery, blacks were relegated to the bottom of the social structure. They were denied their basic human rights and were considered property rather than persons. Slavery destroyed the slaves' African heritage and profoundly transformed one of their most important institutions; the family. Under slavery, family members were separated from each other and sold to different slave masters. Furthermore, slave masters either raped, seduced, or used female slaves for their sexual pleasure, thereby producing illegitimate children. This destruction of the black family unit has left a legacy that is still visible today. The black female-based household that exists today has its root in slavery.

Silberman (1978) views violence among blacks as a function of the black experience in this country--an experience that differs from that of other ethnic groups. Silberman argues that blacks have learned to be violent because of their violent treatment during and after the abolition of slavery. He contends that "Black Americans have discovered that fear runs the other way, that whites are intimidated by their very presence; 350 years of festering hatred has come spilling out" (p. 153) in the form of violence.

Because of historical experience and persistent racism, a segment of the black population resides in residentially segregated poor neighbors, and is undereducated, unemployed, and unemployable. According to Glasgow (1980), "these young blacks, some as young as thirteen or fourteen are already earmarked for failure--they are undereducated, jobless, without saleable skills or the social credentials to gain access to the mainstream life" (p. vii). These young blacks are considered obsolete even before they begin to pursue a meaningful role in society.

The historical past and structural factors of poverty, inadequate education, disorganized and deprived environments, unemployment, and other social ills interact to weaken the bonds that some black youths have to society. The underlying factor appears to be the degree of social integration of the black youths in American society. Social integration is determined by person's significant relationships with social institutions. As a youth's intimacy with social institutions declines, the less integrated that youth will be in society (Friday & Hage, 1976). As level of integration in the society decreases, so does the possibility of delinquency. Many black youths are not socially integrated into the American society.

Given the weakened bonds and this lack of integration into the society, the gang becomes very significant to many black youths, providing status, acceptance, respect and prestige that they might otherwise not receive. In fact the gang in the inner city is believed to have taken over the socialization of the youth by replacing the family, the school, the corporation, and government agencies (Voight et al., 1994). As the saliency of gangs increases, so too does the probability of delinquency. In this perspective, the underlying causes of delinquency are the historical and structural factors that predispose black youths to delinquency, with bonding to delinquent peers serving as an important inducement.

SUMMARY

The chapter reviews biological, psychological, and sociological explanations of delinquency. These explanations are unidimensional, however, and are deficient in accounting for this phenomenon. What is needed is a more comprehensive approach to understanding delinquency among black youths. The chapter also presents a perspective that integrates social and historical factors as an alternative to present approaches. The sociohistorical perspective presented provides a more holistic view of delinquency among black youths.

5

Police and Black Youths

The juvenile justice process begins at the point of referral, when a juvenile is brought to the attention of the juvenile justice system. The police officer is usually the first contact that a child has with the system, but parents and others also can refer the youth to the juvenile justice system. This chapter first discusses the role of the police in the juvenile justice system and then focuses on the relationship between blacks and the police.

DEPARTMENT WITH SEPECIALIZED PERSONNEL UNITS

Most large-city police departments have special units to handle juveniles, but in rural areas all police officers tend to deal with juveniles. Departments with specialized services for juveniles usually have trained juvenile officers, a juvenile unit, or juvenile specialists.

The juvenile crime problem has grown so large that many police departments now assign *juvenile officers* to work solely with juvenile crime. These officers come from the ranks of patrol officers, and, in smaller departments, one officer may be given this special assignment. Unfortunately, many officers do not have the specialized training necessary to work with this age group, and they deal with juveniles in much the same way as with adult offenders.

Large departments often hire *juvenile specialists* who may have specialized training in social work, sociology, psychology, public administration, and the administration of justice. They also may understand child development, the nature of juvenile-parent relationships, the problems of adolescence, identity formation, alcoholism and other addictions, and the consequences of living in poverty-stricken conditions.

Juvenile units found in many large cities have the normal crime-fighting tasks of detecting, investigating, and prosecuting offenders for violations from bicycle thefts to serious felonies. They investigate any crimes believed to have been committed by juveniles, as well as complaints of child abuse, victimization or neglect, and they search for runaway youths. The units refer juveniles to appropriate social service agencies in the community, counsel parents and children, and supervise youth activities in the community. They may also monitor juveniles in high-risk crime areas, and develop and run antidelinquency programs.

Police often use discretion handling juvenile cases informally by either giving a warning, releasing juveniles into the custody of their parents, or referring them to a social agency. If any of these diversions are used, then the case is filtered out of the system and proceeds no further. Diversion is used primarily for nonserious acts; youths accused of serious behaviors, such as rape, murder, and robbery, are referred to the juvenile court system by the police.

THE POLICE AND THE LEGAL RIGHTS OF JUVENILES

Until the 1960s, juveniles were not protected by the Constitution because of the rehabilitative nature of the juvenile justice system. It was in that decade that the U.S. Supreme Court began close scrutiny of the procedures used in the juvenile justice system and moved to protect several constitutional rights of delinquents.

Police Searches and Seizures

Although police are given the authority to enforce the law against juveniles, they are subject to some of the same types of legal limitations that apply to adult suspects.

Within the juvenile justice system, police officers have more latitude when arresting a juvenile than with an adult. Many states allow a juvenile to be taken into custody without a search warrant if the officer believes that the juvenile is a delinquent. Most state statutes suggest that taking a "child into custody" constitutes not an arrest but a form of protection for the juvenile (Davis, 1989). While in custody, however, juveniles are accorded certain legal rights.

The Fourth Amendment gives everyone the right to be secure from unreasonable search and seizure, and searches and seizures must be preceded by a warrant. In the case of *Mapp v. Ohio* in 1961, the Supreme Court reaffirmed this right to adults (*Mapp v. Ohio*, 1961). In the 1967 *State v. Lovery* case, the Supreme Court applied the Fourth Amendment protection against unreasonable searches and seizures to juveniles (*State v. Lovery*, 1967). When taken into custody, juveniles must be presented with a valid search warrant unless they waive that right. If this procedure is not followed, under the exclusionary rule, the evidence obtained can be ruled inadmissible in court. In some situations, however, a warrant is not necessary, only probable cause. These include search in conjunction with an arrest, a stop-and-frisk (pat-down of the outer garment), and the suspect's voluntary agreement to be searched. In addition, parents may grant police permission to search the rooms and belongings of their underage children.

One issue regarding search and seizure concerns whether or not school officials have the right to search students or their lockers. In the case of *New Jersey v. T.L.O.*, the Supreme Court ruled that, although students are constitutionally protected from illegal searches and seizures, school officials only need have "reasonable grounds" to search (*New Jersey v. T.L.O.*, 1985). This important case involved a 14 year-old student whose purse was searched by an assistant principal who observed her smoking a cigarette in the lavatory. When a further search was conducted, marijuana and several items indicating marijuana sales were found. T.L.O. was adjudicated a delinquent by the court, which grants this search latitude to officials in recognition that school officials need to preserve a safe and secure environment for students. The decision still left unanswered the question of whether teachers and other school officials can search student lockers and desks.

While in custody, the juvenile is protected under the Fifth Amendment. which states any person charged with a crime is protected against self-incrimination. Thus, a person is not required to answer any questions that can be used against him or her in court. For most of this century, children were not protected by this amendment, for the purpose of the juvenile justice system was to be rehabilitate rather than punish. However in 1966, a landmark case, *Miranda v. Arizona*, placed limitations on police interrogation procedures used with adult offenders (*Miranda v. Arizona*, 1966). The landmark case in a juvenile proceedings regarding this issue was *In re Gault* in 1967. Gerald Gault was 15 years old and on probation when he was taken into custody for making obscene calls to a neighbor. He was picked up at his home while his parents were at work. At the time of the hearings of the charges against Gault, the complainant was not present, no one was sworn in, there were no transcripts or records of the proceedings, and the officer reported that Gerald admitted to the charges. The defendant and his parents were not advised of their right to remain silent or their right to be represented by counsel. At the conclusion of the hearing, the court committed Gerald to a state industrial school until his twenty-first birthday.

Gerald's attorney filed a writ of habeas corpus with the U.S. Supreme Court. The Court overruled the conviction on the grounds that (1) neither Gerald nor his parents were informed of the charges against him; (2) no counsel was offered or provided for Gerald; (3) no witnesses were present, thus denying Gerald's rights of cross examination and confrontation; and (4) no warning of his right to remain silent was given to him (*In re Gault*, 1976). As a consequence of this case, most states have ordered that police advise juveniles that (1) they need not answer any questions; (2) anything they might say may be used against them; (3) they have a right to have an attorney present during interrogation; and (4) if they cannot afford an attorney, one will be provided for them. In effect, they must be informed of their Miranda rights.

One issue regarding interrogation of juveniles is whether juveniles can waive their Miranda rights. Can a juvenile knowingly and intelligently waive his or her Miranda rights? Juveniles can waive their Miranda rights, but the validity of this waiver is determined by the total circumstances of each case. This means that in order for the court to accept the child's waiver, it must determine whether the child knowingly, intelligently and voluntarily waived those rights. To do this, the court will examine such factors as the age of the juvenile; the education of the juvenile, the juvenile's knowledge of charges and the right to remain silent, whether the interrogation took place before or after the charges were placed, the method of the interrogation, and whether the accused refused to give statements on prior occasions. Some states do not require that parents or attorneys be present for juveniles to effectively waive their Miranda rights while others demand that the parents or an attorney be present when a juvenile is questioned by the police (Siegel & Senna, 1994). In the case *Fare v. Michael C*, the Supreme Court examined the totality of the circumstances before rendering a decision. A youth was arrested for suspicion of murder and, after he was read the Miranda caution, he requested to speak to his probation officer. The request was denied, and Michael confessed to the crime and was later convicted. He appealed the conviction on the ground that the police should have allowed him to speak to his probation officer. The Supreme Court found that police were justified in denying the request, because asking for a probation officer was not the equivalent of asking for an attorney. After considering the "totality of the circumstances," the judge argued that the statements by the accused were admissible in court (*Fare v. Michael*, 1979).

Another important issue regards confessions and the use of force. The Supreme Court ruled in *Brown v. Mississippi* that force may not be used to obtain confessions (*Brown v. Mississippi*, 1936). In this case, police used physical force to extract a confession. Other confessions have been ruled invalid because the accused was too tired; was questioned too long; and was not permitted to talk to an attorney while being interrogated or until they confessed (Davis, 1986). One of the most important cases on this issue is *Haley v. Ohio* in which Haley was arrested five days after a robbery and shooting of a store owner. He confessed after five hours of questioning by five or six police officers, with neither parents nor lawyer present. During the questioning, the officers showed him the alleged confessions of two other youths. The Supreme Court ruled that he was questioned too long, that he had no parent or attorney to advise him, and that the officers coerced the confession from the juvenile. The courts have to follow the voluntary standards for confessions in juvenile proceedings, but the "totality of circumstances" under which the confession was obtained has to be examined. This means that procedures and circumstances leading to a confession are considered before determining the legality of that confession (*Haley v. Ohio*, 1948).

The fingerprinting of juveniles is a very controversial issue. The basic criticism is that the juveniles' records will not be destroyed when they are no longer under the jurisdiction of the juvenile justice system. Some states have passed statutes prohibiting the fingerprinting of juveniles without a judge's permission, and many of these states also require that judges control access to the fingerprints and that fingerprints be destroyed after the juvenile reaches an adulthood. The most important case to reach the court is *Davis v. Mississippi* in which the youth in question was detained by the police without authorization by a judicial officer, was interrogated at the time he was first fingerprinted, and then was fingerprinted again at a later date. The Court ruled that the police should not have detained the youth without authorization by the judicial officer; that the youth was unnecessarily fingerprinted the second time; and that the youth should not have been interrogated at the time when he was first fingerprinted (*Davis v. Mississippi*, 1969).

POLICE-COMMUNTIY RELATIONS WITH BLACKS

The relationship between blacks and police is paradoxical, for, while blacks need the protection of the police more than any other group, they often have the greatest resentment toward law officials. The conflict between police and blacks is greatest among young blacks. Although blacks make up 12% of the general population, they accounted for 29% of all arrests of youths under the age of 18 for Index Crimes in 1992 (Federal Bureau of Investigation, 1993). More black youths than whites are also arrested, harassed, and killed by police.

Blacks' Attitudes toward Police

Blacks consistently give lower ratings to police than do whites. In 1993, national surveys on perceptions of police showed that 23% of blacks compared with 11% of whites rated police "high" for honesty and ethical standards. Similarly, 38% of blacks compared with 47% of whites reported confidence in the police's ability to protect them from violent crimes. Fewer blacks than whites believed that police protection in black neighborhoods was equal to that in white neighborhoods: 18% and 40%, respectively (Maguire & Pastore, 1994). In 1992, 11% of blacks and 29% of whites rated the police as "excellent" in not using force; and 9% of blacks compared with 22% whites rated the police as "excellent" for treating people fairly. Forty-five percent of blacks and 33% of whites reported that there is police abuse in their area (Maguire & Flanagan, 1993). Similar responses were obtained from a survey in Philadelphia, which found that only 53% of blacks compared with 87% of whites gave the police a "good" or "excellent" rating (Philadelphia Police Study Task Force, 1987). Waddington and Braddock (1991) found that Asian and white youths viewed police officers as guardians whereas black boys almost exclusively regarded police as "bullies." Their study also revealed that black youths regarded the police's maintenance of order as oppressive and discriminatory, whereas Asian and white youths felt that police have to be tough.

Joseph (1992) reported that 70% of the black youths in her study expressed negative feelings toward the police. Basically, they disliked and distrusted police because of the way the police often treated them. Smith and associates (1991) found in their study that nonwhites, particularly blacks, living in areas that are racially mixed have less favorable views of police than nonwhites.

Werthman and Piliavan (1967) found that black gang members viewed neighborhood streets as their "turf" or home, but the police did not honor this perception. The boys regarded the police as enemies who enforce the laws produced and supported by the white elite. These laws were seen as attempts to suppress minority group members and to perpetuate patterns of discrimination.

A survey sponsored by the Kerner Commission in the 1960s found that, among police officers in thirteen large cities, 31% felt that most blacks regarded the police as enemies and 42% felt that young blacks viewed the police as enemies. The study concluded that white police officers were more likely to project their own prejudices and fears on blacks, viewing them as hostile. Wilson (1973) suggested that police officers may exaggerate the extent of citizen hostility.

Police Harassment

Racial minorities charge that the police single them out for harassment by stopping, questioning, and frisking them. Joseph (1992) reported that 60% of black juveniles claimed that police harassed them. The harassment included stopping and questioning them unnecessarily, taking away their property, such as jewelry, and verbally insulting them by using racial slurs. According to some of these youths, carrying cash was likely to end up in their being harassed if stopped by the police. A few reported that they were taken to the police station simply because they had "lots" of cash on them, whereupon the police assumed that they were dealing drugs. They, therefore, were taken to the police station to explain how they acquired the money. These youths claimed that if they did not provide an "adequate" explanation, the police confiscated their money even though they were never arrested. Others reported that they were stopped, questioned and frisked if they were just "hanging out" at night with their friends.

Boydstun (1975) reported that in a San Diego field interrogation study, 66% of the people stopped for questioning were black and Mexican-American men, despite the fact that they represented only 30% of the population in the areas studied. All of the people stopped were male, and almost two-thirds were juveniles.

Piliavin and Briar (1964) found that African Americans who dress like "tough guys" receive more police surveillance in their neighborhoods. In town, more surveillance leads to more police intervention, questioning, and harassment. The police justify their behavior by saying that certain neighborhoods, such as the inner cities, are hot spots of crime and that males in these neighborhoods are more likely to participate in delinquency. But the young black males view police questioning as unwarranted harassment; they feel they are being picked on unfairly. They react by being uncooperative when the police ask them questions. The police in turn see this attitude as a sign of "badness" and are, therefore, more likely to arrest them. This increase in arrests leads the police to increase surveillance and harassment in the area, and the vicious circle continues.

Several other factors explain the tendency of the police to stop and question racial minority males at a disproportionate rate. Police officers are trained to look for criminal suspects and police tend to stereotype certain groups of people (Skolnick, 1968). It would appear that police officers' experience may lead them to believe that a higher percentage of young black men than young white men engage in crime and delinquency. Consequently, they stop and harass them more often than they do whites.

The police officer's stopping and questioning procedure is justified when there is probable cause. But a stop based on generalized stereotypes about race, with no evidence of probable cause, constitutes harassment and discrimination. Even when stops are based on the police officer's legitimate suspicions, a policy of aggressive field interrogations can contribute to the community's perception of police harassment.

Arrest Practices

Blacks are disproportionately arrested when compared to whites. Black youths constituted 27% of all arrests for juvenile crimes in 1992. That year 49% of youths arrested for violent crimes and 26% of those arrested for property crimes were blacks, although the black population is only 12% of the general population (Federal Bureau of Investigation, 1993). The crucial question which these statistics prompt is whether this is the result of discrimination by the police, a higher rate of participation by blacks in crime, or other extralegal factors.

A common view held by the black community and many researchers is that the decisions made by law enforcement agents are directly influenced by the race of persons and that the police are biased in their actions toward blacks. In this view, the police act more harshly toward black suspects than they do toward white suspects. This argument has been supported by Krisberg and Austin (1978) who have suggested that police decisions reflect community variations, the socioeconomic and racial backgrounds of offenders, and organizational variations in police departments. Goldman (1963) found that the police referred to court 65% of black alleged offenders in Philadelphia but only 34% of white alleged delinquents. In his study, this differential handling of racial groups was complex. Although nearly the same number of blacks and whites were referred to court for serious offenses, blacks apprehended for minor delinquent offenses ended up in juvenile court much more frequently than were their white counterparts. Thornberry (1973) also found that in Philadelphia police sent more blacks to court than whites. Thornberry concluded that "the striking finding is that racial differences are quite apparent even when the influence of the seriousness of the offense is controlled" (p. 94).

Dannefer and Schutt (1982) found that a juvenile's race was the best predictor of police disposition. Fagan and associates (1987) reached a similar conclusion after studying racial disparities in decision making at six points in the juvenile justice process, from apprehension through judicial commitment decisions. They found that, with respect to police decision making, the offender's race was particularly influential when the alleged offense was relatively minor. Bishop and Frazier (1988) found that race has a direct effect on decisions made at several processing junctures in the juvenile justice process. According these researchers, African Americans are more likely to be recommended for formal processing, and being African American increases the probability of formal police action by 11%.

The contrary thesis that the disproportionate arrest rate of black youths reflects these youths' involvement in serious delinquent acts (Black, 1970; Wilbanks, 1987), considers race to be important only because it is incidentally related to seriousness of an offense. Several research studies support the proposition that the high arrest rates of black youths are strongly influenced by the seriousness of the offenses. With regard to the question, Lundman, Sykes, and Clark (1978) examined about 200 police-juvenile encounters that occurred in a large Midwestern city in 1970-1971 and found that blacks were more often involved in felony complaints than were whites. This is a major reason why greater numbers of blacks were being reported to the court. These studies present a picture of police operating in a relatively legalistic fashion, rather than in terms of prejudices and biases, because they seemed to be more impressed by the nature and seriousness of offenses than by any other factors.

Studies show that the suspect's demeanor determines whether a police officer will make an arrest. Piliavan and Briar (1964) noted that police frequently stopped black youths who are given relatively severe dispositions because they often showed a hostile demeanor toward the police. They stressed, however, that the police concentrated much of their attention on urban ghettos, where they indiscriminately harassed citizens. In turn, black youths responded to the police with hostility or indifference, earning a large number of them a court referral. The high arrest and referral rate for black youths was then taken by the police as evidence in support of the stereotype that most young blacks are potential criminals.

Werthman and Piliavan (1967) claimed that delinquent boys in urban ghettos employed a number of stratagems to avoid contact with the police. For example, they dispersed into smaller units when the police approached, positioned themselves near girls, wore their club jackets inside-out to hide identifying marks, or wore wedding rings so that the police would assume they were married. However, these tactics often failed, so that even these youngsters were drawn into encounters with the police. When they did interact with the police, the juveniles were prone to display hostility and scorn toward the officers, owing to their perspectives on the role of law enforcement in furthering discrimination. This interaction produced high rates of arrest and court referral.

The complainant's race also determines whether or not police will arrest a juvenile. Smith and associates (1984) found that police were more responsive to white victims who complained about black suspects, particularly for property crimes. In an analysis of the Police Services Study, data indicated that the police were more likely to comply with the wishes of white victims complaining against black suspects than with those of black victims complaining against black suspects, particularly in property crimes (Baldus, Pulaski & Woodworth, 1983). However, black complainants requested arrests more often than white complainants and, since in most incidents victims or complainant are the same race as the suspect, more blacks were arrested (Friedrich, 1979). Lundman and associates (1978) argue that black complainants are more likely than white complainants to request the police to arrest the suspect. The police had more contacts with black juveniles in which the complainant is often black. Furthermore, black officers tend to arrest black suspects slightly more than white officers because of the greater responsiveness of black officers to the requests of black complainants (Black, 1980).

The above data are based on from police records and show that the offenders' demographic characteristics are related to police dispositions, since the seriousness of the offense is correlated with background characteristics. Black youths are believed to commit the most harmful and costly acts of lawbreaking. At the same time, some investigations have indicated that the police arrest black youngsters more often than their white counterparts. These discrepant findings likely reflect real differences in police enforcement practices. In some communities with a relatively small black population, race may not be an important factor in police behavior, whereas in larger communities with a large black population race may become significant. In short, selective enforcement in some communities may account for the discrepancy in the studies of arrests of black youths.

The studies discussed in this chapter also appear to indicate that in some communities the police are sensitive to the racial background of offenders, while in others race does not enter into police decisions concerning juvenile lawbreakers. According to some of these studies, police focus on the seriousness of the offense, the demeanor of the suspects, the race of the complainant, and to a lesser extent the racial characteristics of offenders (Bishop & Frazier, 1988; Black & Reiss, 1970; Dannefer & Schutt, 1982; Fagan, Slaughter & Hartstane, 1987; Lundman, Sykes & Clark, 1978; Piliavin & Briar, 1964). In short, it appears with regard to arrest, police respond in a legalistic fashion to black suspects with regard to arrest. There is little evidence that individual police officers operate primarily in terms of blatant racist sentiments or that their actions can be explained principally in those terms. According to Griswold (1978), the evidence tends to show that police do not discriminate against minorities and that factors other than race weigh most heavily in the police decision-making process.

Police Use of Force

Police officers are expected to use reasonable force before, during and after arrests. Although they are given legal authority to use coercive force, including deadly force, the law limits the use of force is limited by law and, when it is employed, it has to be within the guidelines of the law.

In the last decade, the police use of physical force under questionable circumstances has become an important area of tension between police and the black community concerns . Accusations of police brutality, or excessive use of physical force, are among the most frequent issues in police-community relations. In most cities, complaints about excessive use of force comprise the largest number of complaints filed by citizens (Walker, 1992).

The nation looked on in disgust when a videotape was aired on network television in 1991 showing some members of the Los Angeles Police Department beating, kicking, and using electronic stun guns on Rodney King. The police officers were charged but were later acquitted of the abuse. This acquittal ignited several nights of riots, looting, and attacks by some black youths on innocent individuals. The federal government later indicted the officers who had been acquitted in criminal court, and two of them were found guilty and are now serving time in prison. In 1989, a police officer from Long Beach, California, pulled a black police officer from a neighboring town from his car, verbally assaulted him, pushed his head through a glass window and pounded him on the trunk of his car for refusing to answer "properly." These police officers were not aware that this was another officer and that he was accompanied by an NBC camera crew. This evidence of police brutality was captured on camera and was later shown on television. These two publicized incidents highlight the tension and poor community relations that exist between blacks and the police.

Fyfe's (1988) study of police. violence in Metro-Dade County, Florida, found that in nonarrest traffic stops, white officers were twice as likely to use force against black motorists as against white or Hispanic motorists. At the same time, black officers were twice as likely to use force against white and Hispanic motorists as against black drivers. These data suggest complex patterns of action and reaction between police officers and citizens based on race. Reiss (1971) also found that white and black officers were most likely to use force against members of their own race.

Nearly all the studies report that police shoot at more blacks than whites. Here is a sample of the findings:

1. Chicago police shot at blacks 3.8 times more than at whites during the 1970s.
2. New York City police officers shot at blacks 6 times more than at whites during the 1970s.
3. St. Louis police shot at blacks 7.7 times more than at whites during the 1987 and 1991.
4. Memphis police officers fatally shot at blacks 5.1 more times than they did whites from 1969 to 1974; 2.6 times more from 1980 to 1984; and 1.6 times more from 1985 to 1989. For property crimes, Memphis police officers were 9.4 times more likely to shoot at blacks than whites from 1969 to 1974; 13 times more from 1980 to 1984; and were the only property crime suspects shot at from 1985 to 1989 (Geller & Scott, 1992).

Historically, the common-law fleeing felon doctrine has governed the use of deadly force. Under the doctrine, police officers can, if necessary, use deadly force to apprehend any fleeing felony suspect. However, in the case of *Tennessee v. Garner* (1985), the Supreme Court ruled that the use of deadly force against unarmed and nondangerous felon suspects is an illegal seizure of their person under the Fourth Amendment. Edward Garner, a 15-year-old black youth, was allegedly trying to break and enter into a house. The police were called, and on arrival, they pursued the youth, who then tried to jumped over a chain-link fence. The police shouted for him to shop, but the suspect began to climb the fence. Convinced that the suspect would get away, one officer shot him. The bullet struck the suspect in the back of his head, and he later died in the hospital. The police were acting in accordance with Tennessee law and Memphis Police Department policy. In a 6 to 3 decision, the Supreme Court ruled that the Constitution prohibits a peace officer from using deadly force against a fleeing suspect who is neither armed nor dangerous. The Supreme Court stated that police can use deadly force only when (1) it is necessary to prevent the suspect's escape, and (2) the suspect poses a threat of death to the officers or to others (*Tennessee v. Garner*, 471 U.S. 1, 1985). The Supreme court ruling effectively ban all police policy that allowed police to use deadly force against unarmed or nondangerous offenders.

The use of deadly force has been the source of one of the most bitter complaints by minorities, especially blacks. Takagi (1974) stated that police have one trigger finger for whites and another for blacks, suggesting that police deliberately kill blacks. The typical victim of the police's use of deadly force is the young black male (Fyfe, 1978).

Fyfe (1982) in a review of data from 1969 to 1974 in Memphis concluded that police did differentiate racially with their trigger fingers by shooting blacks in circumstances that were less threatening than those in which they shot whites. According to Fyfe, blacks who are unarmed and in a nonassaultive situation are 18 times more likely to be killed in police shootings than whites.

A national review of citizens killed by police from 1965 through 1969 found that 42% were black (Kobler, 1975). In Miami, a study of citizens killed by police between 1956 and 1983 revealed that the majority of the victims were black (*Miami Herald*, 1983). Estimates of the ratio of blacks to whites shot and killed by the police range from a high of 15 to 1 to a low 3 to 1. In one of the first studies of police shootings, Robin (1963) found that, between 1950 and 1960, Chicago police shot and killed blacks at a rate of 16.1 per 100,000, compared with 2.1 whites per 100,000 (for a ratio of 7.4 to 1). In Boston the police shot and killed blacks eight times more often than whites (3.2 per 100,000 blacks compared with 0.4 per 100,000 whites).

Several individual incidents of police use of deadly force against blacks are as follows:

ITTA BENA, MISSISSIPPI--SEPTEMBER 1989: After a high school football game, two black youths got into an argument with a group of whites. After being told of the incident, the police dragged them off the bus, took them to the police station where they were severely beaten and tortured. After hitting and kicking them, police used an electric cattle prod which they placed on their genitals.

CHICAGO, ILLINOIS--AUGUST 1989: Two black teenagers were picked up by white police officers after a White Sox game. The boys who were driven around by the officers were racially insulted, and then physically assaulted before being dropped off in a notoriously racist neighborhood near a white gang. The boys were chased by the gang and one of the youths was beaten unconscious.

TEANECK, NEW JERSEY--APRIL 1990: A sixteen-year-old black youth was shot to death by a white policeman. Two officers responded to a 911 call concerning a youth holding a gun in a school yard. When police arrived on the scene and attempted to search him, the teenager suddenly bolted by running down a driveway behind the school and hopping a hedge, shouting, putting his arms up and saying "Don't shoot." One of the policemen, nevertheless, shot him in the back. This touched off a night of violence in the predominantly black section of Teaneck (Kifner, 1990).

Why do police use deadly force on blacks? Goldkamp (1976) offers two possibilities. One is that a disproportionate number of minority (blacks) shot and killed by police can be explained by selective enforcement and irresponsible use of deadly force. Second, blacks are shot and killed more often because minorities are disproportionately involved in violent crimes and are more likely to carry guns. There is some evidence in support of this claim.

On the one hand, Milton and associates (1977) found that 70% of the people shot by police in seven cities were black, although blacks made up only 39% of the population. Jenkins and Faison (1974) analyzed data on 248 persons killed over a three-year period by New York City policemen found that majority of victims were black. On the other hand, Fyfe's study (1981a) of shootings in New York showed that in many such incidents police officers themselves were killed or wounded. He also found that more minorities more than whites were likely to be involved in incidents in which guns were used.

According to Griswold (1978), the evidence tends to show that police do not discriminate against minorities and that factors other than race weigh most heavily in the police decision-making process. Empey (1982), as well as Krisberg and Austin (1978), however, argue that, although individual police officers probably do not behave in a blatantly racist way toward black suspects, racism may nonetheless be reflected in police actions. Long-standing patterns of racism, which are endemic in American society, operate as a major cause of much delinquency that occurs among black youths, particularly those in inner-city neighborhoods. Moreover, police agencies and the juvenile court often concentrate on poor and minority populations, because these groups are thought to be particularly prone to criminality. The thrust of these observations is that societal forms of racism may play an important factor in police responses to juveniles who are from different racial backgrounds. Racism may, therefore, be responsible for overenforcement of the law in black neighborhoods.

Police Relationship and Other Minority Youths

This section briefly examines police relationships with Asians/Pacific Islanders, American Indians, and Latinos/Hispanics.

The Asians/Pacific Islander designation comprises at least thirty-two distinct ethnic and cultural groups, including Chinese, Japanese, Fijians, Bangladesh, East Asians, South Indians and Malaysians. In 1992, Asian/Pacific Islanders constituted only 2% of juveniles arrested for offenses. They made up 1.2% of all violent crimes and 1.8% for all property crimes (Federal Bureau of Investigation, 1993).

Asians/Pacific Islander conflicts with police have been intensified in recent years by the arrival of new Asians such as the Vietnamese, Laotians, and Cambodians (National Minority Advisory Council on Criminal Justice, 1982). Asians/Pacific Islanders are likely to receive differential treatment by police officers because of their cultural and ethnic backgrounds. Accordingly, they have been subjected to police misconduct and harassment, and a few cases have been reported to the U.S. Commission on Civil Rights (Shusta et al., 1995). Asians/Pacific Islanders are reluctant to report crimes, either because they do not trust the police or they are not knowledgeable about the criminal justice system. Furthermore, many of these groups prefer to resolve their problems in their communities and they do not like to cooperate with police for fear of retaliation from members of their own communities (Shusta et al., 1995. Since there are few Asian/Pacific police officers, law enforcement officers experience difficulties in communicating with this group especially because of differences in language and cultural practises.

In 1992, American Indians constituted only 1% of all juveniles arrested--1% of for violent crimes and 1.1% for property crimes (Federal Bureau of Investigation, 1993). Police officers are in an unusual situation vis-à-vis enforcing the law against American Indians. In the case of Indian reservations, the police may or may not have any jurisdiction, since many Native American tribes deal with crime and punishment under tribal laws.

Not surprisingly Native Americans, who historically have had bad relationship with whites, have a general distrust of police. They view police officers as representatives of the white establishment. For their part, many police officers view American Indians with suspicion and are likely to harass them because of stereotypes of Native Americans (Shusta et al., 1995). Native Americans living near or on reservations have long complained about police abuse and discriminatory treatment and have often reported being stopped for no reason and harassed (Flowers, 1990).

Latinos/Hispanics consist of over twenty-five different ethnic and cultural groups from Central and South America and the Caribbean. Because of their past experiences with police officers in their native countries, some Latinos/Hispanics are reluctant to report crimes to the police. As far back as 1931, a government report concluded that Mexican Americans were subjected to police abuse (Flowers, 1990). In areas such as Los Angeles, with large numbers of Latino/Hispanic Americans, serious conflicts with the police have been reported (National Minority Advisory Council on Criminal Justice, 1982). Latinos/Hispanics are also subjected to police violence. Fyfe (1978) stated that "blacks and Hispanics are everywhere overrepresented among those on the other side of police guns" (p. 29). Very little has changed since then: Latino/Hispanics are still victims of police abuse. For example in August 1990, Chicago police beat a Latino man and threw him down the stairs because he refused to leave his window while another man was being roughed up. In 1989, the San Bernardino police were filmed as they attacked five Latinos while responding to a noise complaint (Brook, 1991).

Although these groups are likely to be subjected to police abuse, blacks appear to be the major target this abuse (Flowers, 1990). Blacks have had a very long history of police conflict which peaked in the mid-1960s when a number of cities erupted in violence (Levin & McDevitt, 1993).

Dealing with Police Abuse

Many studies have shown that, in some cases, police officers deliberately and maliciously use force, false arrest, and harassment against blacks but are rarely criminally prosecuted and, when they are brought to justice, many are acquitted. Often, the incidents occur without any witnesses, and the investigating officer or even the courts are more inclined to believe the police officer than the suspect. Even in the presence of tangible evidence, such as medical records or a visual images of police brutality, as in the Rodney King case, police officers accused of brutality may still be acquitted. A 1987 survey showed that Detroit had a rate of 115 per 1,000 complaints for police abuse, but the substantiated rate was only 7.2 per 1,000. Dallas had a substantiated rate of 10 per 1,000, whereas Houston had 12.7 (*Crime Control Digest*, 1989).

One legal remedy available to persons who believe they were victims of police misconduct is to file lawsuits for civil damages under state or federal law. A number of successful suits against police have been filed over the years. Between 1986 and 1990, the city of Los Angeles awarded $20 million to successful plaintiffs in police-misconduct suits (Skolnick & Fyfe, 1993). The city of Detroit paid a total of $14 million in damages for police misconduct between 1975 and 1980 (Paulsen, 1991). Detriot also paid out $20 million in 1990 alone (Skolnick & Fyfe, 1993). Damage suits compensate the victims, but they are expensive and time consuming. Moreover, for many black citizens, the legal system appears unfriendly or even threatening. Filing a civil suit may beyond their financial capability. In addition, many abused victims do not understand their right to bring litigation against police officers and their departments.

Prior to 1958, the power to investigate police abuse was vested in police departments, in the form of internal reviews. But during the late 1950s and 1960s, this policy came under fire when the United States Commission on Civil Rights found that many blacks felt powerless to do anything about police abuse. These revelations were later confirmed by a number of studies conducted by the American Civil Liberties Union (ACLU), the National Association for the Advancement of Colored People (NAACP), and the University of California, which pointed to a range of dissatisfactions with internal police review (Mendelsohn, 1971). Consequently, police departments were urged to shift investigative responsibility for complaints to citizen-controlled boards; this would provide citizens, including blacks, an avenue of redress against police abuse. Most police departments have long resisted citizen intrusion into their work, and it is not surprising that many of their organizations, such International Association of Chiefs of Police, International Conference of Police Association, the Fraternal Order of Police have fought bitterly against civilian review boards. The popularity of civilian review boards increased in the mid-1980s and by 1993, 33 of the nation's largest 50 cities, including Philadelphia, Washington, and New York City, had established review boards (Newman, 1993).

Improving Community Relations

• To do their jobs, police officers need public as well as good relationships with the community that they serve. Improving community relations has become an important goal of many major police departments across the country. Police departments have tried to improve community relations with blacks by hiring more black police officers, providing cultural diversity training for police officers and changing to community policing.

Black Police Officers

Historically, police departments recruited very few police officers from the black community, despite the large black and other minority population in urban areas are. The effort to recruit more minority police officers started in the late 1960s after the urban riots. The Equal Employment Opportunity of 1972 and affirmative action policies were designed to increase the employment of both minorities and women, who traditionally had experienced tremendous discrimination in employment.

Efforts to recruit blacks or other minority officers have not been very successful, either because departments have not been aggressive in their search, because young blacks have a negative view of law enforcement, or because minorities fail to meet the educational requirements of police work (Cole, 1992). Although Walker (1989) found substantial progress over the five-year period 1983-1988, many police departments are still underrepresented by black and Hispanic police officers. For example, in New York City, the police departments lag in their recruitment of black officers. Blacks comprised 29% of the population in the city, but only 11.6% of the police officers are black. In addition, of the elite corps of 115 captains, not one was black by the end of April 1994. Moreover, in the last decade, the number of black officers has declined in New York City (Kilborn, 1994). Similarly, in Washington and in Atlanta, both of which have black with black populations of about 70%, only 40% of officers in Washington and 56% in Atlanta are black (Cole, 1992). Detroit is one of the few cities in with a representative number of blacks on the police force: the black population is 53.3%, while the number of black police officers constitutes 75.7%. Overall 12% of the police officers throughout the nation are black (Carter, Sapp & Stephens, 1989). Affirmative action appears to have been only moderately successful so far in hiring black officers. It is hoped, however, that recruitment of black officers will continue, especially in cities with a high concentration of blacks.

Some black officers face great difficulties in becoming integrated into existing police systems. Some white officers resent the affirmative action policies, and the result has been friction between some black and white officers. Consequently, black officers have formed their own separate organizations such as the Afro-American Patrolman's League (AAPL) of Chicago, the Afro-American Police (AAP) of New York, National Organization of Black Law Enforcement Executives (NOBLE), and the black Guardians of Bridgeport, Connecticut (Cole, 1992). These organizations provide black police officers with support, cultural pride and a network of persons with similar interests, concerns, and background. More importantly, their memberships "provide emotional sanctuary from stereotypes, hostility, indifference, ignorance or naivete that members encounter within their organization and communities" (Shusta et al., 1995, p. 41).

Within police departments, black officers also experience difficulties in obtaining promotions. The glass ceiling, which is an imaginary barrier that inhibits certain individuals from moving beyond the rank of entry-level positions, has not been broken, and promotional opportunities in law enforcement are still reserved for white males only. This situation creates resentment, disenchantment, frustration, early burnout and resignation (Shusta et al., 1995).

The major argument for hiring more black officers has been that black officer will have a better rapport with the black community. Rossi and associates (1974) found that black officers had more positive attitudes toward the residents in their assigned black districts. However, not all black officers make good "crime fighters" for the black community because not all minority officers have the skills to work with their own cultural or racial group. In addition, not all police officers of the same background as the citizens will be sensitive to their needs (Shusta et al., 1995). Fyfe (1981b), found that when the place of assignment was controlled, black and white officers used deadly force at the same rate. Hampton (1992) also reported that a new black recruit wanted to work in black areas, because he could tell his own people what to do and could not do. This recruit also referred to people from his neighborhood as "maggots." There is little research on the effect of increased employment of black police officers on the attitudes of blacks in their communities (Shusta et al., 1995). Nevertheless, the importance of employing more black police officers for black neighborhoods cannot be overemphasized.

Cultural Diversity Training

Cultural diversity training is designed to create an understanding of different cultural groups. Such training be given to law enforcement officers if they are to function effectively in this multicultural society. The Police Foundation's 1989 study on police training and concluded that courses in cultural diversity can reduce the possibility of potential violent confrontations for officers (Shusta et al., 1995). Most police programs have added a cultural awareness or race-relations segment to their curricula (Shusta et al., 1995); this training has shown to have positive effects on police attitudes. In the San Francisco Police Department, for example, community race-relations training resulted in more positive attitudes toward black residents. Unfortunately, this program has been terminated (Eisenberg et al., 1973). Similarly, an experiment conducted by Metro-Dade County found that officers who included intercultural awareness in their training were better equipped to handle violent encounters than those who lacked this training (Torres, 1989).

Cultural Diversity training for police in many big-city departments is inadequate; much of it, in fact, seems to occur as a quick fix after an incident or a crisis (Weaver, 1992). Instead, this training must be an ongoing process designed to help police officers develop an understanding and an awareness of blacks and other racial groups.

Community Policing

A community relations approach is one way to foster better relationships between police and black residents. Community policing is based on the premise that it not only acts as a deterrent for crimes, but it also gives police a chance to become acquainted with the community.

Police departments have set up police-community relations units, which assign foot patrols to a particular neighborhood. Police get out of the patrol cars and into the streets where they can get to know the public. Hundreds of cities have implemented this program over the last few years with good results in areas such as Newark, Houston, and New York City (*Newsweek*, 1992; Police Foundation, 1981).

Police are also encouraged to work with citizen groups to create a "neighborhood watch" so that the public can develop trust in the police. In addition, innovative programs have been designed to foster community police initiatives and implement drug-reduction efforts at the juvenile and adult levels (Wilson, 1990).

Police-community relations programs have been criticized for their "Band-Aid" approach to serious social problems because they do not attack the sources of the problems. It is also difficult to measure their effectiveness (Clark, 1994). The 1994 crime bill will provide monies to put 100,000 more police officers on the streets (Reno, 1995).

SUMMARY

Data have shown that black youths are disproportionately arrested in comparison to their white counterparts. Studies also show that the decision to arrest is influenced by a number of factors: the seriousness of the crime, the preference of the complainant, the nature of the relationship between victim and suspect, the demeanor of the suspect, and the characteristics of the neighborhood. Some of these factors become confounded with the race of the suspect. Even when these other factors are controlled, there appears to be a pattern of higher arrest rates for blacks, based on discrimination.

The available data also show that black youths are disproportionately physically assaulted or even killed by police. Too many black youths are victimized by law enforcement officers, and this abuse happens far too often, in too many cities, on a daily basis. Police seem to reflect the racism that exists in the society. Programs implemented to improve the relationship between blacks and the police appear to have been limited and not always effective. What is needed is a radical change in the approach to policing the black community. Police need to engage in more race-relations training and cultural sensitivity training before and during their tenure on the force.

6

Black Youths and Juvenile Court

Once a youth is taken into custody, he or she will likely be referred to juvenile court. The court process includes a series of decision points. This chapter examines the critical decision points in the juvenile court process: detention, intake, adjudication and disposition. The effects of the court process on black youths are also discussed.

In 1899, the Illinois Juvenile Court Act created the first juvenile court to handle children who committed offenses. It was based on the premise that the parens patriae doctrine gave the court the right to act in the child's best interest. Because the court's purpose was to rehabilitate rather than punish juveniles, to achieve such a goal, the court employed psychiatrists, psychologists, and social workers to work with delinquents. The juvenile court judges were to assume the "parental" role in a nonthreatening atmosphere in which hearings were to be conducted in an informal, nonadversarial, and nonlegalist manner.

From its inception, the juvenile court system denied children procedural rights granted to adults in the criminal justice system since its operations were based on the goals of rehabilitation and protection of juveniles. As a consequence, conditions had become so oppressive that, in the early 1960s, the U.S. Supreme Court expressed a deep concern about the rights of juveniles and encouraged litigation to extend due process rights to juvenile offenders. Since then, the Court has mandated constitutional rights at virtually every level of the juvenile justice system.

ORGANIZATION OF COURTS

The jurisdiction of the juvenile court is defined by state constitutional amendments or state legislation. Juvenile courts have jurisdiction over a juvenile under the age of majority who commits an offense or is neglected, abused, or dependent. As discussed earlier, the states differ as to the upper age limit for the juvenile court jurisdiction. Some states such as New York, North Carolina, and Connecticut have established the juvenile age as under 16 years. Others, including Georgia, Illinois, and Texas have set the upper age as under 17 years. The most common age, 18 years, is found in New Jersey, Alaska, Indiana, Utah, and the federal districts.

Also as noted earlier, juvenile courts are concerned with rehabilitation and treatment. The court procedure is informal, private, and nonadversarial and also functions as a surrogate parent. It has the legal power to transfer a violent or habitual delinquent to an adult court, to place a child in a foster home, and to transfer a child to a social agency or a special facility for the purpose of treatment.

The juvenile court's structure varies from state to state. In states such as Utah and Wyoming, there are autonomous juvenile courts that are separate from the adult court, and the judges spend all their time in such courts. New York, New Jersey, and Delaware have coordinated juvenile courts wherein the proceedings occur within the family or domestic courts.

There are also designated courts, found in North Carolina, for example, in which the same judges preside over criminal, civil and juvenile matters.

DETENTION

Juvenile detention is basically equivalent to adult jail and is variously referred to as detention, shelter and detention center. Detention is a temporary facility designed to hold delinquents who are awaiting adjudication, or transfer to another facility, or considered a risk to society. Detention workers or probation officers usually make the initial detention decision. Normally, a detention hearing is held within a reasonable time and in order to formalize the detention decision. In 1991, a total of 18,511 youths were detained (Maguire & Pastore, 1994).

An important question regarding detention is the issue of preventive detention, which is often used for repeat, chronic, and violent offenders. In 1984, the *Schall v. Martin* decision of the United States Supreme Court resulted in a change in detention practices. Gregory Martin, a 14-year old, was arrested in New York City in 1977 on charges of robbery, assault and possession of an illegal weapon. He was arrested at 11:30 p.m. He lied about his residence, and so he was kept overnight in detention. When he appeared in family court the following day, the judge ordered him detained before trial, citing his possession of an illegal weapon, the lie about his residence, and the apparent lack of family supervision. Martin's attorneys filed a habeas corpus petition, demanding his release from custody and claiming that his detention denied him his due process rights under the Fifth and Fourteenth amendments. This was an action suit on behalf of all youths subjected to preventive detention in New York. In this case, the Supreme Court ruled that a juvenile can be held in preventive detention if there is adequate concern that the juvenile may commit additional crimes while the case is pending further court action (*Schall v. Martin*, 1984). In other words, the court can deny a youth pretrial release if he or she is perceived to be "dangerous."

Preventive detention raises several questions. First, crime cannot be accurately predicted because one cannot tell in advance whether a juvenile is going to commit another offense, after release. A youth may be considered high risk but may not commit another offense if released; this is an example of a "false-positive" problem. The converse of this is the "false-negative" problem in which a juvenile, considered to be safe, actually commits another offense after being released. Second, the detainee can view preventive detention as punitive, regardless of the stated purpose of the practice. Finally, this practice may become discriminatory in that some youths, especially minority youths, may be detained unnecessarily.

Many juveniles are detained in adult jails, especially in states where no other facility exists or where detention centers are overcrowded. Many jails are in deplorable physical condition, with inadequate plumbing, poor ventilation, and deteriorating buildings, and, in addition, many are fire hazards. Because of the rapid turnover in jails, rehabilitative and recreational programs are often nonexistent.

In 1989, the Juvenile Justice and Delinquency Prevention Act (JJDPA) of 1974 was amended to require states to remove all juveniles from adult jails and lockups. The federal government threatened to take away juvenile justice funds if states did not comply. In 1983, the daily average population of juveniles in adult jails was 1,760, but by 1992, this had risen to 2,527 (Maguire & Pastore, 1994). It is quite clear that a significant number of juveniles are still held in adult jails. In the case of *Hendrickson v. Griggs*, the Court found that Iowa had not complied with the removal of juveniles from jail and ordered local officials to develop a plan to comply with the law (*Henderickson v. Griggs*, 1987). California passed legislation stating that no juvenile can be incarcerated in any jail after July 1, 1989 (Steinhart, 1988). It is anticipated that the federal government will exert increased pressure in the future from the federal government to remove juveniles from jails.

Black youths are detained more often than white youths. For example, in New Jersey in 1992, 65.2% of those detained were blacks (Juvenile Delinquency Commission, 1993). Similarly, in California, African-American juveniles are detained at consistently higher rates than any other racial or ethnic group of juveniles (Austin, Dimas & Steinhart, 1992). Data for Florida show that in 1989-1990, black male juveniles accounted for 57% of all males detained and black females accounted for 42% of all female cases detained (Tollett & Close, 1991). Johnson and Secret (1990) analyzed juvenile statistics for the years 1982-1987 on the juvenile court process in the state of Nebraska and found that blacks were significantly more likely than whites to be detained. In 1991, national official data indicated that 43% of juveniles in detention were white and 40% were black (Maguire & Pastore, 1994). The Hubert Humphrey Institute of Public Affairs (1986) found that minority youths are placed in secure detention facilities at a rate three to four times higher than that of white youths. Klein (1990) found that black youths constituted 50% of all youths detained in Delaware in 1989.

The proportion of black youths detained has increased tremendously over the years. Schwartz and associates (1987) reported that the proportion of black youths detained since the mid 1970s has increased significantly. Britts and Sickmund (1991) reported that the use of detention in cases involving minority (black and Hispanic) youths in 1989 increased 28% compared with 19% for white youths. Given that more black youths are disproportionately detained, the question is whether there is racial discrimination in detention decisions. The results are inconsistent and inconclusive. Some data show that race is not a factor. Frazier and Bishop (1985) found that neither legal variables nor sociodemographic characteristics had much impact on detention and that the detention decisions were based on judicial discretion.

Other researchers suggest that detention decisions are biased against minority youngsters. According to Schwartz and associates (1987), blacks and Hispanic constituted over 50% of youths detained nationally, and this proportion represented a significant increase since the mid-1970s. Furthermore, these researchers have suggested that the increase was the result of discrimination rather than greater involvement of minority youths in serious offenses. In a national study of 2,500 youths, the findings showed that African Americans were likely to be detained even if they lived with both parents, but whites were subjected to detention only when they resided with one parent (Synder, 1990). Thus, race appears to have a substantial effect on detention decisions, with black juveniles more likely to be detained than whites.

INTAKE

The second major decision point in the court process is the intake and the main purpose is to determine whether juveniles accused of law violation should be diverted from the juvenile court. Intake officers are usually juvenile probation officers who are sometimes trained as social workers. They receive most of their referrals from police officers, but school personnel and parents also make such referrals.

During this process, an officer reviews the case to determine whether the alleged facts are sufficient to cause a juvenile court to take jurisdiction or whether some other action would be in the best interest of the child. Several options are available to intake officers. If the referral lacks sufficient evidence or if the juvenile has committed only one minor offense, the intake officer can recommend an informal disposition which includes case dismissal, informal adjustment, informal probation, and consent decrees. Complaints are dismissed if the intake officer determines that the alleged violation is not within the jurisdiction of the juvenile court. Informal adjustment involves a decision to close the case after the juvenile is warned or has met certain conditions, such as paying restitution, attending treatment programs, or by the parents' agreement to improve supervision. Informal probation generally involves a period of informal supervision during which the juvenile is required to fulfill certain conditions, such as attending school or obeying parents. Consent decrees are intermediate steps between informal supervision and formal disposition. Decrees are used to place the child under the jurisdiction of the court without finding that the child is delinquent. It could involve a formal order for treatment or supervision to be provided by the court or another agency. If the intake officers decide that the case warrants formal judicial processing, a formal petition is filed with the court. This is the most severe option available to intake officers.

In 1991, official data showed that 46% of whites who were arrested compared with 58% of blacks were petitioned to juvenile court (Maguire & Pastore, 1994). Goldman (1963) found that only 34% of offenses committed by whites were referred to juvenile court, compared to 65% of those committed by African Americans. In the juvenile court procedure in Florida in 1989-1990, black males were two and a half times more likely to be petitioned for delinquency as compared to white males, and black females were twice as likely as white females to be petitioned to juvenile court (Tollett & Close, 1991). In Nebraska between 1982 and 1987, black youths had a two to three times greater chance of being petitioned to juvenile court than comparable whites (Johnson & Secret, 1990). In New Jersey in 1992, 51% of youths referred to juvenile court were whites, 33% were blacks, 15% were Hispanic, and 1% were other minorities (Juvenile Delinquency Commission, 1993). Joseph (1992) found in her study in Atlantic City that 96% of black juveniles who were arrested were referred to juvenile court.

Does racial discrimination occurs at the intake? This is a concern for researchers and analysts. Several factors, including the race of the juvenile, affect the outcome of the intake process. Tollett and Close (1991) reported that between 1989 and 1990 72% of black males compared with 60% of white males in the Florida juvenile justice system were handled judicially. During the same period, 55% of black females compared with 45% white females were petitioned to juvenile court. These researchers concluded that race was a factor in the use of nonjudicial alternatives. McCarthy and Smith (1986) indicate that during the intake process, black youths have a greater chance than any other group of being petitioned to juvenile court.

Some studies show that the seriousness of the alleged offense also influences the decision to file a petition. Thus, youths who are accused of serious offenses are more likely than those accused of less serious offenses to be petitioned to juvenile court (Bell & Lang, 1985; Cohen & Kluegel, 1978; Fenwick, 1982; Thornberry, 1973). In 1992, 49% of white youths as compared with 63% of minority youths (the majority being black) in New Jersey were referred to the juvenile court. A partial explanation for this disparity in diversions was that minority youths entered the court with more serious offenses (Juvenile Delinquency Commission, 1993).

Prior record is another factor in the intake decision. Youths with prior offenses are more likely to be referred (Bell & Lang, 1985; Cohen & Kluegel, 1978; Fenwick, 1982; Thornberry, 1973). Many of these studies, however, did not examine whether racial discrimination was a factor in the delinquent's prior record because many studies did not attempt to determine how the prior criminal record was achieved (Perry, 1985). Prior record itself can be an artifact of police bias. If the police are more likely to arrest minority youths in the first place, then they are more likely to have a prior record. Once they have a prior record, they are more likely to be referred to juvenile court. Sociologists call this process bias amplification.

ADJUDICATION

Adjudication involves the trial stage of the juvenile justice system. In many jurisdictions, juveniles can be transferred to adult court based on the nature of the offense, the age of the juvenile, and his or her prior delinquent background.

The federal and state constitutions mandate due process of law and protection of defendant rights during trial. For many years, juveniles were denied due process rights in juvenile court because of that Court's treatment philosophy. Consequently, for most of the first sixty years of the existence of juvenile courts, juveniles had no right to an attorney because of the nonadversarial nature of the proceedings; hearsay evidence was accepted, and the court did not have to prove innocent "beyond a reasonable doubt." Instead since the proceedings were conducted in a manner similar to those in the civil court, the commonly applied test for guilt was " preponderance of evidence." However, since the 1960s, the U.S. Supreme Court has provided due process rights for juveniles.

In *In re Gault*, discussed in Chapter 5, the court also dealt with the issue of counsel during judicial proceedings. This case established the following principles with regard to adjudicatory hearing in juvenile proceedings: (1) the juvenile has a right to counsel, and one will be appointed by the court if necessary; (2) the juvenile can present his or her defense and confront witnesses under oath; (3) the juvenile has the right to confront his or her accuser; (4) the juvenile has a right against self-incrimination; and (5) the juvenile has a right to timely notice of the charges against him or her. The *Gault* decision was significant because it changed the constitutional nature of the court (*In re Gault*, 1967).

In *In re Winship* (1970), the Supreme Court ruled that juvenile court has to be sure beyond a reasonable doubt in order to convict a juvenile. Samuel Winship, a 12-year-old boy, was accused of stealing $112 from a woman's purse. The judge made his decision based on the principle of the "preponderance of evidence" rather than the "proof beyond a reasonable doubt" required in criminal court. Winship was found guilty and was placed in a training school for eighteen months. The defense attorney appealed to the Supreme Court and, in a 6-to-3 vote, the Supreme Court ruled that, before a juvenile could be convicted, the evidence should prove guilt "beyond a reasonable doubt" (*In re Winship*, 1970).

One of the most controversial issues in the area of juvenile rights is the right to a jury trial during the adjudication procedures. The most significant case regarding this matter was *McKeiver v. Pennsylvania* in 1971. Joseph McKeiver was a 16-year-old juvenile who was charged with robbery, larceny, and receiving stolen property. At the hearing, McKeiver requested a jury trial, but his request was denied. He was later adjudicated delinquent and was placed on probation. The defense appealed the case on the grounds that the right to a jury trial was denied. The Supreme Court in a 9-to-0 decision ruled that juveniles did not have a right to a jury trial for the following reasons: (1) not all rights constitutionally assured to adults are given to juveniles; (2) jury trials would make juvenile court proceedings adversarial; (3) a jury trial is not necessary to have a fair trial; and (4) a jury trial would result in delays, formality, and the possibility of a public trial. The court, however, recommended that states experiment with the jury trial concept in their jurisdiction (*McKeiver v. Pennsylvania*, 1971).

The juvenile statistics for New Jersey in 1992 show that 49% of white youths referred to juvenile court were adjudicated as delinquent compared with 73% of black youths (Juvenile Delinquency Commission, 1993). Official national statistics for 1991 show that 58% of white and 57% of black juveniles petitioned to juvenile court were adjudicated as delinquent. Black youths were more likely than white youths to be waived up to adult court, with 1% of whites versus 2% of blacks (U.S. Department of Justice, 1993e). Joseph (1992) found that 93% of the black youths in her study who were referred to juvenile court were adjudicated as delinquents. A six-week observational study of juvenile proceedings in a juvenile courtroom in a racially diverse community in New Jersey presented some alarming and frightening situations. Over 90% of the youths were black, and many of their offenses were drug related. One of the youngest to enter the court during those six weeks was a 12-year-old boy who was charged with attempted murder. It was shocking to see this young boy paraded into court shackled at the hands and feet. Further investigation revealed that he had a 15-year-old brother in detention with him awaiting trial on a different charge and an older brother in prison. This 12-year-old boy had been in the juvenile justice system since he was about 8 years old and had over twelve previous charges. Although his 15-year-old brother appeared to understand what he had done, the 12-year old did not seem to comprehend the seriousness of the charges. Both boys were adjudicated as delinquents. Interestingly, the 12 year old's behavior was that of a typical twelve-year-old child.

Some data suggest that whites are not consistently treated more leniently than blacks with regard to adjudication. Brown and associates (1990) in their study of 500 previously adjudicated delinquents in Dauphin County, Pennsylvania, found that race was related to the type of disposition rendered by the juvenile court at first referral. Their analysis revealed that white youths were more likely than minority youths to be adjudicated as delinquents at first referral to juvenile court, whereas minority youth were more likely to be adjudicated only after subsequent referrals. Dauphin County, wishing to see how well the respective groups fared as adults, initiated a general policy that favored adjudicating white youth early and minority youth late. White youths who were adjudicated at first referral were less likely as adults to have a conviction record. Minority youths who were not adjudicated at first referral were more likely than other minority youths to have a conviction record as an adult. Conversely, minority youth who were adjudicated at first referral, like white youth, were less likely as adults to have a criminal conviction.

Johnson and Secret (1990) found that in Nebraska between 1982 and 1987, whites, rather than blacks, had a greater chance of being found guilty in juvenile court. They concluded that since blacks were more likely than whites to be detained and to be handled by petition, these earlier decisions seemed to work to their advantage at the adjudication stage.

DISPOSITION

Disposition is basically similar to sentencing in the adult court and is concerned primarily with rehabilitation. Prior to the disposition, the judge often requests a predisposition report, which consists of information from interviews with the juvenile, his or her parents, and school officials. In addition, the predisposition report also includes results of psychological or psychiatric evaluations and intelligence tests. It assists the judge in deciding which disposition is best for the child; it provides information about the juvenile; and it aids the juvenile probation officer in designing treatment strategies for the juveniles in cases where appropriate. Some states make the predisposition report mandatory, whereas others request it only when there is a possibility that the juvenile will be sent to an institution. The probation officer, who compiles the predisposition report, usually recommends a disposition to the presiding judge, who often accepts the recommendation.

The juvenile court judge may choose any of dispositional options. Juvenile probation, which allows the child to remain in the community under supervision, is the most frequently used disposition. The juvenile can be required to pay restitution, or a fine, or perform community service. The child can also be placed in either a foster, group, or family group home, a community treatment facility, or home detention. The judge can also commit the child to a training school. Finally, the judge can dismiss the case and release the child to his or her parents or guardians.

Black youths often receive more severe dispositions than white youths. Minority youths were nearly four times as likely as white youths to be incarcerated in 1992 (Juvenile Delinquency Commission, 1993). Krisberg and his associates (1987) reported that black males were committed to training schools at a rate almost five times that of white males in 1982.   In California, African-American juveniles are sentenced to secure public facilities at a rate of four times their representation in the state youth population (Austin, Dimas, & Steinhart, 1992).   The 1991 national data showed that 25% of white youths and 35% of black youths were placed out of the home; the rates for black and white youths placed on probation were 58% of white youths and 55% of black youths (Maguire & Pastore, 1994).

One explanation for the disparity in dispositions is the legal argument which posits that blacks receive more severe dispositions because of their legal status, which includes type of offense, prior record, seriousness of the offense, and the number of charges.   This argument is supported by several researchers (Aday, 1986; Clarke & Koch, 1980; Cohen, 1975; Cohen & Kluegel, 1978; Eaton & Polk, 1961; Liska & Tausig, 1979; Staples, 1987; Terry, 1967). Krisberg and his associates (1978) reported that black youths have higher rates of arrests for offenses such as robberies, rapes, aggravated assaults, and simple assaults.   Official arrest data for 1992 also support the fact that blacks are arrested far more than whites for serious crimes of murder, rape, and assault (Federal Bureau of Investigation, 1993).   The assumption is that more serious sanctions are imposed on blacks because blacks on the whole commit more serious and violent offenses than whites.

A second argument for the differential in disposition of black and white youths is the interactional process between the defendant and the judges.   This includes extralegal factors such as age, demeanor, family intactness, economic status, rates of delinquency in the neighborhood, and level of educational achievement.   Since many of these factors relate to race, racial differences will appear in dispositional decisions.   These social cues result in negative consequences for black delinquents (Liska & Tausig, 1979; Tittle & Curran, 1988). Smith, Alexander and Roberts (1980) concluded that race and ethnicity may be subtly or indirectly related to decision making because factors such as dress, demeanor, and verbal abilities of defendants contribute to judicial decisions.

The third argument for the disparity in dispositions between black and white is discrimination in the juvenile justice system.   Consequently, black youths receive harsher sentences because of their race.   Some research supports the notion that race is a significant factor in disposition decisions in juvenile court. After controlling for relevant legal factors, several research studies have shown that race is a predictor of dispositions in juvenile court (Arnold, 1971; Bishop & Frazier, 1988; Bortner & Reed, 1985; Fagan, Slaughter, & Hartstone, 1987;   Marshall & Thomas, 1983; McCarthy & Smith, 1986; Thornberry, 1973, 1979).   In Georgia, black youths are prosecuted and locked up at higher rates than whites accused of comparable crimes.   Black youths represent 61% of those in juvenile institutions in Georgia.   The disparity between blacks and whites widens as they move from complaint to prosecution to disposition (Hansen, 1988).   In Florida between 1989 and 1990, the number of black males committed to delinquency programs increased from 45% to 60% of the total of male cases, and the proportion of black females committed to these programs increased from 42% to 52% of all female cases. The proportion of white youths, both males and females, committed to delinquency programs decreased, while that of black youth increased (Tollett & Close, 1991).

Ferdinand and Lutchterhand (1970) examined a subsample of 228 first-time offenders for whom police disposition was available. Controlling for offense, age, and gender, they discovered that African-American males were referred to juvenile court more often than whites. However, when they compared the juveniles who were third-time offenders, both black and white youths were treated in a similar fashion. Their conclusion was that when a youth had extensive involvement in the juvenile justice system, the disposition was based primarily on the offense. But when a first-time offender was involved and when the offense was relatively minor, race was a factor in the disposition decision.

Other researchers, on the other hand, have found little or no racial effect on dispositions (Bailey & Peterson, 1981; Bortner & Reed, 1985; Fagan, Slaughter, & Hartstone, 1987; Horwitz & Wasserman, 1980). Still others have found racial effects in some circumstances and jurisdictions but not in others (Dannefer & Schutt, 1982; Peterson, 1988). Tittle and Curran (1988), in a study of thirty-one counties in Florida, showed that when there are large proportions of youths and minorities in the juvenile court, minorities are treated more severely because their youthfulness is threatening to adults.

According to Bortner and Reed (1985), the issue of race and disposition is complicated by the fact that the discrimination that occurs in earlier processing decisions may mask later discrimination. To illustrate this point, there is considerable evidence that detained juveniles are more likely than nondetained juveniles to receive severe dispositions. Since detention affects the severity of dispositions (because judges often give longer sentences to detained juveniles), race can have an indirect effect on dispositions. To the extent that detention decisions are biased against minority and lower class youngsters, dispositions will be discriminatory even if juvenile court judges do not take race into account in deciding the dispositions of cases.

Reed (1984), after examining racial differentials in juvenile court decisions, argued that court personnel allow personal and social characteristics to influence their recommendations or decisions. This bias works to the disadvantage of the minority youth.

An analysis of black youth in juvenile court would not be complete without a comparison of other minority youths. Data for the New Jersey juvenile court in 1992 indicate that 39% of the juveniles adjudicated as delinquents were black, 13% were Hispanic, and other minority groups constituted less than 1% (Juvenile Delinquency Commission, 1993). Intensive analysis of minority youth representation in secure facilities in four target counties in California confirmed a statewide pattern of overrepresentation of African Americans, even representation of Latinos and underrepresentation of Asian and other minority youth (Austin, Dimas, & Steinhart, 1992). African Americans are ten times more likely to be sentenced to the California Youth Authority than any other racial or ethnic group (Austin, Dimas, & Steinhart, 1992).

Arnold (1971) found that African Americans were more likely than Hispanics to have formal hearings in juvenile court and to be committed to a youth authority. Bell and Lang (1985) found no difference between African Americans and Hispanics with regard to procedures in juvenile court. Leiber (1992) found that because black youths were perceived as dangerous, they received more severe outcomes than did Native Americans.

Leiber (1994) studied the processing of minority youths through the Iowa court system and found that minority youths received disparate treatment in comparison to white youths. Contrary to his expectations, he found that Native Americans received more lenient outcomes than did African Americans. A major factor contributing to this disparity was the belief of some juvenile court employees that African Americans are less trustworthy than other minority groups and are more unwilling to cooperate with officials. Consequently, diversionary or informal methods of dispositions may be withheld because of the lack of cooperation. Another explanation for the differences in court decisions between African Americans and Native Americans was the stereotypical belief by some court officials with regard to African-American youths that black youths were more likely than any other minority groups to be affiliated with gangs. Finally, Native American youths could be diverted through the Indian Youth of America, an agency that specializes in handling Native American youths.

POLICY IMPLICATIONS

The available data suggest that racial bias affects the processing of black youths at major points in the court process. The finding of racial bias presents some critical issues for the court system.

There is a need for sensitivity training for court personnel. Judges, prosecutors, intake officers, probation officers, and public defenders should receive regular minority and ethnic sensitivity training in cultural, racial, and ethnic differences. This training should be part of the basic ongoing training for court personnel. Training programs, workshops, and conferences focusing on the needs of minority youths should be developed, implemented, and attended by key juvenile justice practitioners, including judges (Council of Juvenile and Family Court Judges, 1990; Johnson & Secret, 1990; National Council on Crime and Delinquency, 1992.)

Although police departments have made attempts to recruit black police officers, the courts have been slow to employ black personnel in key court positions. Greater representation of black personnel is needed in the juvenile court for those in the critical decision-making ranks of the juvenile process and those involving developing and implementing important policies (Council of Juvenile and Family Court Judges, 1990; Johnson & Secret, 1990; National Council on Crime and Delinquency, 1992).

Clear and specific guidelines need to be established as to the criteria on which decisions, such as petitions to juvenile court, adjudication, and dispositional decisions, are based. This may necessitate curtailing the level of discretion in the juvenile court, especially among judges. In addition, a system of accountability is needed to ensure that the guidelines are followed (Johnson & Secret, 1990). Accountability, especially judicial, could prevent arbitrary decision making and introduce more fairness into the system.

Increased use should be made of alternative and nonlegal dispositions for black youths. There appears to an underutilization of diversionary programs with black youths. Diversionary programs for black youths should be tailored to their needs. In this regard, the juvenile court could elicit the assistance of black organizations and institutions in the community. The black church is a very powerful institution in the black community, and diversionary programs could be established with the church. In conjunction with these programs, more intervention programs operated by the court for black youths should be instituted. Such programs, if properly implemented, will decrease delinquency over time and will eventually save the state time and money. The black youth's family and community should be regarded as important factors when making decisions in the court.

Attempts should be made to eliminate racial bias in the courts because a "racially biased juvenile justice system is not only indefensible, it is potentially self-defeating in every function the juvenile justice system is designed to perform. Moreover, such a system undermines the legitimacy of the system" (Johnson & Secret, 1990: 181).

SUMMARY

Black youths are overrepresented at every point in the judicial process. Some research has shown that legal factors account for the overrepresentation of black youths, while others indicate that racial discrimination plays a major part in the juvenile justice process. Despite the claims of some researchers, such as Wilbanks (1987), that the criminal or juvenile justice is not racist, clear evidence exists that in some cases racial discrimination is a factor in juvenile court decision making. This fact calls for significant changes in the juvenile court process, especially for black youths.

7

Juveniles and Adult Court

One of the most significant actions that occurs in the early processing of a juvenile offender is the transfer process. Otherwise known as a waiver, this process involves transferring a juvenile to adult court. As violent crime rates increase among juveniles, more and more juveniles are being transferred to juvenile court.

TRANSFER TO ADULT COURT

Many legislative proposals have been made to take certain juveniles out from under the jurisdiction of the juvenile court. States, of course, vary widely in how they achieve waiver. Some states focus on the age of the offender, whereas others focus on the offenses. Fifteen states, including Florida, Indiana, and Maine, and federal districts have no specific age at which juveniles may be tried as adults. Nebraska and New York do not permit any waiver for juveniles, and the remaining thirty-three, as well as the District of Columbia, have a minimum age of waiver that ranges from the ages of 10 to 16 (see Table 7.1). Three methods have been used to waive juveniles to adult court: legislative waiver, judicial waiver, and prosecutor's waiver.

Legislative Waiver

Legislative waiver is accomplished in five ways. The first occurs when legislatures, such as those in Arizona or Maine, exclude certain felonies from juvenile court jurisdiction. Any youth, then, who commits a specified offense automatically goes before the adult court. The second method lowers the age over which the juvenile court has jurisdiction as in states such as California and Oregon. For example, if a state's age of juvenile court jurisdiction is 18, the legislature may lower it to 16. This approach focuses entirely on the age of the juvenile but ignores the offenses committed. The third form of legislative waiver specifies that juveniles of specific ages who commit specific crimes are to be tried by adult court. States with such stipulations include Alabama, Indiana, North Carolina, and Colorado. This method of legislative waiver focuses as much on the offense as it does on the age of the offender. The fourth method of legislative waiver, in states such as Florida and Kansas, involves statutes that simply state that anyone who commits a specific crime may be tried in an adult court. The fifth method is for state legislatures to grant both the juvenile and criminal court concurrent jurisdiction. Thus, juvenile court shares jurisdiction over juveniles with the criminal court. Under this procedure, the prosecutor or judge in the adult court usually makes the decision as to which court will try the juvenile. States like Georgia and Utah have such a statute.

Judicial Waiver

Judicial waiver involves the actual decision-making process that begins when the juvenile is brought to intake. Intake personnel or judges can make the decision as to whether or not to transfer the juvenile to adult court. Typically, the criteria used often include the age and maturity of the child, the seriousness of the referral incident, the child's past record, the child's relationship with parents, school, and community, the issue of whether the child is considered dangerous, and the matter of whether court officials believe that the child may be helped by juvenile court services.

Many state laws also permit states to send youths who are over the maximum age of jurisdiction back to the juvenile court if the adult court feels the case is appropriate for juvenile court jurisdiction.

Prosecutor's Waiver

In states with concurrent jurisdiction, prosecutors have the discretion to file charges in either juvenile or adult court. Some of these statutes apply only to capital offenses, others to all felonies or only to specified classes of felonies, and some to all offenses. Other forms of prosecutorial discretion relate to the prosecutor's charging authority to decide what the final charge will be. Some prosecutorial waiver statutes contain clear, specific, and restrictive criteria for their application, whereas others provide vague guidelines. Prosecutorial waiver statutes have been the subject of great criticism. One criticism of this waiver is that it grants too much power to the prosecutor and can result in arbitrary and discriminatory decisions.   Second, prosecutorial waiver statutes expand the powers of prosecutors who have, in general, traditionally supported retribution rather than rehabilitation, the main philosophy of the juvenile court (Bartollas & Miller, 1994).

At present, twelve states have prosecutor's waiver; thirty-six states have legislative waivers, by excluding certain offenses from juvenile court jurisdiction; and forty-eight states, the District of Columbia, and the federal government have judicial waiver provisions (Bureau of Justice Statistics, 1988).

Table 7.1
Youngest Age at Which Juvenile May Be Transferred to Criminal Court by Judicial Waiver[a]

Age	State[b]
No specific age	Alaska, Arizona, Arkansas, Delaware, Florida, Indiana, Kentucky, Maine, Maryland, New Hampshire, New Jersey, Oklahoma, South Dakota, West Virginia, Wyoming, federal districts
10 years	Vermont
12	Montana
13	Georgia, Illinois, Mississippi
14	Alabama, Colorado, Connecticut, Idaho, Iowa, Massachusetts, Missouri, North Carolina, North Dakota, Pennsylvania, South Carolina, Tennessee, Utah
15	District of Columbia, Louisiana, Michigan, New Mexico, Ohio, Oregon, Texas, Virginia
16	California, Hawaii, Kansas, Nevada, Rhode Island, Washington, Wisconsin

[a]Many judicial waiver statutes also specify offenses that are waivable. This table lists the youngest age for which waivers can be obtained without regard to the offense.
[b]Forty-eight states, the District of Columbia and Federal Government have judicial waiver provisions.
Source: Bureau of Statistics (1988), Report to the Nation on Crime and Justice, 2nd ed. (Washington, D.C.: Department of Justice).

DUE PROCESS IN TRANSFER PROCEEDINGS

Although state statutes provide the courts with the basis for waiver, those making waiver decisions have a great deal of discretion. In the past, the youth was waived to adult court without a hearing, without reasons being given for the waiver, and without the youth having the benefit of an attorney. However, in the cases of *Kent v. United States* (1966) and *Breed v. Jones* (1975), the U.S. Supreme Court ruled that juvenile court procedures for waiver were inadequate and that juveniles were guaranteed many of the same due process rights as were adults.

The *Kent* case declared a waiver transferring the youth to adult court in the District of Columbia as unconstitutional. Morris Kent was first arrested in 1959 at the age of 14 for housebreaking and was freed on probation. In 1961, during an investigation of theft, Kent's fingerprints were found at the scene of the crime. The juvenile judge, after considering the charges against Kent, decided to waive jurisdiction and transferred the case from juvenile court to adult court without stating a reason to the youth or his parents. Kent stood trial as an adult and received a sentence of thirty to ninety years in prison. If Kent had appeared in juvenile court, the maximum sentence for the 16-year-old boy would have been five years (since the jurisdiction did not extend beyond age 21). The case was appealed to the Supreme Court, and in 1966 the Court ruled that Kent's due process rights under the Fourteenth Amendment had been violated. In handing down its decision, the Court ruled that (1) a hearing must be held in juvenile court on the issue of transferring a juvenile case to adult court; (2) the juvenile is entitled to counsel at the waiver proceeding; (3) counsel is entitled to have access to all of the social records of the juvenile prepared by the staff of the court for use in their decision to waive jurisdiction; and (4) it is incumbent upon the juvenile court that a statement of reason accompany the waiver order (*Kent v. United States*, 1966).

In the *Breed* case, the Supreme Court declared that the child was granted protection from the double-jeopardy clause of the Fifth Amendment after he was tried as a delinquent in the juvenile court. Allen Breed, a 17-year-old juvenile was arrested and charged with robbery with a deadly weapon. The juvenile was ordered to be detained pending an adjudication on the delinquency petition. The juvenile court sustained the delinquency petition, finding that the juvenile had committed robbery, and ordered a dispositional hearing. At this subsequent hearing, the juvenile judge ruled that the juvenile was not amenable to the care, treatment, and training program of the juvenile court and, therefore, remanded the juvenile to the adult court for a new trial. Despite the defendant's objections that such an action would constitute double jeopardy, the juvenile was tried and convicted in adult court.

A petition was filed in federal district court, but the federal district court denied the petition stating that juvenile proceedings were civil and not criminal in nature. The case was then taken to the U.S. Supreme Court of Appeals, which ruled that the double-jeopardy clause was applicable to juvenile proceedings as well. The Supreme Court ruled that for a waiver to adult court to occur legally, juvenile court must transfer youths to the adult court jurisdiction before any adjudicatory hearings are held on these cases. In handing down its decision, the Supreme Court broadened the concept of double jeopardy beyond the traditional meaning of double punishment to include "potential or risk of trial or conviction" (*Breed v. Jones*, 1975).

The Supreme Court stated that when making waiver decisions the juvenile court should consider:

1. The seriousness of the alleged offense to the community and whether the protection of the community requires waiver.
2. Whether the alleged offense was committed in an aggressive, violent, premeditated or willful manner.
3. Whether the alleged offense was against persons or against property, greater weight being given to offenses against persons, especially if personal injury resulted.
4. The prosecutive merit of the complaint, that is, whether there is evidence upon which a Grand Jury may be expected to return an indictment.
5. The desirability of trial and disposition of the entire offense in one court when the juvenile's associates in the alleged offense are adults who will be charged with crime in the [criminal court].
6. The sophistication and maturity of the juvenile as determined by consideration of his home, environmental situation, emotional attitude and pattern of living
7. The record and previous history of the juvenile.
8. The prospects for adequate protection of the public and the likelihood of reasonable rehabilitation of the juvenile (if he is found to have committed the alleged offense) by the use of procedures, services, and facilities currently available to the juvenile court (Davis, 1986).

Today, states have transfer hearings that provide specific requirements for transfer proceedings. Due process of law for transfer hearings require that there be (1) a legitimate transfer hearing, (2) sufficient notice to the child's family and defense attorney, (3) the right to counsel, and (4) a statement of the reason for the court order for transfer.

PROBLEMS WITH WAIVER

Waivers are infrequent, accounting for 2% of juvenile court outcomes in 1991 (Maguire & Pastore, 1994). However, as a result of the current "get tough" policy of conservatives, the number of waivers seems to be increasing (Juvenile Justice Bulletin, 1989). Champion's study of waivers in Georgia, Mississippi, Tennessee, and Virginia found that, between 1980 and 1988, the number of waiver hearings in these states rose from 228 in 1980 to 466 in 1988, an increase of more than 100% (Champion, 1989).

Juveniles who are waived to adult courts are not always the most serious or violent offenders. Bishop and associates' (1989) examination of 583 prosecutor's waivers of 16 and 17 year olds in Florida from 1981 to 1984 revealed that most juveniles were low-risk juveniles and property offenders. In addition, many minor and nonthreatening offenses, such as public order offenses and violations of traffic and fish and game statutes, are sent to adult court (Bortner, 1986; Hamparian et al. 1982). In 1991, 2.2% of violent crimes, 1.1% of all property crimes, 4.0% of all drug cases, and 1% of public order cases nationally were waived to adult court (Maguire & Pastore, 1994). It would appear that property and nonserious offenses are transferred to adult court to create the impression that the juvenile justice system is tough on delinquents or to get rid of troublesome delinquents (Bortner, 1986; Rubin, 1985; Rudman et al., 1986).

One alleged shortcoming of the waiver is that there is inconsistency in the handling of juveniles in adult court. Some juveniles who are found guilty in adult court receive severe penalties, including the death penalty. However, several studies have found that a high level of leniency has been granted to juveniles in adult court. The practice in New York, for example, has been criticized on the grounds that 70% of children arraigned in adult courts are waived to juvenile court, wasting both time and money; 40% who are sentenced are placed on probation and only 3% of those tried in adult court received longer sentences than they would have been given in juvenile court (Allinson & Potter, 1983).

In many states, even when juveniles are tried in criminal court and convicted of the charges, they may still be sentenced to a juvenile institution rather than an adult prison. The laws may allow them to be transferred to an adult prison when they have reached a certain age.

A major objection to the waiver is that transfer decisions can be politically and administratively motivated. By singling out a small portion of juveniles to be transferred to adult court, the politicians and administrators of the juvenile court system can convince the public that they are concerned with public safety, thereby deflecting public criticism (Bortner, 1986). Another problem is that transfer to adult court is not made with fairness and justice. Racial disparity is shown in the administration of the waiver, and minorities are overrepresented in this waiver process.

The trend to treat juvenile delinquents as adult criminals, especially violent offenders, defeats the principal philosophy (rehabilitation) of the original juvenile justice system. Moreover, when juveniles are held in detention, the criminal justice system treats them very harshly, and such a practice is contrary to the treatment philosophy of the juvenile justice system.

Black Youths and Waiver

Race is a factor in transfer decisions, as shown by the more frequent waiver of black youths than white youths to adult court. In 1991, official statistics showed that 2% of black youths while 1% of white youths were waived to juvenile court (Maguire & Pastore, 1994). In Florida between 1980 and 1990, the percentage of black male youths transferred from juvenile court to adult court increased from 47% to 55%. During the same period, the percentage of black females transferred to adult court rose from 42% to 48%. This means that the proportion of cases involving whites transferred to adult court decreased from 1980 to 1990 (Tollett & Close, 1991). In 1989, 86% of youths waived to adult court were black (Klein, 1990).

Thomas and Bilchik (1985) evaluated the first year of New Jersey's revised statutes on waiver and reported that 73% of the waivers filed in 1984 were against minority youth. Fisher (1985) also concluded that significantly more black 15 and 16 year olds were processed for waiver than were white or Hispanic juveniles of the same age. Hairston (1981) estimated that 71% of the youths transferred to adult court in New York were black. Similarly, Hays and Solway (1972) reported that 83% of the youths considered for transfer to adult court in Harris County, Texas, were black. Hamparian et al. (1982) found that in 1978, 38% of youths, nationwide, transferred to adult court were black.

The question that arises is whether transfer decisions are discriminatory. Fagan, Forst, and Vivona (1987) studied 225 chronically violent delinquents who were adjudicated in juvenile court for a major felony from four urban areas between 1981 and 1984. Their comparison sample was 201 delinquents, for the same period, who were considered for transfer to criminal court. In both samples, nearly four out of five black juveniles were charged with murder (79% for each sample). After analyzing the two samples, Fagan, Forst, and Vivona (1987) concluded that age and offense were consistent discriminators of transfer decisions. Race was indirectly a factor in that more minority youths compared to white youths were charged with murder. Moreover, the age at first arrest was earlier and length of career was longer for minority youths. Eigen (1981) analyzed determinants of transfer decisions in homicide cases in juvenile court in Philadelphia and found that race was a direct predictor only in cases where the homicide was interracial. Black defendants were transferred significantly more often if the victim was white. Keiter (1973) studied sixty-four cases transferred in 1970 from Chicago Juvenile Court in Cook County. The Illinois statutes at that time provided little guidance on the criteria or procedures to inform the judicial waiver decisions. Keiter found that 92% of the youths transferred were black, although white youths had more serious criminal involvement. He also reported that the threshold of "dangerousness" for transfer was lower for minority youth.

The findings on race and transfer decisions are very inconsistent based on the few studies that do exist. Some studies show a direct relationship between race and transfer decisions, while others have failed to demonstrate that such a relationship exists. More comprehensive studies will have to be conducted before it can be determined whether there are racial determinants in juvenile court transfer decisions.

Youths in Adult Facilities

Adult institutions are substantially different from juvenile institutions. Many adult facilities are large, greatly overcrowded, and violent, and offer few rehabilitative programs. Juveniles institutionalized in these facilities are subjected to rape, exploitation, and exposure to drugs and disease. Given their age, juveniles can become easy prey for adult inmates when placed in such institutions.

Juveniles convicted in adult courts are subjected to the same range of dispositions as are adults. Cases may be dismissed or offenders may be found guilty. If found guilty, youths may be released to the care of their parents, placed on probation, fined, ordered to pay restitution, or referred to a social agency qualified to deal with their problem. Placement of youths in adult correctional facilities is very controversial, however.

The National Correctional Reporting Facilities Program (NCRP) collected data on persons entering state prisons from thirty-three states, the District of Columbia, the Federal Bureau of Prisons in 1987. The National Correctional Reporting Facilities Program reported that 2,957 persons under the age of 18 entered correctional facilities in jurisdictions participating in the study. Of these, 97% were males and 83% were age 17 at admission. Texas and North Carolina accounted for nearly one-third of the reported admissions to NCRP. The ethnicity data were missing for 40% of the cases, but those available showed that 14% were Hispanic. Over half (54%) of these youths were black, 35% were white and the race for the remainder was unknown (Krisberg & DeComo, 1993).

Hamparian and associates (1982) found that only two states, Delaware and Kentucky, at the time of their study prohibited the placement of juveniles in state adult institutions. Some variations on the practice of confining a juvenile in an adult institution do exist among the states. In some jurisdictions, states have no alternative but to place juveniles in adult institutions if the courts require incarceration. Some states, under special circumstances, can place youths in either juvenile or adult institutions, and still other states can refer juveniles back to juvenile court for their disposition. In some instances, very young juveniles are sent to juvenile facilities but are then transferred to adult institutions when they come of age. Recognizing the dangers and inadequacies of placing juveniles with adults, some jurisdictions have developed special institutions for these younger adult offenders.

Hamparian et al. (1978) have proposed that a youthful correctional system be developed for young adults (16 to 19 years of age). In these institutions, programs would emphasize work readiness, job training, and work experience. They would also attempt to establish close ties between the youths in the institution and the community to which the youth would return; to employ flexible staff who would act as positive role models; to enforce the rules strictly; to provide opportunities for decision making, with consequences clearly and fully related to the choices made; to provide opportunities to enhance self-esteem; to create a continuity of care between the program/treatment sequence and integration into the community to which the youth would be returning; and to offer supportive services in the community after completion of the program/treatment sequence as long as the youth needed them.

With the rise of drug-trafficking street gangs across the nation and the violence related to gang activity, it is likely that increased numbers of juveniles will be sentenced to prison sittings (Siegel & Senna, 1994; Regoli & Hewitt, 1994).

Joseph, in 1993, interviewed a young black male, who was confined to an adult training school, about the difficulties of being so young in an adult prison. The youth was one of four youngsters accused of killing an elderly white lady. According to the youth, he was not present at the time of the crime, but he was nevertheless charged with murder and transferred to adult court at the age of 15. At the age of 18, he was convicted and sent to one of the toughest prisons in New Jersey for life. At the time of the interview in 1993, he was 23 years of age, and he explained that he had been beaten and raped and suffered other forms of violence in prison. He did not believe that delinquents should serve time in adult prisons with hard-core criminals.

In 1991, 0.6% of inmates in state prisons were delinquents, and in 1992 only 0.1% of the prisoners in federal prisons were delinquents (U.S. Department of Justice, 1993f). In 1989, black juveniles were incarcerated in adult prisons at a rate of eight and one-half times that of white juveniles in Florida. In addition, black delinquents were sent to adult facilities at an earlier age (Tollett & Close, 1991). Given the fact that black youths are more likely than other youths to be transferred to criminal court, their numbers in adult institutions would be expected to be higher than any other group.

JUVENILES AND DEATH PENALTY

The United States is one of only three countries in the industrialized world that execute criminals; the two other countries are Japan and South Africa. Of the thirty-seven states and the federal government authorizing the death penalty, only twenty-two permit the execution of persons who committed murder under the age of 18 (Siegel & Senna, 1994). One outcome of the waiver is the sentencing of juveniles to death. The laws that permit juveniles to be tried as adults also permit them to be executed in the states that have capital punishment.

The first documented juvenile execution in North America occurred in 1642 when a 16-year-old youth boy was executed in Roxbury, Massachusetts, for the crime of bestiality (Teeters & Hedblom, 1967). In 1992, Texas executed Johnny Garrett who committed his offense as a juvenile (Regoli & Hewitt, 1994). Executions for crimes committed by youths under the age of 18 accounted for 363, or 1.3% of all executions carried out between 1642 and 1986 (Streib, 1987). From 1890s to 1930, fewer than thirty juveniles were executed in any given decade, but in the decades of the 1930s and 1940s, forty to fifty such executions did take place in each decade (Regoli & Hewitt, 1994).

Nearly two-thirds (64%) of all the executions of juveniles occurred in the South with Georgia carrying out the highest number of executions. It was found that 65% were blacks; 55% were 17 years of age at the time of the crime; 26% were 16 years old; and 19% were 15 years old or younger. Also 80% were convicted of murder; 9% of the victims were black, while 87% of the victims were white (Regoli & Hewitt, 1994; Streib, 1990).

On April 20 1994, there were 2,848 residents on death row, and of these 50% were white, 40% black, and 10% others (Maguire & Pastore, 1994). The youngest person on death row in 1991 was a black prisoner in Florida born in 1975 and sentenced in October 1991. The oldest person on death row in 1991 was a white prisoner in Missouri born in 1914 and sentenced to death in May 1991 (U.S. Department of Justice, 1992c).

As of 1993, there were thirty-six residents on death row in United States who were juveniles at the time of the crime but were waived up to adult court for trial and sentencing. Of these, 75% are awaiting execution in the South, and all of them are male; 52% of the victims are female (Regoli & Hewitt, 1994).

The Constitutionality of Capital Punishment for Juveniles

The United States Supreme Court had an opportunity to settle the question of the constitutionality of the death penalty for juveniles in the 1982 case of *Eddings v. Oklahoma*. Monty Lee Eddings, a 16-year-old male, killed a highway patrol officer and was sentenced to death. Upon appeal, the Court overturned the lower court ruling but avoided the constitutionality issue; instead it sent the case back for resentencing after full consideration of all mitigating factors. On the issue of the offender's youth, however, the Court did hold that "the chronological age of a minor is itself a relevant mitigating factor of great weight" (*Eddings v. Oklahoma*, 1982: 116).

The U.S. Supreme Court had the opportunity to consider the constitutionality issue again in the case of *Thompson v. Oklahoma* in 1988. Wayne Thompson was only 15 years old when he brutally murdered his former brother-in-law by beating him, cutting his throat, stabbing him in his chest, and shooting him twice. He was transferred to adult court where he was convicted and sentenced to die. Upon appeal, the U.S. Supreme Court ruled that execution of juveniles under the age of 16 was unconstitutional (*Thompson v. Oklahoma*, 1988).

In its ruling on the *Thompson v. Oklahoma case*, the U.S. Supreme Court left unanswered the question of whether the death penalty is unconstitutional for juveniles who were 16 or 18 at the time of their crimes. The Supreme Court was confronted with this issue in the cases of *Wilkins v. Missouri* and *Stanford v. Kentucky* in 1989. Heath Wilkins was 16 years of age when he committed the murder, while Kevin Stanford was 17. In another extremely close decision, the Court rejected this argument and left the minimum age at 16. The Supreme Court stated that states were free to impose the death penalty on juveniles who commit murder at the age of 16 or 17 (*Wilkins v. Missouri*, 1989; *Stanford v. Kentucky*, 1989). Determining the legality of capital punishment for juveniles is thus left to each individual jurisdiction. The only constitutional mandate is that each jurisdiction must permit consideration of mitigating circumstances.

As a result of the above decisions, the thirty-seven states that have the death penalty are allowed to set the minimum age for execution at 16, 17, or 18 years. About half of these states do not allow the death penalty for persons who committed their crimes under the age of 18. Of the remaining states, four have set the minimum at 17, while others use age 16 or have no specific age identified in their death penalty statutes (Regoli & Hewitt, 1994).

ISSUES REGARDING THE DEATH PENALTY

The death penalty has always been a controversial issue; one of the most emotional challenges facing society today is its appropriateness for juveniles. Many opponents of the death penalty maintain that it is barbaric and that civilized societies should not allow it for anyone, let alone juveniles. Among the major issues surrounding the death penalty are retribution, deterrence, the danger of mistakes and the arbitrary use of executions.

A primary reason why society strongly supports the death penalty in general is retribution, defined broadly as a sense of justice and the need for legal revenge against the offender. Supporters of the death penalty believe that society should impose the most severe punishment for the most heinous crime, murder. They believe in the "eye for an eye" philosophy. Opponents disagree with this revenge mentality and argue that, although crimes committed by youths may be just as harmful to victims as those committed by older persons, they deserve less punishment than those committed by older persons because their degree of culpability calls for less severe measures. The death penalty is too harsh for juveniles, who should not have the same legal responsibility as adults (Streib, 1990). Joseph (1994) suggested that an alternative prison system could be provided for juveniles who commit murder, or a separate justice system could be developed for youths between the ages of 16 and 19.

Another argument for the death penalty is deterrence. The deterrence theory assumes that an individual makes a rational choice to commit crimes, and, therefore, the pain of the punishment should override the benefits of crimes. There is individual deterrence, which prevents the individual from committing future crimes, and the death penalty is the ultimate individual deterrence. The purpose of general deterrence is to prevent potential murderers from killing, but there is some question as to whether or not general deterrence really works. The empirical evidence regarding the general deterrence element of the death penalty is inconclusive. Some researchers find little evidence that executions affect the rate of homicides (Bailey, 1980; Sellin, 1980; Zeisel, 1976). On the other hand, Ehrlich (1975) reported that executions do have some deterrent effect, because such executions prevent eight to twenty murders. His study, however, was criticized on methodological grounds. Recently, researchers have been examining the relationship between the publicity of executions and the homicide rate. The results have been contradictory since some studies show a deterrent effect (Phillips, 1980; Stack, 1987) while others have found that neither newspaper nor television publicity of executions has a deterrent effect on homicide rates (Bailey, 1990; Bailey & Peterson, 1989; Peterson & Bailey, 1991). Moreover, the death penalty will not necessarily be a greater general deterrent to murder than is long-term imprisonment (Bowers, 1984).

The death penalty is irreversible and, if mistakes are made, there is no recourse. Unlike imprisonment, executions cannot be changed. Those who oppose the death penalty argue that the possibility that an innocent person can be executed is justification to abolish the death penalty. Supporters, on the other hand, argue that there are enough safeguards in the criminal justice system to avoid executing innocent persons (Territo, Halstead, & Bromley, 1992). Moreover, they argue that, although the risk of executing an innocent person exists, there are few documented cases that this has occurred in recent times. However, Radelet and Bedau (1988) recently completed a comprehensive study on capital punishment, and they reported that during this century, 350 defendants were either erroneously convicted of a capital offense or were convicted of crimes that never occurred. (In seven cases, for example, the "murder victim" showed up alive after a conviction had been handed down.) Wrongful convictions do occur as in the case of James Richardson, who served twenty-one years in prison for murders he did not commit. Randall Adams (depicted in the docudrama "The Thin Blue Line"), also spent years on death row for a murder he did not commit.

One argument against capital punishment is the arbitrariness with which it is instituted. As of April 1993, 40% of residents on death row were black. Most of those on death row are indigents--too poor to afford proper counsel. Opponents of the death penalty argue that capital punishment is imposed unfairly. Supporters counter with the argument that the overrepresentation of certain groups in the death penalty statistics does not indicate discrimination. Rather, they say, it indicates that some groups are more involved in murder more than others (Johnson, 1989; Territo, Halstead, & Bromley, 1992).

The issue of the discriminatory administration of the death penalty was addressed by the Supreme Court in *Furman v. Georgia* in 1972. William Furman had been sentenced to death for murder in Georgia, and his attorney argued that the death penalty as imposed by the trial court was unconstitutional because it was imposed disproportionately against blacks, other minorities and poor people. In this case, the Supreme Court ruled for the first time that the death penalty, as administered, constituted cruel and unusual punishment, thereby voiding the laws of thirty-nine states and District of Columbia

(*Furman v. Georgia*, 1972). In response to *Furman*, thirty-five states and the federal government enacted new death penalty legislations designed to remove the discrimination and arbitrariness. These laws took two forms: some states removed all discretion from the process by mandating capital punishment on the conviction of certain offenses; other states also instituted a bifurcated trial, or two-stage trial, in capital cases. The first trial stage involves the determination of guilt or innocence. If the defendant is convicted, the jury begins the second stage of the process to decide whether the death penalty or life imprisonment should be imposed.

The new laws were tested in 1976 in the case of *Gregg v. Georgia*. Troy Gregg was charged with robbery and the murders of two men in 1973 and he justified the killings on the grounds of self-defense. The jury, however, found Gregg guilty of two accounts of armed robbery and two counts of murder. He challenged Georgia's two-step trial procedure. The Supreme Court struck down the mandatory death penalty provisions but upheld those provisions requiring judges and juries to consider mitigating and aggravating circumstances. It also upheld the two-tier procedure of new capital punishment laws (*Gregg v. Georgia*, 1976).

The constitutionality of the death penalty was challenged in 1987 in the case *McCleskey v. Kemp*. In this case, Warren McCleskey, a black man, was convicted of two counts of armed robbery and one count of murder and was given the death penalty in Georgia. McCleskey appealed his sentence, arguing that the death penalty in Georgia was unconstitutionally administered in a racially discriminatory way. When his case was presented to the Supreme Court, his attorneys cited research conducted by Professor David Baldus and his associates to show that a disparity in the imposition of the death penalty based on the race of the victim and to a lesser extent, the race of the defendant exists in Georgia. By a vote of 5 to 4, the justices rejected McCleskey's assertion, arguing that in order to show that Georgia's law was administered in an unconstitutional way, McCleskey had to prove that the decision makers had acted in a discriminatory manner in his case and not in general. Furthermore, the Court ruled that if racial discrimination exists, it is at a tolerable level. It is unfortunate that the Court made such a statement because *no* form of racial discrimination should be tolerated, especially in the event of a sentence of death.

The death penalty prohibits rehabilitation, the primary concept on which the juvenile justice system is based. There is always the possibility that delinquents will change their behavior as they mature. The death penalty rules out the possibility of rehabilitation. To reject rehabilitation for youths is to deny them the opportunity to change their delinquent behavior (Streib, 1990).

Blacks and Capital Punishment

Aguirre and Baker (1990) have reviewed empirical data on racial disparities in the death penalty and have found that the death penalty continues to be imposed against blacks in a discriminatory manner. At present, there are thirty-six persons on death row who committed their crimes while under the age of eighteen and 47% are African-Americans and 75% are in the south. All are males, and 52% of the victims were females (Streib, 1993). In addition, 65% of all juveniles who have been executed since 1642 were African Americans (Streib, 1986).

Streib (1990) examined death penalty sentences between 1982 and 1987 and reported that 61% of the offenders were black and 39% were white. He found that during that period, 57% of juveniles were from the South and 70% of those outside the south region were black. Thus sentencing black youths to death is not unique to the South.

It has been argued, for example, that black youths are overrepresented on death row because they disproportionately commit murder. However, this assumption does not explain the current practice in the imposition of the death penalty.   The common tendency in juvenile court is to impose the death penalty if the victim is white and the offender is black, but white-on-white and black-on-black homicides are more likely to result in incarceration. Streib (1990), for example, found that 69% of juveniles executed up to 1987 were black, but only 9% of their victims were black, while 89% were white. Louisiana, for example, executed eight juvenile offenders, and all offenders were black, the victims were white, and all eight juries were white as well (Streib, 1990). Baldus, Pulaski, and Woodworth (1983) found that in Georgia, white-victim cases were about eleven times more likely to produce a death sentence than were black-victim cases. When they examined cases tried in Georgia in 1970s, 22% of black defendants who killed white victims were sentenced to death; 8% of white defendants who killed white victims were sentenced to death; 1% of black defendants who killed black victims were sentenced to death and 3% of white defendants who killed black victims got the death sentence.   Keil and Vito (1990), after extensive examination of black-on-white homicides in Kentucky, concluded that racism cannot be ruled out in death penalty decisions. Of the juveniles on death row in 1987, 55% were black and 80% of the victims were white (Streib, 1990). Between 1973 and 1977 in Florida, a black person convicted of the murder of a white person was seven times more likely to receive the death sentence than a black who killed a black, while a white person who kills a white was almost five times more likely to be sentenced to death than was a black who killed a black person (Bohm, 1991). Moreover, a white person convicted of murder of a black person rarely receives the death penalty. These data seem to suggest that the killing of a white, regardless of the race of the offender, is treated more seriously than the killing of another person.   Basically, the offenders more likely to receive the death penalty are young black males who kill whites (Streib, 1990).

Without doubt, many of the states use "victim-based" racial discrimination in the imposition of the death penalty. There is glaring discrimination as to how the death penalty is imposed in the United States. Racial discrimination in the sentencing of criminal defendants violates the equal protection clause of the Fourteenth Amendment (Aguirre & Baker, 1990).

Some observers disagree that the criminal justice system is practising a "victim-based" form of racial discrimination. One such person is Laurence Johnson (1989), who argues that the criminal justice system does not practice a victim-based discrimination in the imposition of the death penalty because whites are disproportionately represented on death row. Of the 2,737 persons on death row on April 20, 1994, 50% were white, 40% black and 10% others. In addition, of the 157 murderers executed between 1977 and 1991, 56% were white, 40% were black, and 4% were other (Maguire & Pastore, 1994). Between 1977 and 1990, 71% of black persons were executed for killing a white and 29% for killing a black, although, in general, murder is intraracial (Death Row, U.S.A., 1991). The above data show that under post-Furman statutes, the greater number of persons sentenced to death and executed have been white. However, this does not mean that racial discrimination against blacks does not exist. In fact, since the post-Furman statutes have been instituted, a white person has yet to be executed for the murder of a black person; yet they do kill blacks (Bohm, 1991). These data seem to suggest that offenders who kill whites are more likely than those who kill blacks to receive the death penalty, especially in the South.

The Future of the Death Penalty

The number of persons sentenced to death row is increasing. There was a 11% increase in the number of persons sentenced to death between December 31, 1992 and April 20, 1994 (Maguire & Pastore, 1994). At present, judges and juries are sentencing murderers to death at a rate of about five or six a week, and the number of persons executed (31) in 1992 more than doubled the number (14) executed in 1991 (Anderson & Newman, 1993; Greenfeld & Stephan, 1993). Between 1977 and 1992, only 188 persons were executed or an average of 13 per year (Maguire & Pastore, 1994).

Many people appear to be concerned about the slow rate of executions and the seven and a half year gap between the time of sentencing from the court and the actual execution. Furthermore, the Supreme Court has become frustrated by the death-row inmates' use and perhaps the abuse of the appeals process. In a strong move to reduce delays in executions, the Supreme Court, in the case of *McCleskey v. Zandt* in 1991, limited the number of appeals a death-row inmate can file in the courts. The Court established a two-prong criterion for future appeals. According to *McCleskey*, in subsequent petition beyond the first, the capital defendant must demonstrate (1) why the claim now being made was not included in the first filing and (2) how the absence of that claim may have harmed the petitioner's ability to mount an effective defense (*McCleskey v. Zandt*, 1991). Congress has attempted to introduce legislation to limit the number of appeals available to murderers on death row but has failed. The present administration will once again try to pass similar legislation.

The states' death penalty laws are continually being revised. In 1992, five states revised their statutory provisions relating to the death penalty. Nearly all the changes related to specification of the circumstances under which capital punishment may be applied, some broadening and some narrowing provisions in the previous laws. In Tennessee in 1992, the state Supreme Court in *State v. Middlebrooks* struck down those parts of the death penalty relating to the application of aggravating circumstances for felony murder (*State v. Middlebrooks*, 1992). Tennessee also revised its death penalty statutes to grant a person who is given the sentence of death for first-degree murder the right to direct appeal to the court of criminal appeals. Montana amended its statute preventing juveniles under 16 years of age from being confined in a state prison, but a minor could still be tried in adult court. The judge could also consider the death penalty for juveniles, but age is a mitigating factor in such cases. New Jersey amended its constitution to include "bodily harm causing death" as an interpretation of "knowingly or purposely causing death," thereby broadening the constitutional definition of intent to cause death. South Carolina revised its capital punishment statute to define mental retardation and to specify it as a mitigating circumstance in punishment for murder, but this provision applies only to defendants who were mentally retarded at the time of the crime. Finally, Utah amended its capital punishment statute from death or life imprisonment to death or life imprisonment without parole (Greenfeld & Stephan, 1993).

The future of capital punishment for juveniles rests primarily with the legislature, but legislatures are often motivated by public opinion. It appears that the death penalty for juveniles will be around for a long time. First, the conservative Supreme Court has ruled that capital punishment for juveniles does not violate the Eighth Amendment concerning cruel and unusual punishment. Second, it has ruled that the states could execute juveniles 16 years of age years and over. With murderers getting younger and the Clinton administration's "get tough" policy, it is doubtful that the Supreme Court will abolish the death penalty for juveniles in the near future.

The following case gives a clear picture of capital punishment in action.

The Case of Willie Francis

This story began in November 1944 when Andrew Thomas, a pharmacist from Matinsville, Louisiana was found shot five times. The police found his watch and wallet containing $4 missing. During the search for Thomas's murderer, the police arrested a fifteen-year-old black youth named Willie Francis--mistakenly thought to be a suspected drug dealer.

During interrogation, Francis admitted to the murder of Andrew Thomas. Francis was then turned over to Louisiana authorities and tried for murder. Although there were no witnesses to the crime and the murder weapon was lost, the prosecution had a strong case, because Francis had voluntarily confessed twice. During the trial, his court-appointed attorneys did not call any witnesses in his behalf.

The jury found Francis guilty of murder. No transcript of the trial was taken, there was no request for a change in venue, no motion for a new trial was entered and no appeal was filed. Francis was sentenced to die.

On May 3, 1946, Francis age seventeen, was strapped into an electric chair. Captain E. Foster of Louisiana State Penitentiary checked his dials, bid Francis goodbye and then pulled the switch. For a fraction of second nothing happened. Then Francis jumped and groaned. But he did not die. The switch was thrown again and again for about two minutes. Yet nothing happened. Francis did not die.

The electrodes were moved from Francis' body and he managed to get to his feet. He later said that he felt only a small amount of electricity. The story caught the public's attention all across the country, and the public wrote the governor of Louisiana imploring him not to send the youth through the experience again.

Francis appealed to the Supreme Court of America asking the court to forbid Louisiana from trying to execute him a second time because it constitutes "cruel and unusual punishment" in violation of the Eighth Amendment. The court refused stating that the fact Francis had been subjected to a current of electricity does not make his subsequent execution more cruel in the constitutional sense than any other execution. The court further stated that the cruelty against which the Eighth Amendment protects a convicted person relates to the method of execution, and not necessarily to the suffering involved in any method. The court further stated that an unforeseeable accident preventing the prompt consummation of the sentence did not add an element of cruelty to any subsequent execution. On May 9, Willie Francis was strapped again into the electric chair. This time he died. (*Louisiana ex. rel. Francis v. Resweber*, 1947; Prettyman, 1961)

SUMMARY

There are three types of waivers: legislative, judicial and prosecutorial. Although only about 2% to 3% of juveniles are sentenced to death, capital punishment is a controversial issue (Streib, 1990). There is support for and against the death penalty for juveniles. Conservatives also believe that juveniles who kill deserve to be killed. Many opponents believe that the death penalty for juveniles is inappropriate for a "civilized" society such as the United States. Moreover, many who oppose the death penalty believe that rehabilitation should be the focus since the offenders are young and still within the formative years of their lives.

Research has also shown that black youths are disproportionately transferred to adult court or sentenced to death. Racism will continue to plague the criminal and juvenile justice systems if society does not try to eliminate it. Racial discrimination against blacks in the imposition of the death penalty seems to indicate a subtle form of genocide of young black males. This is a very repressive response to the problem of crime by black youth.

Transferring black delinquents to adult court or sentencing them to death will not solve the problem of violence, especially murder. The solution to this kind of behavior lies not in imposing severe penalties but in eliminating the root causes of violence. This will necessitate intervening in family life, and providing more economic opportunities and social programs for black youth. Long-term policies to deal with violent youths are needed.

8

Juvenile Institutions

Several options are available to the juvenile court judge once a juvenile has been adjudicated a delinquent. The juvenile justice system has developed a variety of methods to treat delinquents, including community-based programs and institutionalization. This chapter examines correctional aspects of institutionalization programs for delinquents. The final section of this chapter discusses black youths and institutionalization.

HISTORY OF JUVENILE INSTITUTIONS

Until the early 1800s, juvenile offenders were confined to adult prisons. Physical conditions in these prisons were so horrible that social reformers advocated the establishment of separate institutions for juveniles. One of the first such institutions was the New York House of Refuge which opened in 1825 to house vagrant, dependent, and delinquent children and which was sponsored by a philanthropic group called the Society for the Prevention of Pauperism. Not long afterward, the states began to establish *reform schools* for juveniles.

The first reform school for boys was opened in Massachusetts in 1846, followed by New York in 1849 and Maine in 1853. Reformatories were fortress-like in physical design and housed a large number of delinquents. These schools stressed schooling and inmate labor, which eventually became very exploitative. By 1900, thirty-six states had reform schools (Bartollas & Miller, 1994; Siegel & Senna, 1994).

In the second half of the nineteenth century, there was a shift from massive reform institutions to the *cottage system*. Under this system, juveniles were housed in a series of small cottages, each one holding twenty to forty youths. The first cottages were log cabins; later cottages were made of brick. Each cottage was supervised by cottage parents who attempted to create a family atmosphere for the youths. It was felt that this kind of environment would be more conducive to rehabilitation and treatment. The first cottage system was introduced in Massachusetts in 1855 and the second in Ohio in 1858, and quickly spread throughout the country. This form of organization was applauded as an improvement over the earlier reform or industrial schools and is the basic design for many juveniles facilities today (Bartollas & Miller, 1994; Siegel & Senna, 1994).

The early twentieth century brought several changes in the structure and the operation of juvenile institutions. For example, in the 1940s reception and classification centers were introduced in order to place juveniles in the proper facility.

Since the 1970s, several additional reforms have been made in juvenile institutions. The federal government passed the Juvenile Delinquency Act in 1974 which began the process of removing status offenders from institutions, including pretrial detention. Also initiated was a decarceration policy which mandates that the court use the least restrictive alternative for status offenders. Today, many states have separate facilities for status offenders, although, in some states, they are still housed with delinquents. From the 1980s to the present, the "crime control" period, the juvenile courts and the public have become very conservative and emphasize incarceration for repeat and serious offenders. This conservatism is evident in the attempts by many states to incarcerate more and more delinquents, as well as to execute them (Clear & Cole, 1994).

TYPES OF INSTITUTIONS

There are three types of institutions, based on level of security: minimum, medium, and maximum. Medium-security facilities usually are designed as dormitories or cottages. They house more serious offenders than those found in minimum-security facilities. Maximum-security institutions are the most secure facilities and house violent and repeat offenders. Many of these institutions often have one or two wire fences and even a wall surrounding them, and institutional security is the primary emphasis. These facilities have a variety of treatment programs consisting of recreational, educational, religious, medical and dental programs. Training schools exist in every state except Massachusetts, which abolished them in the 1970s.

Public and Private Institutions

Public institutions are operated by the state and by local agencies such as social service departments, departments of corrections, child welfare departments, or youth service departments. In 1993, New Jersey placed all juvenile correctional institutions under the authority of the Department of Human Services.

Private institutions are supported by contributions, donations and charitable organizations. They function under state authority and must comply with minimum standards regarding health, sanitation, residential care and institutional programming. Because they are private, they tend to select youths from affluent backgrounds, and often they are able to capitalize on young people who have medical insurance. As a result of their selection practices, the majority of residents in private institutions are white, while most of those in public institutions are minorities. Private institutions, like public institutions, range from relatively large institutions to small group homes and even wilderness programs.

With the high cost of operating juvenile institutions, some states are turning more and more to the privately run programs. For example, the Eckered Foundation took over a 400-bed facility in Florida in 1982 (Mullen, Chabotar, & Carrow, 1985). Privatization can reduce the cost of juvenile programs, since businesses are likely to run programs more cheaply than public programs. It is also easier to terminate a contract with a private company than to close an institution. However, private companies, in their quest for profits, may not operate effective programs; they may avoid dealing with serious and high-risk offenders and they have to be monitored carefully to ensure that the terms of the contract are carried out.

In the United States in 1991, there were 1,076 public juvenile public institutions: 506 state institutions and 570 local institutions. These institutions held 57,661 youths under the age of 21; and the Western region had the highest number of juveniles in institutions with 21,821. In 1991, the custody rate for juveniles held in public institutions was 221 per 100,000. In addition, there were 2,032 private institutions holding about 36,190 juveniles in 1991 (Maguire & Pastore, 1994).

Institutional Treatment

Nearly all juvenile institutions use some form of treatment program for their residents, including educational and vocational training, recreational programs, religious programs, counseling, and therapy. The purpose of these programs is to rehabilitate the youths so that they can lead productive lives when they leave the institutions, thereby lowering their chance of returning.

One form of treatment is *psychotherapy*, an outgrowth of Freudian psychoanalysis, which involves an extensive analysis of the individual's past childhood experiences. The therapist helps the client to understand how childhood experiences affect his or her present behavior. The best clients for psychotherapy programs are those who are amenable to treatment.

Reality therapy, a common treatment program used in institutions, was developed by William Glasser, who advocated that juveniles should take responsibility for their behavior.   Glasser believes that it is necessary to emphasize the present behavior if clients are to take responsibility for that behavior. The therapist develops a positive relationship with the client because the success of reality therapy depends on the therapist's warmth and concern. The objective of this therapy is to make the individual more responsible and confident. This approach has been criticized as being too simplistic.

Behavior modification assumes that all behaviors are learned through a system of rewards and punishments, which are given as reinforcements. If behaviors are to be changed, a relearning process must take place that will provide a set of rewards and punishments that will evoke appropriate behaviors in the clients. The simplest form of behavior modification techniques is "good time" credits, which are designed to promote good behavior in the institution. In an extreme form, aversive therapy can create physical pain for the client as in the case of electric shocks. This is used in many juvenile institutions. Behavior modification techniques are effective in controlled settings, but once the youths leave the institution and the reinforcements no longer exist, their good behavior sometimes ceases.

Group therapy requires a group of clients who have similar problems. Group therapy is useful because members in the group provide support and hope for each other. Group members advise each other in dealing with difficult, emotional-based problems.

Educational programs can assist delinquents with their post-release efforts to avoid delinquent behavior. Delinquents are now also able to graduate from state-accredited high schools while confined in an institutions. All training schools have educational programs. Some institutions allow residents to attend school in the community while others attend school in the institution. · Although some juveniles do acquire their general education diploma while in the institutions, there are some problems associated with these programs. These programs are inadequate and many of the youths are retarded or have low intelligence or learning disabilities. In addition, some youths dislike school and may act out in the program (Siegel & Senna, 1994).

Vocational programs are used to teach juveniles a skill they can use after release.   Programs offered include auto repair, woodworking, mechanical drawing, and plumbing for boys and secretarial training, hairdressing, laundry, sewing and cooking for girls. Vocational programs for delinquents include job counseling that provides clients with career opportunities and attempts to build self-confidence. One problem with vocational programs is that they are based on gender. Although, the recent trend is to allow the teaching of nontraditional male and female vocations in some institutions, the majority offer gender-based training programs. Another problem with these programs is that some of the skills are taught on outdated machinery; as a result, much of the training is obsolete when the delinquents return to the society.

Recreational programs, such as basketball, weightlifting and football, are offered in many institutions. Recreational programs are pursued individually or as a group. Many juvenile institutions have athletic teams in basketball, football, and baseball that compete against outside teams. Regardless of the specific type of activity, recreation can be extremely rewarding because it allows residents to alleviate the stress and frustration of institutionalization.

THE RIGHTS OF INSTITUTIONALIZED JUVENILES

An important goal of juvenile corrections is to rehabilitate delinquents. The children's rights movement and proponents of due process rights argue that delinquents confined in an institution should have rights such as the right to treatment and freedom from cruel and unusual punishment (Bartollas & Miller, 1994).

Several cases have focused on treatment. The *White v. Reid* (1954) case ruled that juveniles could not be kept in institutions that did not provide treatment. The case of *Inmates of the Boys' Training School v. Affleck* examined the conditions in institutions that violated the rights of juveniles, and concluded that (1) the true purpose of juvenile institutions is rehabilitation and, without that goal, due process rights are violated, and (2) juveniles have a statutory right to rehabilitative treatment (*Inmates of Boys Training School v. Affleck*, 1972). In a class civil rights action suit filed on behalf of the Indiana Boys' School, a state institution, alleging that the officials' practices and policies violated the Fourteenth Amendment rights, the Seventh Circuit Court of Appeals in Indiana ruled that inmates have a right to treatment even in a closed institution (*Nelson v. Heyne*, 1974). In *Morales v Turman*, the U.S. District Court for the Eastern District of Texas ruled that all juveniles held in the state of Texas have a constitutional right to treatment; the court established a number of criteria to be followed by the state of Texas (*Morales v. Turman*, 1973).

Some courts have applied the Eighth Amendment right against cruel and unusual punishment to juveniles. In the *Morales* case in Texas, the district court found conditions of brutality, such as tear gassings, excessive use of solitary confinement and lack of proper medical services to be inappropriate, and it established standards for incarcerated juveniles in Texas (*Morales v. Turman*, 1973). In the *Pena v. New York State Division for Youth* which challenged the practices in Goshen Annex Center, the federal court held that the use of isolation, hand restraints, and tranquilizing drugs was punitive and antitherapeutic and, therefore, violated the Eighth Amendment right of protection against cruel and unusual punishment (*Pena v. New York Division for Youth*, 1976). In the Mississippi case of *Morgan v. Sproat*, a federal district court found that confining youths to padded cells with no windows and furnishings and with only flush holes for toilets and denying them access to many programs was unconstitutional (*Morgan v. Sproat*, 1977). In *State v. Werner*, a federal also court found that residents were kicked, slapped, beaten, and sprayed with mace by staff, required to scrub floors with a toothbrush, and stand and sit for prolonged periods without changing position. The Court ruled these practices to be unconstitutional (*State v. Werner*, 1978).

CONDITIONS OF JUVENILE FACILITIES

Overcrowding is a serious problem in juvenile institutions. A study conducted by the Office of Juvenile Justice and Delinquency Prevention (OJJDP) to assess the conditions of confinement for juveniles from 1987 to 1991 found that overcrowding was a pervasive problem in the facilities and that crowding was more common in the larger facilities. In order to eliminate crowded sleeping rooms, the study estimated that slightly over 11,000 juveniles would have been removed from confinement (Parent et al., 1994). Some states have responded to crowding by restricting intake. Other states have closed public facilities and now house most of their juvenile populations in small, privately operated facilities. Colorado, West Virginia, and Oregon, Pennsylvania, and North Dakota are increasing their use of community-based programs and reducing institutionalization (Siegel & Senna, 1994).

Security is a problem in juvenile institutions. Security practices in juvenile facilities are intended to prevent escapes and to ensure safety for the residents. The Office of Juvenile Justice and Delinquency Prevention found that between 1987 and 1991 81% of juveniles were confined in facilities that were required to have three or more facility-wide counts every day, but that only 62% of the facilities classified juveniles on the basis of risk and used classification for making housing assignments. Larger facilities were more likely than smaller facilities to conform to counts and classification criteria, whereas smaller facilities were more likely to conform to staff-inmate ratio criteria. Only 20% of confined juveniles were in facilities that conformed to all national standards. Youth are deprived of security if the residents outnumber the staff. In male institutions, there is the constant threat of violence, especially with the introduction of gang members into training schools.

OJJDP found that suicidal behavior is a serious problem in juvenile facilities. Only half of confined juveniles were in facilities that monitor suicidal juveniles at least once every four minutes. About three-fourths were in facilities that screen juveniles at least once for indicators of suicide risk at the time of admission, and about three-fourths were in facilities that train staff in suicide prevention. Almost 90% were in facilities that had written suicide prevention plans. However, only 36% of confined juveniles were in facilities that conformed to all the criteria. The researchers recommended that juveniles be screened for risk of suicide immediately upon admission and that suicidal juveniles be constantly monitored by staff and transferred them to a medical health if necessary (Parent et al., 1994).

Lack of proper health care services is yet another problem in juvenile institutions. OJJDP found that health screenings at admission and health appraisals that ought to be done within seven days of admission were seldom completed in a timely fashion. Over 90% of confined juveniles did get health screenings at some point, but only 43% got them within one hour of admission as required by national standards. Although 95% did get health appraisals at some point, only 80% obtained them within a week. Large facilities were more likely to conform to the appraisal criteria, whereas small facilities were more likely to conform to the health screening criteria. The researchers recommended that juvenile justice agencies act to ensure that health appraisals are completed within one week and that agencies should provide adequate training for nonmedical staff who perform the health screenings (Parent et al., 1994).

The National Advisory Commission of Criminal Justice Standards and Goals recommended that states refrain from building more state institutions for juveniles, and that the states should phase out present institutions over a five-year period (National Advisory Commission on Criminal Justice Standard and Goals, 1973). It was not until the passage of the Juvenile Justice and Delinquency Act of 1974, however, that states started removing juveniles from jails. In addition, the conditions of institutions and the negative impact they may have on juveniles have prompted liberals to advocate the *deinstitutionalization* of juveniles.

Deinstitutionalization

Deinstitutionalization refers to reducing the number of delinquents in secure correctional facilities; it began in Massachusetts in 1972 under the leadership of Jerome Miller. The principal premise of this approach was that institutions for juveniles were of little or no value to many offenders. The deinstitutionalization movement gained popularity in the early 1970s and is still advocated by many today. Utah, Maryland, Vermont, and Pennsylvania have dramatically reduced their reform school populations and instead provide a wide range of community programs for juveniles.

Deinstitutionalization attempts to offer a less restrictive option by treating juveniles in the community; certainly, it is a more humane alternative to institutionalization. It decreases the negative contact between juveniles and the juvenile justice system. It is also cheaper. It costs between $25,000 and $47,00 a year to house a juvenile in an institution. For this money, a juvenile could attend a private prestigious school (Fox & Stinchcomb, 1994).

Deinstitutionalization, however, raises several questions. First, there is the issue of safety. Once the institutions are closed, the state may not be able to protect the community from juvenile criminals. Many observers are concerned about delinquents remaining in the community and committing further crimes. Others are concerned that deinstitutionalization will not have a deterrent effect for delinquents. Perhaps, some juveniles will not view remaining in the community as punishment. There is also the issue of community acceptance of such a policy. At present, some communities are showing resistance to community-based programs that tend to house less violent offenders. There will definitely be community resistance to placing violent and habitual offenders in the community. If community support is not available for these programs, they will likely fail.

BLACKS AND JUVENILE INSTITUTIONS

The percentage of blacks in juvenile facilities far exceeds that in the general population. In 1989, national statistics showed that 40% of youths in public facilities were white, 42% were black, 16% Hispanic, and 2% were American Indian and Asian American. A one-day count in public and private facilities showed that the rate for blacks was 558 per 100,000, while whites had a rate of 149, Hispanics 126, and others 295. In private facilities, the rate for blacks was 257 per 100,000, for whites 118, for Hispanics 94, and for other groups 105. Black youths had a rate of 815, whites 260, Hispanics 220, and others 399 (Krisberg & DeComo, 1993). Between 1987 and 1991, the proportion of blacks in juvenile facilities increased from 37% to 44% (Parent et al., 1994). In 1991, 57% of youths in private facilities were white, 32% were black, 9% Hispanic, and 2% others (Maguire & Pastore, 1994). The juvenile in a public facility is most likely to be an African-American male between the ages of 14 and 17 years. On the other hand, the juvenile most likely to be in a private institution is a white male between 14 and 17 years of age (Siegel & Senna, 1994).

Blacks are more likely than whites to be confined to secure facilities. For example, in 1991 32% of incarcerated black delinquents compared with 16% of whites were in secured facilities (Maguire & Pastore, 1994). Although the data show that the majority of youths in institutions are white, Krisberg et al. (1987) found that minority youths are incarcerated at a rate three to four times that of white youths. Krisberg et al. (1987) argued that the overrepresentation of minorities, especially blacks, in juvenile institutions was not the result of differentials in their arrest or crime rates, thereby implying that discrimination exists in the juvenile justice system. These authors found that racial disparity in juvenile disposition was a growing problem.

Black youths are overrepresentated in institutions in several states. For example, in Georgia, although blacks account for half of all delinquent acts, they represented 61% of those in institutions (Hansen, 1988). In New York, a preponderance of black children was admitted to the state juvenile correctional system (Kaplan & Busner, 1992). Young African-American males are more than twenty-three times more likely than young white males to be locked up in prisons in New York. The sad truth is that two times as many young black males are incarcerated in New York's institutions than are enrolled full time in New York colleges (Gangi & Murphy, 1990). In Arizona, black juveniles are treated differently from nonblack juveniles, and this results in overrepresentation of blacks in the juvenile institutions. Also because of the lack of private residential facilities, blacks remain in institutional facilities for longer periods of time (Bortner et al., 1990).

The Governor's Juvenile Justice and Delinquency Prevention Advisory Committee of New Jersey studied the overrepresentation of minority youth in state-run training schools, residential treatment centers, and correctional day-centers. The committee found that the percentage of black and Hispanic youths who were sent to juvenile institutions has escalated over the years. For example, in 1984, the three institutions operated by the Department of Corrections and the Division of Juvenile Services had a total of 664 youths with a racial makeup of 23% white, 63% blacks, and 15% Hispanic. In 1986, the racial makeup in these institutions was 17% white, 65% black, 17% Hispanic, and 1% other, although those adjudicated delinquent consisted of 45% white, 42% black, 9% Hispanic, and 1% (Governor's Juvenile Justice and Delinquency Prevention Advisory Committee, 1990). The committee argued that neither the public nor the private sector was dealing adequately with the unique problems presented by minority youth. It reported an urgent need for more public and private efforts that would focus on minority youths, in an effort to reduce their involvement in the juvenile justice system. The committee suggested that community-based alternatives for minority youths be explored (Governor's Juvenile Justice and Delinquency Prevention Advisory Committee, 1990). In 1992, however, minority youths (72% black) were still four times more likely than whites to be incarcerated, once adjudicated as delinquent in New Jersey. On December 31, 1992, 75% of juveniles in New Jersey's Juvenile Complex facilities were black, 14% were Hispanic and 11% were white (Division of Policy and Planning Office of Policy Analysis and Planning, 1991).

Minority youth did enter juvenile court in New Jersey in 1992 with more serious offenses than those of white youths. However, even when the type of offense was controlled, minority cases were diverted less than white cases. For example, 51% of cases for white youths were diverted compared with 27% of cases for black youths (Juvenile Delinquency Commission, 1993).

In institutions in New Jersey, visited by Joseph, the resident population consisted of an overwhelming majority of blacks. It seems clear that very little has changed in New Jersey since the Governor's Juvenile Justice and Delinquency Prevention Advisory Committee's report in 1990. Black youths are still overrepresented in juvenile institutions in New Jersey. The new governor of New Jersey, Christine Todd Whitman, has recently established a committee to examine the problems of the state's present juvenile justice system.

In California, between 1982 and 1989, the number of minority youth incarcerated in California increased by about 50%, while the number of incarcerated Anglo-American youth decreased by approximately 10% (Austin, Dimas, & Steinhart, 1992). For example, 37% of the incarcerated youths were African Americans in 1989, although only 9% of the state population was African American. The index of overrepresentation of African Americans in California's public juvenile facilities was, therefore, slightly more than four times their representation (37% divided by 9%). By contrast, Anglo-American juveniles were underrepresented in secure public facilities, representing only 27% of incarcerated youths, but constituted nearly 47% of the state youth population. Thus, the Anglo-American index of incarceration was only 0.6 (27% divided by 47%). In 1989, the rate per 100,000 for African-American youths committed to the California Youth Authority was 529; Latinos had a rate of 116, Asian Americans/others 60, and Anglo-American youths 47. African-American females had the highest incarceration rate of any female minority groups of juveniles (Austin, Dimas, & Steinhart, 1992).

The National Juvenile Corrections System Reporting Program selected six test states to study the admission and release of juveniles in those states. Some of the results from those states are presented in Table 8.1.

Table 8.1 shows that black youth had the highest representation of youths taken into custody, except in California and Texas. The greatest disparity between blacks and whites was in New Jersey, with 72% versus 16%, respectively. Table 8.2 shows that black youths had the highest rate of custody than any other racial or ethnic group in all six states.

Austin, Dimas, and Steinhart (1992) reviewed several explanations for the overrepresentation of minorities in the California juvenile justice system. One possible explanation they posited was institutionalized racism within the juvenile justice system--racism in the form of racial stereotypes, which in turn led to over incarceration of black youth. Poverty and joblessness affecting minority youth was another possible explanation. Black youths lack adequate job opportunities and instead turn to illegal economic pursuits, such as drug selling. Poor economic and social opportunities result in low self-esteem, which contributes to criminal and delinquent behavior. Lack of resources needed to effectively respond to the delinquency of minority youths was yet another explanation proposed by Austin and his associates. Diversion and alternative disposition programs in California that used to be available have disappeared, leaving the juvenile justice system with fewer options and thus contributing to the high rate of incarceration of blacks and other minorities.

Debate over why black youths are overrepresented in juvenile institutions has continued for many years now. It is not quite clear whether this overrepresentation is due to the black youths' involvement in more serious offenses or discrimination in the juvenile justice system. With regard to the overrepresentation of blacks in prison, Blumstein (1982: 1280) observed:

As the seriousness of the offenses decreases, blacks are disproportionately represented in prison. This does suggest that blacks become increasingly disadvantaged as the amount of permissible criminal-justice discretion increases, and discrimination must remain a plausible explanation for an important fraction of that effect.

The apparent discrimination in the adult criminal justice system probably exists in the juvenile system as well. What is clear, however, is that as black youth move through the juvenile justice system, their overrepresentation increases.

INSTITUTIONAL LIFE

Once black youths are institutionalized, how do they adapt to institutional

Table 8.1
Characteristics of Juveniles Admitted to State Custody in Six States, by Race and Ethnicity, 1989

Race	California	Illinois	New York	Ohio	Texas	New Jersey
White	54%	46%	29%	50%	65%	16%
Black	40%	53%	58%	49%	34%	72%
Native American	1%	1%	0%	0%	0%	0%
Asian American	4%	0%[a]	1%	0%	0%	0%
Unknown	1%	0%[a]	13	0%	1%	12%[b]

[a]Less than 1%.
[b]Because of the separate coding in the data elements for New Jersey, 12% unknown Hispanics could not be identified as belonging in the white or black categories.
Source: Barry Krisberg & Robert DeComo (1993), *Juveniles Taken Into Custody: Fiscal Year 1991.* Washington, D.C.: Office of Juvenile Justice and Delinquency Prevention.

Table 8.2
Juvenile Admission Rates by Race and Ethnicity in Six Test States per 100,000, 1990[a]

Race	California	Illinois	New York	Ohio	Texas	New Jersey	Total
White	70	80	71	136	164	28	97
Black	352	343	488	878	426	530	477
Native American	57	450	120	0	57	0	78
Asian American	33	3	24	0	0	0	23
Other	2	8	274	109	6	285	44
Hispanic[b]	76	88	203	236	201	129	129

[a]Rates are calculated per 100,000 youths aged 10 to the upper age of court jurisdiction.
[b]Persons of Hispanic origin may be of any race.
Source: Barry Krisberg & Robert DeComo (1993), *Juveniles Taken Into Custody: Fiscal Year 1991.* Washington, D.C.: Office of Juvenile Justice and Delinquency Prevention.

life? The few studies that are available indicate that they achieve a dominant status in the institutions.

Black juveniles in institutions appear to control the infrastructure of the inmate subculture. Bartollas, Miller, and Dinitz (1976) found that an exploitation matrix exists in the institution they studied. The inmate leader labeled a "heavy," was a black youth with three or four black lieutenants who made up the second ladder of the matrix. The third ladder consisted of a top half made up mostly of blacks who were called the "alright guys" and a bottom half consisting of whites who were referred to as "chumps." The lowest group were the "scapegoats." These researchers also reported that power was identified with blackness because the inmates were predominantly black, as was the staff. Consequently, blacks exploited whites, but whites seldom or never exploited blacks. They also found that blacks were more cohesive than whites because they resented the whites. Black residents would "get even" with white residents when they physically abused their black "brothers."

Research has shown that there is a different response to institutionalization based on race. Bartollas, Miller, and Dinitz (1976) have suggested that black juvenile inmates follow a different normative code from that used by institutionalized white inmates. While a general inmate code exists for all inmates, there is a specific code for black residents. The general code for all inmates includes statements such as "Don't trust anyone," "Don't kiss ass," "Don't rat on your peers," "Be cool," and "Don't get involved in another inmate's affair." Black inmates tend to have the following norms: "Exploit whites," "No forcing of sex on blacks," "Defend your brother," and "Staff favors whites."

Bowker (1977) examined the dynamics of interracial contacts in Ohio and found that blacks exploited whites. During the initiation to test new inmates, blacks try to pressure whites into sexual encounters, and, if the new inmate fails, he or she will be exploited further. In addition, white residents were disorganized while black residents stuck together.

One explanation for the behavior of black residents in the institution is role reversal (Bartollas & Sieverdes, 1981). In many juvenile institutions, unlike the larger society, black youths outnumber white youths, and black youths assert power and control over the white inmates as a way of paying them back for what society has done to blacks. This situation creates racial tension in juvenile institutions.

SHORTCOMINGS OF JUVENILE INSTITUTIONS

Institutional programs isolate the offender from the society, and producing alienation from and further delinquency (McGee, 1981).

Many sources of delinquency, such as poor education, dysfunctional family life, and lack of accessibility to legitimate opportunities, exist in the community. However, the system seldom addresses these problems. As noted, the initial philosophy of the juvenile justice system was rehabilitation, but it appears that institutional treatment has had very little impact on delinquency.

Many believe that training or reform schools could have a negative effect on juveniles. Many of these juveniles may, therefore, leave these facilities as more hardened criminals. Furthermore, such institutions stigmatize the delinquents, making it difficult for society to accept them once they leave the institutions (Gibbons & Krohn, 1991).

POLICY IMPLICATIONS

Research on juvenile corrections clearly indicates that black youths receive harsher penalties than whites and are disproportionately found in secure facilities (Bishop & Frazier, 1988; Tittle, & Curran, 1988; Krisberg et al., 1987). These findings pose important questions. What criteria do judges use to send a black youth to a secure facility? States should consider establishing clearly defined and culturally and racially unbiased criteria for sentencing. In addition, states should devise methods to ensure compliance with these criteria.

The data clearly indicate that whites are more likely than blacks to be referred to community-based corrections. The question is, Why are alternative programs not used more extensively with black youth? Black youths can derive the same benefits from these programs as do white youths. States need to increase the involvement of black community groups and organizations, such as black citizen groups, churches, and service organizations, to assist with nondangerous offenders. Black community groups could have more of an impact on black youths than white groups because members of black groups have a better understanding of the values and problems of black youth.

The states should employ more minority professionals in corrections, for correctional agencies should have staff representative of their client populations. In addition, states should provide cultural sensitivity training so that nonminority professionals who administer these correctional programs can be sensitized to the needs of minority youth. States also need to establish more culturally sensitive community-based programs that are multicultural in nature. One major deficit of juvenile correctional programs is their lack of cultural diversity.

Juvenile corrections should change policy and invest in community-based programs and reduce expenditures for incarceration (Austin, Dimas, & Steinhart, 1992). Institutionalization should be used only as a last resort. Deinstitutionalization, which is used primarily with status offenders, should be employed more extensively with non-serious delinquents, especially minority delinquents. The states should also attempt to keep more nonserious and nonviolent juvenile offenders in the community; this approach will save the sates money because deinstitutionalization is cheaper than incarceration.

More efforts should be made to treat all youths, especially blacks, and to address the causes of their delinquent behavior, rather than taking punitive measures. Chronic and violent delinquents who are released from the juvenile justice system with little or no treatment will continue to be a menace to society.

States need to develop a larger number of early intervention programs and preventive measures for black youth (Governor's Juvenile Justice and Delinquency Prevention Advisory Committee, 1990). Prevention programs designed to reduce the likelihood of juvenile delinquency entail giving black youths more legitimate opportunities, such as employment, income, education and proper housing conditions, to black youths. This society tends to focus on remedial measures rather than preventive measures. Early intervention programs can stop further involvement into further delinquency. More programs for "at risk" youths are vital.

SUMMARY

Juvenile facilities include both public and private institutions. Public institutions accept anyone, whereas private institutions are more selective of their clients. Although the main purpose of juvenile corrections is rehabilitation and treatment, the effects of confinement can be harmful to many juveniles. The movement toward deinstitutionalization is an alternative to the failure of juvenile facilities.

Black youths are disproportionately represented in secure facilities, such as training schools. It is not quite clear whether the higher proportion of black offenders can be fully explained by their higher arrest rates. What is quite clear, however, is that their overrepresentation increases as they progress further into the juvenile justice system. Given the problems inherent in the training schools today, it is questionable whether they meet the rehabilitative needs of black youths. States need to examine this problem seriously and take appropriate action to reduce the number of black youths in juvenile corrections, especially institutions. Measures to be taken should include reducing discrimination in the juvenile justice system, training professionals in the system to be culturally sensitive, increasing the employment of more black professionals, utilizing black community organizations and groups, increasing the use of diversionary and alternative dispositions for black youth, and developing more prevention and early intervention programs for black youths. This society tends to regard the problems of black youth as a black problem. In reality, problems in one segment of the society are problems for everyone.

<u>9</u>

Community-Based Treatment Programs

Several states have initiated ways to keep delinquents out of the juvenile justice system and to treat them in the community. This chapter focuses on intervention programs, primarily community-based treatment programs, such as diversion programs. The discussion encompasses specific programs that serve black youths.

HISTORY OF COMMUNITY-BASED TREATMENT PROGRAMS

The institutionalization of juveniles in a training school is the juvenile justice system's most severe penalty. In many cases, this harsh punishment can do more harm than good to the delinquent. Furthermore, the juveniles are stigmatized as a result, and such labeling can push the juvenile deeper into delinquency. Because of the problems associated with institutionalization, several agencies, such as the National Council on Crime and Delinquency and the American Bar Association, have recommended that institutionalization should be used only as a last resort and that, wherever possible, delinquents be treated in the community.

Community treatment programs utilize the resources in the community to treat delinquents and enable youths to work out their problems in a community environment. These programs can be effective in reintegrating delinquents into their communities and in enabling them to adapt to their environment.

In 1969, under the direction of Jerome Miller, state commissioner of youth services and Director of Youth Services, Massachusetts was one of the first states to remove juveniles from institutions and place them in the community. Massachusetts closed most of its institutions and began a massive deinstitutionalization of juvenile offenders, and today it operates a community-based correctional system. In the last two decades, several other states have closed many of their secure institutions in favor of nonsecure community-based facilities (Blackmore, Brown, & Krisberg, 1988).

In the 1980s, community-based programs were faced with several challenges. First, as juvenile offenses became more violent, many members of the public shifted their preference in crime control from rehabilitation to "get tough" sentiments. The shift now threatens the existence of community-based programs. Second, the Law Enforcement Assistance Administration's funding for these programs ended, leaving many communities unable to finance these programs. Third, some communities had developed elaborate network services, while others were not able to do so. Those communities with elaborate networks of services had more effective programs than those without such services.

There are two main types of community-based treatment programs: nonresidential and residential treatment programs.

Nonresidential Treatment Programs

Nonresidential treatment programs provide treatment and supervision for juveniles, but the delinquents are allowed to remain at home. These programs monitor the delinquents and provide intensive counseling, family therapy and educational counseling; job placement may also be part of the program. These court-mandated programs are popular because they are more economical than residential placements. They do not provide living and sleeping quarters and accommodation; they make parental participation easier; fewer staff members are required; and they focus on treatment rather than punishment. Such programs include probation, restitution, house arrest and electronic monitoring, and aftercare and day-treatment programs.

Probation

Probation is the primary form of nonresidential community-based program. It involves a conditional release into the community under the supervision of a probation officer, who assists the offenders in their efforts to follow the conditions set by the court. Probation is very useful because it is an alternative to institutionalization, allows the offender to escape the negative impact of incarceration, and promotes the rehabilitative philosophy of the juvenile justice system.

Several forms of probation are used for juveniles. One type is *informal probation*, which occurs at intake where officers have the authority to place the juvenile on a short period of probation without an adjudication of delinquency by the court. There is also *shock probation*, which allows the sentencing judge to order a defendant to a short stay in prison and then releases that person to supervised probation. This form is widely used in states such as Kentucky, North Carolina, Texas, Indiana, Idaho, and Maine (Bartollas & Miller, 1994).

Community-Based Treatment Programs

Another type of probation, which emerged in the 1980s, is *intensive supervision probation*. Delinquents who would normally be sent to institutions are placed on probation under the close scrutiny of probation officers. This scrutiny may include increased contacts with a probation officer, mandatory curfews, mandatory drug and alcohol testing, and employment or school attendance. Alabama, Georgia, New Jersey, Ohio, Oregon, and Pennsylvania are among the states with such programs.

In 1991, 57% of juveniles adjudicated as delinquents in the United States were placed on probation (Maguire & Pastore, 1994); thus, probation is the most common disposition in the juvenile justice system. It is cheaper and more humane than imprisonment, and probationers thereby avoid the negative effects of incarceration. It also increases the opportunity for rehabilitation because probationers are able to take advantage of services offered in the community. Probation is not without problems, however. It is designed for low-risk offenders, but sometimes dangerous offenders are placed on probation, and they become a risk to the community.

Restitution

Restitution requires that the offender pay for all or part of the damage he or she inflicted on crime victims. Restitution can take the form of *monetary restitution* in which a juvenile is required to pay back monies for the damage; this is the most common form of restitution. *Service restitution* requires that the offender provide service to the victim or to the community. Presently, all fifty states, as well as the District of Columbia, have legislations authorizing restitution programs for juveniles.

Restitution programs can be used at various stages of the juvenile justice process. They can be a method of informal adjustment at intake, they can be a condition of probation, or they can be part of a diversion program prior to conviction.

Restitution has both advantages and disadvantages. It provides the court with an alternative disposition that is cheaper than institutionalization; it offers direct compensation or service to the victim; and it can provide rehabilitation because it forces the offender to take responsibility for his or her actions. One problem it poses, however, is that it can be punitive for offenders rather than rehabilitative, especially if they have to pay back the original value of the damaged property (Klein, 1980). Furthermore, not all juveniles make restitution to their victims. For example, one study found that only 40% to 88% of juveniles ordered to pay restitution actually do so (Schneider & Schneider, 1984).

House Arrest and Electronic Monitoring

House arrest, which confines the juvenile to his or her home for specific periods of time, is usually monitored by the juvenile court probation department.

Juveniles under house arrest are allowed to leave during the day for school, employment, and important appointments. Surveillance consists of personal daily contacts with youth by surveillance officers.

Electronic monitoring is a variation of house arrest. Under this method, juveniles are confined to their homes and are monitored by means of computer-monitoring devices. Electronic monitoring was initiated in New Mexico when a district court judge read a comic strip in which Spiderman was tracked by a transmitter affixed to his wrist. Electronic monitoring is of two types--active and passive--and the juvenile can wear the electronic device on the ankle, neck, or wrist. Active monitoring involves a transmitter that sends a constant signal from the juvenile's home to a central computer. If that signal is broken the juvenile will have violated house arrest. Passive systems send electronic signals in response to computer-activated calls to the offender. The juvenile responds by inserting a special plug into a transmitter as well as answering the telephone for voice verification by the computer (Siegel and Senna, 1994).

House arrest and electronic monitoring are less costly than institutionalization. They prevent the breakup of the family by allowing the offender to remain at home. The offender also escapes the stigma of incarceration. Reviews of house arrest and electronic programs indicate some success in reducing recidivism among juvenile offenders (Ball, Huff, & Lilly, 1988; Vaughn, 1989). However, several criticisms can be made of house arrest and electronic monitoring. First, these programs may widen the net of social control by including low-risk offenders, who otherwise would not have been brought into the juvenile justice system. Second, these programs are viewed as a violation of privacy because a person's home is considered "his castle." Third, there is concern that these programs will change the role of parents and turn them into "wardens" or "keepers" of their children. Fourth, there is the fear that electronic monitoring can extend to other aspects of our lives and create a Big Brother atmosphere (Ball, Huff, & Lily, 1988).

Aftercare

Aftercare is similar to parole in adult corrections. After being released from an institution, delinquents are placed on aftercare through which they are supervised for a period of time by an aftercare worker. The objective of aftercare is to slowly reintegrate confined juveniles into the society. More recently, aftercare or parole has been used to alleviate overcrowding in training schools. The authority for making aftercare decisions for juveniles rests with the state, namely, the executive branch of government, probation officers, state boards, or juvenile judges. If aftercare is successful, the juvenile is then released from the supervision of the juvenile justice system.

One type of aftercare is Intensive Aftercare Supervision (IAS), which is operated in cities such as Philadelphia, Boston, Memphis, Newark, Detroit, and New York (Palmer, 1992). The participants in this program have frequent contacts with an aftercare worker. The program also focuses on job training, education, and the development of social bonds.

One problem with aftercare is its high failure rate which varies from 25% to 40% (Chambers, 1983; Champion, 1992). Another problem is the large caseloads that aftercare workers have to manage, making it impossible for them to supervise their clients effectively. Despite this, aftercare can be effective if combined with therapeutic treatment (Siegel & Senna, 1994).

An example of a day-treatment program that offers services to youths who have committed serious offenses is *Project New Pride* in Denver, Colorado. Most of the youngsters involved in the project, which has been designated as an exemplary project by Law Enforcement Assistance Administration (LEAA), are African Americans or Chicanos. Each youth receives intensive services in the program for the first three months and then continues treatment geared to individual needs and interests for a nine-month followup period. Academic education, counseling, employment, and cultural education are the four main areas of services provided in Project New Pride. For education, youths receive alternative schooling and are then integrated into the public school system. Job preparation is heavily emphasized; youths attend a job skills workshop and then receive on-the-job training. The purpose of the cultural education is to expose youths to a range of experiences and activities in the Denver area (Project New Pride, 1985).

Project New Pride has established four primary goals in working with its difficult clientele: (1) reduction of recidivism, (2) job placement, (3) school reintegration, and (4) remediation of academic and learning disabilities. The project has had some success in achieving the first three of these goals but less success with educational remediation. The success of this project has been replicated in Chicago, Los Angeles, San Francisco, Boston, Washington, D.C., Haddonfield, New Jersey, and Providence, Rhode Island (Project New Pride, 1985).

Black Youths and Nonresidential Programs

Of all the juveniles petitioned to juvenile court in 1991, national statistics show that 60% of whites and 57% of blacks were adjudicated as juveniles. Of those youths convicted in juvenile court, 55% of black youths and 58% of white youths were placed on probation (Maguire & Pastore, 1994).

In New Jersey in 1992, 42% of white youths compared with 44% black youths, 13% of Hispanic youths and 1% of other youths were granted probation. Although the probation rates for blacks and whites were about the same, there was a disparity in out-of-home placement between the two groups. Blacks were twice as likely as whites to receive an out-of-home placement in 1992 (Juvenile Delinquency Commission, 1993).

Turning It Around is a community-based nonresidential program located in Trenton, New Jersey, sponsored by the Urban League of Metropolitan Trenton. This is one of the affiliates of the National Urban League whose mission is to assist African Americans and other minorities in achieving social and economic equality. The goal of the project is to reduce the number of juveniles incarcerated by providing a comprehensive, individualized alternative program. Referrals for this project come from the family court, the probation department, and the Trenton Police Department Youth Division. Intake is managed by a treatment team consisting of a psychologist, project counselor, project director, and representatives from probation, family court and police. The project seeks to provide community-based alternatives to secure detention and incarceration; to design individualized education, treatment, and referral services; and to provide job skills. An important component of this project is the availability of twenty-five mentors, who become role models for the fifty or so youths in the program (State of New Jersey Commission of Investigation, 1993).

Family Ties began an alternative to incarceration for minority youth aged 7 to 16 in a pilot project in Brooklyn in 1989. The program has since expanded to the Bronx and Manhattan. Family Ties identifies the needs of each delinquent child and works to strengthen family networks so that the delinquent can stay at home. This program has been recently established in California, Kentucky, and Michigan (Juvenile Justice Bulletin, 1993).

Evaluation of Nonresidential Programs

Nonresidential programs are the preferable way of handling young minor offenders. They are more economical, more humane (as they permit the juvenile to live at home), and less coercive and punishment-oriented than residential facilities. The conflicting findings on their success with hard-core offenders make them a somewhat questionable placement for the serious juvenile delinquent. Some juvenile recidivists seem to require more secure placements to gain control over themselves and their antisocial behaviors (Bartollas & Miller, 1994).

Residential Community-Based Treatment Programs

Residential treatment programs include foster homes, group homes, foster group homes, boot camps, and outdoor programs.

Foster homes are homelike environments in which a family provides care and supervision for juveniles who are neglected and abused or who are nonserious delinquents. Foster parents usually care for one or two juveniles and are reimbursed by the state for expenses. The foster parents must meet state certification and inspection standards and are given subsidies for clothing, shelter, and food. The success of the foster placement depends on the compatibility of the parents and the juveniles, but, despite good selection criteria, some foster placements have been disastrous.

Group homes are nonsecure residential facilities, each housing six to fifteen youths. They are staffed by child-care professionals who provide counseling, job training, and therapy. Juveniles who reside in group homes are still part of the community, and so they attend regular schools and participate in community activities (Finckenauer, 1984).

Group homes have several purposes. They are an alternative to institution-alization, and they attempt to reintegrate delinquents into society. They are also used as short-term residences, and they can be used as "halfway-in" houses for juveniles on probation or as "halfway-out" houses for juveniles who are returning to the community from an institution and who do not have adequate home placement.

Foster group homes are a combination of the foster and group home, and are operated by single families rather than professional staff. Foster group homes can give troubled youths a family-type relationship and teach them how to get along within a "family." Like group homes, they provide counseling, treatment and therapy. These homes can be found in states such as Florida, Oregon, and Minnesota (Lawder, Andrews, & Parsons, 1974).

Boot camp programs, frequently called "shock incarceration," require the offenders to serve a short term in a community-based facility with a military-style approach. Boot camps combine discipline, physical training, education and counseling for juveniles for up to 180 days. The intent is not only to "get tough" with juveniles but also to "shock" them out of committing further crimes. Youths are recommended and then can opt to attend a boot camp instead of a training school. Most of the participants have been convicted of drug offenses. After successful completion of the program, the juvenile is released back into the community. If the youth fails to complete the program, he or she will have to complete the sentence in a secure facility, primarily a training school. Boot camps for juveniles are used for young offenders and juveniles who have been waived to adult court in Georgia, Florida, Mississippi and Kansas (Siegel & Senna, 1994).

Boot camp programs can deter crime by threatening the juvenile with insti-tutionalization for future offenses. The experiences in boot camps are designed to build high self-esteem and self-control. The program is more severe than probation, and it keeps the offender out of the community for a while. These programs are also cost effective compared to incarceration (Parent, 1989).

Boot camps have come under a great deal of criticisms recently. Morash and Rucker (1990) have noted that boot camps are vulnerable to increased aggression and abuse of power. They also argue that boot camps foster a "we-versus-they" mentality that can be counterproductive to rehabilitation. Demeaning or dehumanizing epithets, such as "scum," used by officers are likely to further lower self-esteem, which in turn can cause recidivism.

Outdoor programs are minimum-security facilities usually reserved for first-time nonserious offenders and include forestry camps, ranches, and wilderness programs. Juveniles usually spend two to three months in *forestry camps*,

working in state parks and attending school daily. These provide an outdoor
environment for treatment, and juveniles may make one or two visits home
each month. *Ranches* are widely used in California and other western states.
They offer recreational, work, and treatment programs. One of the main requirements of the ranches is for residents to take care of the livestock. Horse-
back riding is a popular form of recreation. These facilities also stress life
skills, responsibility, confidence, self-worth, pride, and trust in others
(Bartollas & Miller, 1994; Finckenauer, 1984).

Wilderness programs or outdoor programs, used as alternatives to incarcer
ation, provide an open-air environment for treatment. Wilderness programs
take streetwise youths and attempt to change them by placing them in an environment where they have to learn to survive on their own. There are several
wilderness programs such as Outward Bound and Vision Quest. Outward
Bound started in Colorado, situated in the Rocky Mountains, but can now be
found in states such as Minnesota, Maine, Oregon, and North Carolina. It includes mountain walking, backpacking, high-altitude camping, and rock
climbing. The purpose of these activities is to help juveniles gain self-re-
liance, self-worth, discipline, and survival skills.

Vision Quest started by Robert Ledger Burton in 1973 in Tucson, Arizona,
offers a wide variety of programs, including wilderness training, a mule and
horse wagon train, an alternative school and home-based counseling. This
program lasts between one twelve and eighteen months. It has been severely
criticized for its use of physical abuse and placing youths in potentially dangerous activities, such as voyaging on a sailing boat or cross-country travel on
a wagon train (Greenwood & Turner, 1987).

Black Youths and Residential Programs

One residential program for black youths is the *House of Umoja*, founded
by Sister Falaka Fattah and David Fattah who have played a remarkable role in
defusing gang violence in Philadelphia. When the Fattahs found out that their
son was a member of a gang, they invited the gang members to live in their
home. They were able to bring together gang leaders and other members to
resolve their problems. Former gang members who were in prison were also
enlisted because the younger youth respected them. Eventually the House of
Umoja included youths who were referred by the Philadelphia juvenile court.
Sister Falaka Fattah and her husband created an African-style extended family
in which gang members could find positive values to contrast with those of
their street-life culture (Woodson, 1981).

The program provides special education, social, and skills training in an intensive family environment, all within a framework of African-inspired black
consciousness. The Fattahs received help from local community groups and
churches and expanded the program. There are now have twenty-two homes
for gang youths and more than 500 gang youth have been involved in this gang
mediation project. Sister Fattah's influence is so extensive that she has been

able to sponsor city-wide gang conferences. The program has also sponsored the Black Youth Olympics, cultural exchange programs with boys from Belfast, Ireland, and local cultural programs (Woodson, 1981).

Evaluation of Residential Programs

Residential programs usually provide more structure and supervision for court-ordered residents than do other community-corrections efforts, such as probation and aftercare. Since facilities often require residents to participate in a variety of programs, they are likely to have a better success rate than non-residential programs.

The difficulties that these programs face is neighborhood acceptance. Most residential programs are located in the least desirable environments because property owners in more desirable sites, fearing victimization and declining property value, exert strong pressure to prevent these programs from opening. Such resistance has forced many residential programs to relocate in nonresidential areas or high-crime areas. Residential programs can offer much to the juveniles, but results concerning effectiveness are mixed (Stojkovic & Lovell, 1992).

DIVERSION

Juvenile justice is constantly finding new ways to deal with juveniles. Perhaps the most significant reform in the juvenile justice system has been the adoption of diversion. The exact meaning of this term is ambiguous, for it can be used to refer either to general policies or to a single act of removing alleged delinquents from the formal processing of the juvenile justice system. In many cases, however, it refers to the development of programs for dealing with delinquents outside the formal processing of the juvenile court. These programs range from informal strategies to well-organized programs.

The modern era of diversion within juvenile justice can be traced to the 1967 President's Commission on Law and Enforcement and the Administration of Justice which made several recommendations for improving the juvenile justice system. One of those recommendations focused on the policy of diversion. Consequently, in the late 1960s and early 1970s, diversion programs exploded on the scene. One reason for the sudden and great growth of diversion programs was the rationale that the labeling and legal processing of juvenile offenders would result in stigmatization and further delinquency. This premise was based on labeling theory, which argued that persons who are negatively labeled have a tendency to become what they are labeled. A second reason for the sudden increase in diversion programs was the system's inability to handle the juveniles referred to it. Diversion offers a viable alternative for some youths. The third reason for the growth of diversion programs was the availability of federal funds (Klein et al., 1976).

Early diversion programs include St. Louis Diversion Program, the Baltimore Diversion Project, and the Sacramento County 601 Diversion Project. The St. Louis Diversion Program was established in 1971 and provided home detention as an alternative to incarceration in crowded detention centers. Probation officers worked directly with juveniles, their families and school representatives. The Baltimore Diversion Project served juveniles between the ages of 15 and 17 who were charged with nonserious offenses. The program focused on job counseling and placement. The Sacramento County 601 Diversion Project started in 1970 as an experiment to reduce both cost and recidivism rates. This project combined crisis intervention and family counseling.

The Nature of Diversion

Diversion offers several benefits. It reduces the number of cases in the juvenile justice system, it costs less than institutionalization, and it also helps youths avoid the stigma of being labeled a delinquent.

Diversion can be used for specific types of juveniles. Sarri and Vinter (1975) argue that first-time offenders charged with status offenses or minor misdemeanors, or youths known to be receiving treatment in the community, are suitable candidates for diversion. In addition, diversion can be used for predelinquent youths who appear to be heading for trouble.

Juveniles can be diverted to several social agencies in the community--to schools, welfare agencies and police departments--with the hope that they will gain positive life experiences. Ideally, these programs should stress youth involvement, treatment, and rehabilitation, and they should also offer group and individual counseling.

Juveniles can be diverted at several points in the juvenile justice system-- during apprehension, court intake, or after adjudication and before disposition. The point of diversion often depends on the seriousness of the offense. Those diverted at apprehension are more likely to have committed less serious offenses than those diverted at intake. Similarly, the diversionary strategy may depend on the point at which the juvenile is diverted. For example, a juvenile diverted at the initial stage of the system may receive a warning from the police, whereas one diverted at the intake may have to be sent to a treatment program.

Different Types of Diversion Programs

Police officers use several types of diversionary methods. The most common type *is diversion without referral* which entails diverting the juvenile from the system without further significant action; police give a warning or counseling. Police also use *diversion with referral*, which is dictated by the police department or by written agreement between police and community agencies.

It involves transferring the juvenile from police custody to some other agency. The police can also transfer the juvenile from one unit of the department to another unit that can better handle the juvenile. The police also have *recreational diversion programs*, the most common of which is the Police Athletic League (PAL). Through athletic activities, the PAL clubs attempt to keep juveniles off the streets and encourage them to channel their energies in positive and constructive ways. There are also informal probation programs in which the police and the juvenile work out a deal that allows the child to go free, but requires the juvenile to report to the officer at the police station on a regular basis for a period of time (Regoli & Hewitt, 1994).

Court diversion programs are also available. Formal juvenile court processes are commonly suspended prior to filing a petition in order to allow a juvenile to be handled informally. This occurs at intake and is referred to as an informal adjustment. Most states have statutory provisions for informal adjustment. Mediation is another form of court diversion. Some cases that come before the court are not suited for formal adjudication and can be settled through mediation, which requires that the complainant and juvenile meet with a neutral hearing officer. The officer helps the juvenile and the complainant reach a mutually acceptable solution, which can be written or verbal. Mediation is very useful in conflict resolution in minor disputes.

Several *school-based diversion programs* are designed to deter youths from committing further delinquent acts. One such program is the police officer liaison program, which involves maintaining a police presence in the schools. These programs also attempt to foster a better relationship between police and juveniles by using police officers as counselors and by improving the communication between police and school officials. The earliest program of this type was developed in Flint, Michigan, in 1958; a number of police departments and school officials are now involved in these programs. Alternative education programs are also used as a form of diversion. These programs serve marginal students who cannot function in the regular school system, and they involve skills training, community internships, and student input into the curricula (Short, 1990).

Community diversion programs include youth service bureaus, community youth boards and wilderness programs. The establishment of *Youth Service Bureaus* was recommended by the President's Commission on Law Enforcement and Administration of Justice in 1967. The goals of the Youth Service Bureaus are to divert juveniles from the juvenile justice system, advocate and develop services for youths and their families, and involve youths in treatment decision making. Community Youth Boards usually consist of volunteers who conduct informal hearings to determine what services should be provided for children referred by the school, court, police, or parents (Regoli & Hewitt, 1994). Youths are expected to obey the orders of the board. One such program in New Jersey is the Juvenile Conference Committee, which works with minor offenders. The committees act as extensions of the court and attempt to resolve matters without further court involvement. Members of the Juvenile

Conference Committee supervise community work sites, coordinate services with service providers, and provide feedback to the court (State of New Jersey Commission of Investigation, 1993). In addition, some programs are targeted at youth and their families who are in need of intervention. These services deal with several types of juveniles and provide individual as well as family counseling.

Black Youth and Diversion Programs

Diversion programs are designed to assist all youths, but Bloomberg (1984) suggests that the juveniles who are most often diverted tend to be middle-class youths. Consequently, lower class youths are often excluded from this process. The same may be said for black youths. Latessa, Travis, and Wilson (1984) point out that when nonlegal factors such as race, social class, age, and gender become part of diversion decisions, due process rights may be ignored. As established in earlier chapters, black youths are less likely than other youths to be diverted. For example, in New Jersey in 1992, 56% of white youths were diverted at intake compared with 27% of black youths (Juvenile Delinquency Commission, 1993). Nonetheless, some programs do serve black youths, either because of their location or their focus. Some of these programs are as follows.

Mediation and Restitution Services (MARS) is part of the Ceninela Valley Juvenile Diversion Project in Englewood, California, in the inner city. MARS uses mediation by negotiating a settlement between first-time juvenile offenders and their victims, outside of the court system. Once the terms of the resolution are agreed upon, MARS helps the juveniles find employment and encourages counseling. Since its inception in 1992, the majority of participants have experienced no further arrests, and only one was arrested again for the same crime (Abner, 1994).

Project Youth Options Unlimited (Project YOU) is an alternative educational program administered by the New York City Board of Education. In 1989-1990, there were two sites--the Mission Society in the Bronx and the Bushwick Youth Center in Brooklyn. About half of the participants were referred by the court, and the other half by community school districts. Project YOU hopes to decrease the negative consequences of official labeling for those youths referred by the court and to provide an educational option for those who have had difficulties in school. Project YOU offers coursework up to the tenth grade level and GED preparation for older students with the goal of assisting students make an appropriate choice for high school (Goldstein, 1991).

The *Andrew Glover Youth Program* is a privately funded organization operating in New York's Lower East Side. It serves a large number of black and Hispanic youths by working with the police, courts, youth services, and social services. The program provides counseling, gang mediation, family counseling, and housing assistance. The Youth workers spend most of their time on the streets and are available for assistance twenty-four hours a day (Drowns & Hess, 1995).

Evaluation of Diversion Programs

The primary goal of diversion is to reduce delinquency and recidivism, and to date the success of these programs has been mixed. Based on their study from their study of 766 juveniles diverted from the Pima County, Arizona, juvenile court, Rojek and Erickson (1981/1982) concluded that there was little evidence of any behavior change among juveniles diverted to community agencies. Brown and associates (1989), in a followup study of youths referred to two Pennsylvania juvenile courts, reported that postponement of adjudication (early diversion) appeared to increase the likelihood that these delinquents would continue to become criminals, whereas early court adjudication reduced that probability. Other researchers also support the above contention (Frazier & Cochran, 1986; Rausch & Logan, 1983; Spergel, Reamer, & Lynch, 1981). On the other hand, some studies report positive results. Duxbury (1973) claimed that diversion led to lower levels of arrests. Quay and Love (1977) found positive results in an evaluation of diversion services in Florida. More recently, Regoli, Wilderman, and Pogrebin (1985) examined six diversion programs in the Denver, Colorado, area by comparing youths in the diversion programs with youths who were processed through the normal juvenile justice system. They found that the rate of recidivism for youths in diversion programs was lower than that for youths processed through the courts. Several other studies have also reported positive results (McPherson, McDonald, & Ryer, 1983; Palmer & Lewis, 1980; Pogrebin, Poole, & Regoli, 1984; Whitaker & Severy, 1984).

Another goal of diversion is to reduce the number of juveniles who come into contact with the juvenile justice system. However, studies have shown that diversion has resulted in *net widening*--the practice of bringing youths, who would otherwise be left alone, into the juvenile justice system (Anderson & Schoen, 1985; Austin & Krisberg, 1981; Frazier & Cochran, 1986; Gibbons & Blake, 1976; Rausch & Logan, 1983). Police and intake personnel, for example, are dealing with and diverting youths who would normally be ignored by the system (Cohen, 1979; Klein et. al., 1976). Rojek (1982) views the problem of net widening as a form of self-aggrandizement, because increased numbers of juveniles in the agencies can provide "proof" that they are doing something. Other researchers report that diversion actually increases court caseloads (Barton & Butts, 1990; Gibbons & Blake, 1976; Klein et al., 1976; Polk, 1984).

Another intended purpose of diversion programs is to reduce the official stigma of being processed through the juvenile justice system. However, research indicates that these programs have negative consequences for some youths. For example, Latessa, Travis, and Wilson (1984) suggest that some of these programs worsen the behavior patterns of some youth.

There is also some evidence that diversion does not reduce the time spent in the juvenile justice system. Frazier and Cochran (1986), after reviewing data gathered from volunteer services in eight counties in Florida between 1977 and 1980, concluded that diverted youths were in the system longer than nondiverted youths. In addition, they found that diversion was widening the net for black youths. These findings appeared to have been related to the fact that many of the professionals in diversion programs were trained in counseling or social work and preferred more intervention in people's lives rather than less (Regoli & Hewitt, 1994).

PROBLEMS WITH COMMUNITY-BASED TREATMENT PROGRAMS

Community-based treatment programs are more economical than residential programs because they allow the juvenile to reside at home. They are also humane and rehabilitative rather than punishment-oriented. However, critics question the reintegrative philosophy behind them, especially when it is used for violent offenders. They believe that juveniles are delinquent because they fail to abide by society's rules and, therefore, should not remain in society. In other words, institutionalization is the punishment they deserve (Bartollas & Miller, 1994).

Communities often resist the establishment of community-based programs. Although some people believe in community-based programs for offenders, they do not want the programs to be placed in residential communities. In some instances, community members sign petitions opposing the construction of group homes or day-treatment programs for juveniles in their communities. Some people may be downright hostile about having community-based programs in their communities for "criminals." These individuals may view community-based programs as insufficiently punitive for juvenile offenders.

Controversy has also arisen over the selection of youths placed in community-based programs. The conservative approach advocates that only those youths most likely to be helped should be placed in these programs because if the wrong type of youth is admitted, the survival of the programs can be jeopardized. The opposing viewpoint argues that, except for the hard-core recidivists, all delinquents should remain in the community, because their problems originated in the community. Furthermore, they suggest that institutionalization makes them worst offenders (Bartollas & Miller, 1994).

There are also conflicting results on the success of community-based programs. Some researchers have found that community-based programs, both residential and nonresidential, usually affect recidivism rates only to a limited extent (Andrew et al., 1990; Garrett, 1985; Izzo & Ross, 1990; Ohlin, Miller, & Coates, 1976; Whitehead & Lab, 1989). Other researchers have found that some of these programs can be as or more effective than incarceration in reducing postrelease recidivism (Empey & Erickson, 1972; Empey & Lubeck, 1971; Gottfredson, 1987). Gottfredson and Barton (1993) studied three groups of youths: a group that was in the Montrose Training School in Maryland during the period when it was being closed (the transition group); a group that completed a stay at Montrose before it was closed (the preclosing group); and a group after Montrose was closed (the postclosing group). Their research indicated that the postclosing group's recidivism was significantly higher than that of the institutionalized groups both for serious offenses and for property offenses. These findings imply that the alternative programs to which the postclosing group was sent were less effective than institutionalization of the youths in Montrose.

More than fifteen years ago, Massachusetts closed down all its large training schools and developed a network of small secure treatment centers for violent and chronic offenders. All other delinquents were placed in community-based programs (Schwartz, 1989). A recent evaluation of the Massachusetts juvenile correctional system by the National Council on Crime and Delinquency reports that juveniles placed under the authority of the Department of Youth Services following the reforms committed fewer offenses after entering the correctional system. This was particularly true of violent offenders. The overall rate of recidivism was low, and the number of juveniles waived to adult court declined steadily over the years. Furthermore, the correctional programs are cost effective, preserve the public safety, and provide rehabilitation (Krisberg, Austin, & Steele, 1989).

POLICY IMPLICATIONS

Community-based programs face several challenges with regard to black youth. First, the selection process needs to include more black youths for referral to community programs. There appears to be a lack of community-based programs for youths in general, but especially for black and other minority youths. Two proposals of the 1992 Reorganization Plan of juvenile corrections in New Jersey were that a Task Force pay special attention to urban and minority issues and examine the array of community services that should be available for juveniles adjudicated as delinquents as well as for youth "at risk" of involvement in the court (Juvenile Delinquency Commission, 1993). Hubert Williams (1991) has stated that there should be alternatives to imprisonment for youthful black offenders in New Jersey. He suggests a program of modified incarceration in an environment offering treatment, discipline and job placement. It should involve the business, government and the health-care community.

The National Council on Crime and Delinquency has recommended that California invest in local community-based programs as alternatives to punitive state training schools in which minority youths are overrepresented. Suggested programs include day programs, mentor programs, work service programs and drug treatment programs (Austin, Dimas, & Steinhart, 1992). The National Council of Juvenile and Family Court Judges (1990) recommends that judges should provide leadership in developing community-based alternatives to secure detention for minority youth.

These community-based programs should also include cultural sensitivity training and employ more black professionals. Cultural sensitivity will provide juvenile justice personnel with the required knowledge to deal effectively with black youths as clients, and the employment of more black professionals will provide black youths with persons who can understand their background and with whom they can identify.

The black community needs to take some responsibility in creating more community-based treatment programs for black youth. Black leaders and community workers should take the initiative in establishing some of these community-based programs rather than depending solely on the government. These programs do cost money, but joint ventures and partnerships between organizations could make these programs a reality. The role of the black community in community-based programs is significant because such programs can be tailored to meet the needs of black youths. An Afrocentric approach rather than a Eurocentric approach to treatment is the preferred approach for blacks. The role of the black community in creating and establishing these programs will be pivotal to their success or failure. After the state governments establish and approve these programs, police, intake workers, judges, and correctional personnel will have to utilize the programs effectively.

SUMMARY

Community-based treatment programs are supported by advocates of the reintegration philosophy. Some states have even closed many of their training schools in order to focus more on community-based programs.

Evidence regarding the effectiveness of community-based programs is conflicting. In addition, community-based programs are threatened by the present "get tough" policy at the federal and local levels. However, because of the continuing increase in juvenile offenses, overcrowded institutions, and the cost of incarceration, these programs may well survive.

Data have consistently shown that black youths are overrepresented in juvenile institutions. The critical question for the juvenile justice system is how to reduce the number of incarcerated black youths. Community-based programs will have to be utilized more extensively for black youths. Unfortunately, there are not enough community-based programs for delinquents, especially for minority youth. This continues to be a major challenge for the juvenile justice system in the 1990s.

10

Delinquency Prevention

The general approach in this society to juvenile delinquency is reactive, with state and federal governments spending millions of dollars to arrest, prosecute, and punish delinquents. This approach has failed to reduce delinquency substantively for the recidivism rate is high, delinquents are younger, and the offenses are more violent. Common sense dictates that prevention of delinquency is the more realistic way to deal with delinquency rather than reacting to it after it has occurred. Some attempts, though not enough, have focused on prevention. The analysis in this chapter begins with a discussion of different types of prevention programs and concludes with policy implications for preventing delinquency among black youths.

FEDERAL PREVENTION INITIATIVES

In 1967, the Task Force on Juvenile Delinquency and Youth Crime of the President's Commission on Law Enforcement and Administration of Justice advocated prevention as the most efficient way to deal with crime. Subsequently, this idea became codified in law with the Juvenile Prevention Acts of 1972 and 1974, which provided for the coordination of federal delinquency programs and established delinquency prevention as a national priority. The act established the Office of Juvenile Justice and Delinquency Prevention (OJJDP) and, within that office, a National Institute for Justice and Delinquency Prevention (NIJJDP) as its research, evaluation, and information center. The OJJDP funds several delinquency prevention and control programs across the country and operates at the state and local levels, many of which are innovative in their approaches. Since 1980, federal initiatives for crime prevention have decreased, and a shift in focus has occurred as well. As is true of many states, the federal government is focusing on punishment rather than rehabilitation and prevention--a greater emphasis on justice (Olson-Raymer,

1983). Despite this shift in focus, some federal programs continue to operate. Federal prevention programs are still available, however.

Traditionally, many of these programs concentrated on status and minor offenders rather than on serious, habitual offenders. Since 1984, however, more emphasis has been placed on serious and habitual offenders in response to the creation of the Habitual Serious and Violent Offender Program. This program provides for special diagnostic assessment, treatment plans, and management after conviction (Cronin et al., 1988).

The OJJDP, in conjunction with the Department of Education, has supported the growth of the National School Safety Center (NSSC), which seeks to expand training resources in school safety and delinquency prevention; to assist schools in developing techniques for involving businesses, criminal justice professionals, and community leaders in school safety; and to collect and disseminate information on school safety and delinquency prevention, criminal law, and procedures in federal, state and local jurisdictions (Speirs, 1986).

TYPES OF PREVENTION AND PREVENTION PROGRAMS

The three levels of delinquency prevention are primary, secondary, and tertiary. Primary prevention is directed at modifying the circumstances and situations that lead to crime. Secondary prevention seeks early identification and intervention into the lives of individuals or groups that are considered "at risk" for delinquency. The idea is to prevent delinquency acts before they occur by identifying juveniles who appear to be "predelinquent." Tertiary prevention focuses on preventing further delinquent acts by youths already identified as delinquents.

Lejins (1967) discusses three types of prevention: punitive, corrective, and mechanical. Punitive prevention is the threat of punishment and assumes that punishment will prevent the act; corrective prevention refers to the attempt to eliminate potential causes, factors, or motivation before delinquency occurs; and mechanical prevention emphasizes making it difficult or impossible for the potential delinquent to commit an offense, for example, through curfew regulations.

Delinquency is a complex problem and so requires a multifaceted approach to its prevention. Delinquency prevention encompasses many factors, especially poverty, poor housing, and unemployment, and it also involves the influence of social institutions. Several prevention programs focus on various social factors; they are as follows.

Family-based Prevention Programs

One very interesting family-based prevention program is the *Girl Scouts in Prison* project which is funded jointly with the National Institute of Justice, the Maryland Division of Corrections, and the Girl Scouts of Central Maryland. The program targets daughters, from ages 5 to 17, of incarcerated women and attempts to strengthen family bonds between mothers and daughters. The program is based on documented research showing that children of mothers who are incarcerated suffer emotionally, exhibit poor performance, and become truant or pregnant. The program also hopes to reduce the trauma the girls experienced because of the separation from their mothers, as well as to improve the mothers' parenting skills so as to increase communication between mothers and daughters.

Through this program, the mothers and their daughters meet every two weeks for Girl Scout meetings in the prison library. Girl Scout volunteers not only coordinate and escort the daughters to the meeting, but also provide transportation. The Guide Scout volunteers offer the mothers Girl Scout leadership and adult development courses twice a month before the girls arrive. Because the girls meet on alternate weeks in the community with a volunteer leader, the children have much to tell their mothers about their field trips. The program appears to have been helpful because deeper levels of understanding and trust have developed between mother and daughter. The enthusiastic response from the participants of this two-year-old program has led other states to express interest in a similar program (Moses, 1993).

School Programs

Schools have always been considered pivotal in delinquency prevention. Not only does delinquency occur in school, but also the acts of delinquency within the school have become more violent. Schools can assist in delinquency prevention in two ways. One perspective suggests that the schools are healthy institutions that have to deal with unruly, undisciplined, and predelinquent youths, who are ill prepared to meet the demands of schools. This is often referred to as the "rotten kids" view (Gibbons & Krohn, 1991). To play a role in delinquency, the school will have to concentrate on those youths who are at risk for delinquency.

Gangs in school are a very serious problem, and several states have developed programs to prevent gang delinquency in their schools. These programs are targeted at youths who are "at risk" for delinquency. One such program is Portland's Gang Prevention Program called Gang Awareness and Intervention Activities and is integrated into the curriculum. It combines the teaching of gang information with group discussion and exercises to teach values and social skills. Lessons in Grades 3-5 focus on teaching gang characteristics and presenting alternatives to gang involvement. The lessons in Grades 5-7 focus on such topics as choosing appropriate friends, responding to peer pressure, solving problems through cooperation, and setting positive goals. Audiovisual aids are used in the classroom, and films that depict real-life gang violence and its impact are shown to reinforce the dangers of gangs (Gaustaud, 1991).

Schools across the country have also developed strategies and tactics to prevent the spread of gangs and gang violence in schools. Some schools have demanded that gang graffiti be painted over immediately once discovered on school property. Clothing has also been targeted. Some schools have banned shoelaces, bandanas, and some types of hats which indicate gang membership (Gaustaud, 1991). However, the problem is that more and more gang clothing and symbols have become teen fashion (Stover, 1986). Recently, professional athletic jackets have become popular with gang members; this makes it difficult to determine gang members since all youths like these kinds of jackets. Schools are also promoting gang awareness among their staff and parents by distributing information concerning dress codes and school regulations. They have also attempted to keep nonstudent gang members off the school campus and to provide gang monitors who are trained in antigang techniques (Gaustaud, 1991).

The second perspective, the "rotten schools" argument, assumes that the schools themselves are defective, creating alienation and adjustment problems for lower class and minority youths, especially black youths, which in turn can lead to delinquency (Gibbons & Krohn, 1991). If one accepts the "rotten schools" argument, then the prevention of delinquency will have to focus on the structure and organization of the schools. This entails modifying the curriculum, creating innovative teaching strategies, eliminating the tracking system, and changing the role of intelligence and other standardized tests. Unfortunately, this is a difficult task, and not enough emphasis has been placed on these tactics.

Although extensive overhaul of the educational system is yet to be attempted, a few programs which have been set up to create a positive environment for students. One such program that has attempted to prevent delinquency by altering the learning environment was Project PATHE (Positive Action Through Holistic Education). It operated in four middle and three high schools in South Carolina for three years as part of the Juvenile Justice and Delinquency Prevention's Alternative Education Initiative (Gottfredson, 1986). Project PATHE attempted to prevent delinquency by strengthening the youth's commitment to school and by providing positive experiences in school through participation in school activities and attachment to positive members of the school community. The program created teams consisting of teachers, students, parents, and community members who were trained to implement changes and revise policies. Mini-courses on such strategies such as note taking and listening and reading for an hour were also initiated in this program. Extracurricular activities were expanded, and peer counseling and rap sessions were introduced, as was counseling for children with special needs.

Gottfredson (1986) evaluated the program and found that the program resulted in a moderate reduction in delinquency and school misconduct, but the services for high-risk youths did not reduce their level of delinquency.

Some school-based prevention programs are centered around mediation. In such programs, students are trained by teachers to be mediators who work with their fellow students in negotiating the settlement of disputes. One such program is the Resolving Conflict Creatively Program (RCCP), which seeks to create a climate of nonviolence in schools. The program started in New York in 1985 and can be found in the Anchorage school districts (Alaska), the New Orleans public schools (Louisiana), the South-Orange Maplewood School District (New Jersey), and the Vista United school districts (California). The program stresses the need for nonviolent alternatives for dealing with conflict, negotiation, and other conflict resolution skills. The lessons involve role playing, interviewing, group dialogue, brainstorming, and other experiential learning techniques. An important aspect of the program is parent training through a Parent Involvement Program component. This consists of a team of two or three parents per school, who are trained for sixty hours in family communication and conflict resolution (Sherman, 1994).

Evaluation of the program indicates that teachers are enthusiastic about the program, and they report decreased levels of violence among the students in the program. Students in the program report that they are now able to resolve their conflict without violence, and they have fewer fights and name-calling (Sherman, 1994).

A number of other strategies are used in schools to prevent delinquency. For example, Lab (1988) reported on programs that have attempted to raise intelligence levels through remedial education. Some of these programs have been successful in reducing recidivism, especially among disabled youths.

Police Programs

Police departments have developed a variety of programs to prevent delinquency. For example, the Los Angeles United School District developed the Drug Abuse Resistance Education (DARE) project. The project uses uniformed officers who go into the elementary school to teach students in fifth and sixth grades. The officers teach the students to say "no" to drugs, as well as ways to say "no," and they help them build high self-esteem. The officers also teach how to make positive decisions and to resist peer pressure.

DARE is based on the concept that youths need social skills to resist peer pressure to take drugs. More than 40% of all school districts have incorporated it into their curriculum as a standard part of their curriculum. The program also now begins in kindergarten and goes through to grade 12. New addition to the DARE program is the DARE Parent Program (DPP) created to motivate parents to participate in preventing substance abuse. Through a series of meetings, parents learn about the DARE program, how to recognize signs of drug use, and how to communicate effectively with their children.

Problem-oriented Policing

In this innovative police approach to crime, the police, instead of simply responding to crime, interviewing victims and witnesses, and arresting delinquents, identify and develop a profile of high-crime areas of the city. In collaboration with schools, businesses, service agencies, and citizens, they then develop a range of possible solutions to the problems. One such problem-oriented program is the Serious Habitual Offender Drug Involved (SHODI) program which concentrates on chronic youthful offenders in Ventura, California, Colorado Springs, Colorado, and Jacksonville, Florida. In these programs, police have access to full data on the delinquents' arrest records so that they can check records by computer if a youth is stopped and questioned. Once a juvenile offender has been identified and has been arrested four times within a year, police officers keep a closer watch on him or her (NBC News Special, 1987).

Community Programs

The first community-oriented delinquency prevention programs focused on changing the environment. One of the earliest of these project was the Chicago Area Project, which was based on the theories of Shaw and McKay who argued that the neighborhood conditions contribute to delinquency. The project focused on the high-crime areas of Chicago and tried to mobilize the support of those neighborhoods to prevent delinquency. The project sponsored recreation projects, community improvement, and other activities. Delinquency decreased in three out of the four communities where the project was implemented, but since the project did not have control groups, it was difficult to measure its effectiveness adequately.

Another early federal community-based prevention project was the "War on Poverty," which was initiated in New York by President Kennedy, who did not live to see it fulfilled; President Johnson continued and expanded the project. This project was based on the opportunity theory of Cloward and Ohlin (1960) and consisted of four major programs. These included Head Start, Job Corps, Vista, and Community Action Program which are still in operation.

The Juvenile Awareness Project inspired the documentaries "Scared Straight" and "Scared Straight: Ten Years After." The program, which was designed to prevent delinquents from committing further delinquency (tertiary prevention), started in 1976 at Rahway State Prison in New Jersey. It exposes youths who have been adjudicated delinquents to the realities of prison life by allowing the delinquents to be face to face with prisoners. The hope is that this contact and exposure will deter youths from further delinquent behavior. The basic approach used by the Lifers Group at Rahway is to scare the juveniles by means of harsh confrontations with prisoners. A documentary film entitled "Scared Straight" of the program was produced in 1978 and was shown on television throughout the country. Soon after the film was shown, similar programs were started nationwide. Although the program still exists today in Rahway State Prison, it presents several problems. Finckenauer

(1982) points out that the claim by the Lifers Group's claim that 90% of the juveniles who participated in the program have gone straight is questionable, since the group did not keep very good records. According to Finckenauer, of the 10,000 to 15,000 youths who have participated in the program, most were recruited from local high schools, and the students were under the impression that they were going on a field trip. Thus, there is no good evidence to indicate that these youths were delinquents. In addition, there are no follow-up services once the juveniles leave the prison setting. Finckenauer questions the credibility of the film and concludes that the project has failed to reduce delinquency.

Black Youths and Prevention Programs

Some programs serve black youths, especially those living in the inner city. One of these programs, *Black Achievers*, is a YMCA community-based program serving up to forty inner-city black youths in Trenton, New Jersey. The goals of the club are to fulfill the objectives of the participants in five areas-- career, leadership, education, social activity and religious development. Activities provide the young men with an opportunity to experience at first hand what they can achieve for themselves. The program is partially funded by the Department of Human Services Minority Males Community Challenge (State of New Jersey Commission of Investigation, 1993).

Second Street Youth Center Teen Rap-port Program, located in Plainfield, New Jersey, provides structured activities for up to fifty minority males, aged 13 to 17, who are considered at risk. Hands-on counseling is made available to combat low self-esteem, substance abuse, illiteracy, and recidivism. These counseling services include life skills instruction, role models, mentoring a group on an individual basis, and basic academic skills improvement. The center encourages client-business and client-law enforcement relationships as a means of breaking down the barriers of hostility and mistrust. The Team Rapport program is funded by the Department of Human Services Minority Males Challenge Grant (State of New Jersey Commission of Investigation, 1993).

Afri-Male Institute, located in Willingboro, New Jersey, is a nonprofit agency that provides services to the black community. The institute prepares young African-American males to become responsible members of the society through several services. Males from ages 12 to 19 are trained in human sexuality, social responsibility, family values, healthy living and public speaking. The institute also provides career counseling and assists seniors in high school to prepare for college (State of New Jersey Commission of Investigation, 1993).

Rites of Passage, located in Cedar Rapids, Iowa, addresses minority over-representation in the juvenile justice system. It attempts to reduce the delinquency rate among middle-school African-American males who are in high-risk situations. The project involves tutoring, mentoring, crisis intervention, individual and family counseling, and recreational activities. The development of self-esteem and responsibility is emphasized. The participants and their mentors view the project as worthwhile, and it has been successful in improving the participants' family lives and academic performance (Allen, 1993).

Bright Future Project is a delinquency prevention project located in Memphis, Tennessee, and provides academic and social support to African-American youth aged 5 to 15. This project provides study resources to help these youths complete their homework assignments. Reading and comprehension testing and prescribed tutoring are available for a limited number of youths. Rap sessions and discussions are also provided, and youths also participate in neighborhood improvement projects.

The project serves about 30 youths a day during the school year, about 330 youths take advantage of the after-school tutoring, and 22 young people have participated in the special testing and remediation program. The quality of the participants' schoolwork has improved, and the program has gained the respect and confidence of the community (Allen, 1993).

The Children at Risk (CAR) program seeks to prevent inner-city youth from joining gangs and using drugs by providing them with intensive activities which include after-school and summer and programs, counseling, tutoring, and mentoring. The CAR project operates in conjunction with schools, police, and other criminal justice agencies. The Center on Addiction and Substance Abuse manages the project, which has been implemented in Austin, Texas, Memphis, Newark, Savannah, and Seattle (Herbert, 1993).

Evaluation of Prevention Programs

As previously indicated, delinquency prevention programs usually focus on individual treatment or on reforming society. Neither approach has been easy to implement. Individual treatment programs are of two kinds. The first deals with youths who already have had contact with the juvenile justice system, and it attempts to prevent further contact. This approach makes it difficult to rehabilitate juveniles once they have engaged in delinquent behavior. Even if the youth completes the program, it is difficult to determine whether that person was truly deterred from further delinquency or was simply pretending to have changed. Many of these individual treatment programs are not multidimensional, and they focus on one or two factors in isolation from other factors. For example, a prevention program that is school or peer-oriented, with little emphasis on the family, may not be successful if the youths come from a dysfunctional background. What is needed is a holistic approach to delinquency prevention.

The second type of individual treatment program is designed to identify youths who are at risk for becoming delinquent. These programs are called early identification programs or predelinquency programs and are intended to work with juveniles before they get into trouble. These programs can create problems, for by focusing on certain youths for treatment, these programs are also singling them out as potential delinquents. This is a form of labeling which, according to labeling theorists, can lead to the very behavior that these programs are designed to prevent.

POLICY IMPLICATIONS

The number of delinquency prevention programs for black youths is insufficient, and many of them focus on males to the neglect of females. Although a significantly greater number of black males than females are involved in delinquency, the number of black delinquent females has increased in the last several years. Furthermore, female delinquents have special problems, such as teen pregnancy and sexual abuse, but few programs respond to these needs, especially to those of minority females. Therefore, more delinquency prevention programs that single out the special problems of black females should be made available.

Joseph and Greene (1994) found that there were few programs for black delinquents even in institutions. The incarcerated youths complained about the lack of constructive programs and about too much free time. Chesney-Lind and Shelden (1992) also reported that programs to meet the needs of females delinquents are inadequate in most states.

Many delinquency programs do not get to the roots of the problem. Many of them ignore the sources of delinquency and are little more than Band-Aid programs. The roots of crime and delinquency are complex, but only by attacking the causes will society begin to address the problem of delinquency. The society would not have such a serious crime problem if delinquency prevention programs were effective in the first place, for the majority of adult criminals were once delinquents.

Programs designed to change society are complex and costly, and the results are often observed only in the long term. These programs, however, may be more effective than individual prevention programs. Unfortunately, less money and time has been spent on these programs as compared with individual treatment programs. Since individual prevention programs have failed to significantly reduce delinquency, more emphasis should be placed on eliminating the factors that contribute to delinquency.

In 1994 the Senate approved the President Clinton's Crime Bill which advocates 100,000 more police officers, life sentences for some third-time felons, expansion of the death penalty, and a ban on nineteen asasult-type weapons (Phillips & Hasson, 1994). The president seems to view this bill as the answer to the crime problem. One issue over which some of the Republican senators and the president fought very fiercely was the crime prevention measures included in the bill. Originally, $6.9 billion was allocated for prevention programs (Phillips, 1994), but this sum was reduced in the final bill passed by the Senate. The objection to the prevention programs was that too much federal money was allocated to these programs, or as one senator referred to it to "pork spending" (Phillips, 1994). Instead, some of these senators wanted stronger mandatory minimum sentences. Such short-sightedness on the part of some politicians is unfortunate. A "get tough" strategy is not the answer to the crime and delinquency problem. It may keep serious criminals and delinquents off the streets for a while, but it will not attack the roots of the problem. Although crime control is important, crime prevention is equally important, if not more so, and should be given more attention than it is given at present. Stiffer penalties, increased law enforcement, and gun control will not have a significant impact on crime and delinquency if more emphasis is not placed on the factors that contribute to crime and delinquency. In particular, meaningful prevention programs are needed for black youths in the inner cities. Several researchers have identified the factors that contribute to delinquency, and these are the factors that need the attention of politicians and communities.

The school is an important source of delinquency, and so a serious modification in the educational system is needed. The educational achievement of black youths lags behind that of white youths, and their dropout rate is significantly higher than that of white youths. Because some black youths feel alienated in a school system that is designed for the white middle class, they often drop out and engage in delinquency. Many of these schools, by the very nature of their structure, create problems for many black youths. Furthermore, schools in the United States are segregated owing to segregated housing patterns. Most schools for black youths are located in poor urban areas, and the standards tend to be lower than those in predominantly white schools (National Research Center, 1989). The educational system needs to be changed so that it will meet the needs of black youth.

The federal government has sponsored many programs aimed at improving educational opportunities for disadvantaged youth. These programs are also designed to decrease the likelihood of delinquency among youth "at risk." One such program is Head Start which is based on the belief that lower class children are more likely to fail in school because they enter ill prepared. Therefore, the goal of Head Start is to assist disadvantaged youth so that they can "catch up" in their preschool years. In 1991, more than $2 billion was spent on Head Start programs in all fifty states (Kantrowitz & McCormick, 1992). Without this program, many children from culturally deprived environments would not succeed or would drop out by the time they reached high school. However, findings from a 1992 study showed that children who attended Head Start programs between 1967 and 1977 in Chicago scored higher than the national average in 1974, but 10 years later, they scored lower and only 62% eventually graduated from high school (Regoli & Hewitt, 1994). These results indicate that lower class children need much more than these programs offer. They may need long term academic support throughout their school careers, not just during the early years.

The school curriculum needs to be more inclusive of black cultural values and experiences so that black children can have a sense of belonging rather than a feeling of alienation, thereby lowering the dropout rate among black youths. This society is multicultural, and the school curriculum should reflect this diversity. Changes in school practices are also necessary. The practice of screening black youths into nonacademic or noncollege tracks needs to be eliminated. Students in noncollege preparatory tracks, compared with those in college tracks, experience greater academic failure and higher dropout rates, engage in frequent misbehaviors, and commit more delinquent acts (Schafer, Olexa, & Polk, 1972; Waitrowski et al., 1982). Another outcome of tracking is the labeling and stigmatization of youths in noncollege tracks as academically inferior or underachievers (Kelly & Grove, 1981).

Poverty is a significant factor causing delinquency among black youth. As was discussed in Chapter 2, blacks are significantly poorer than whites. Another factor identified as contributing to the disproportionate representation of minority youth, especially African Americans, in the California juvenile justice system, is joblessness (Austin, Dimas, & Steinhart, 1992). One recommendation is to create new economic opportunities for minority youths.

The federal government has created several initiatives to assist unemployed youths; these include the Manpower Development and Training Act, Job Corps, and youth opportunity centers. The underlying assumption of these programs is that youths who are employed are less likely than those who are unemployed to be involved in delinquency. The federal government efforts are commendable, but they are not enough. More importantly, the states need to create more occupational opportunities for black youths. Vocational training and employment programs should be offered as alternatives to street gangs and delinquency (Austin, Dimas, & Steinhart, 1992). New economic incentives are needed to increase the labor force participation of black youths, who are among the most chronically unemployed. Businesses should become involved in the black community in order to provide long-term jobs for black youths, and government should provide more economic opportunities for black youths. The problem of joblessness among black youths is very complex and so requires complex solutions. A massive investment in providing economic opportunities is needed if the problem of delinquency is to be curtailed.

The family is often a source of delinquent behavior. This relationship is very critical today because the traditional family is changing. The nuclear family structure is showing signs of being replaced by new family forms, such as single-parent, blended, or hybrid families.

Many black families are headed by females, and the plight of many of the children in these families is compounded by poverty. Many of these families are forced to reside in poverty-stricken environments, with poor housing, high crime rates, chronic unemployment, and unhealthy conditions. Moreover, many of these families cannot afford health care, do not eat regular meals, and are subsidized by government assistance (Children Defense Fund, 1992).

Several family processes seem to be related to delinquency. Children from broken homes are reported to be more involved in delinquency than those from intact homes (Brady, Bray & Zeeb, 1986; Hongeller, 1989; Toby, 1957).

Families suffering economic hardships often experience a great deal of stress and conflict, which in turn can contribute to delinquency. Other family factors include poor discipline, family size, family conflict, and parental criminality (Loeber & Stouthamer-Loeber, 1986).

Since the family can be an important contributor to delinquent behavior, it follows that improving the family can help prevent delinquency. More early childhood prevention programs are needed, especially for mothers who are poor. Counseling and workshops in proper child-rearing practices should be provided to pregnant women who may lack such skills.

Continuing education on parenting should be made available in the black community in such agencies as health-care centers, schools, and community centers.

The states need to provide services that emphasize the prevention of unwanted pregnancy, teenage pregnancy, and divorce. Early intervention services for families at risk of family discord and conflict are a necessity for all states. In addition, states should provide adequate child-care facilities for parents who need them. The states should provide more economic and social opportunities for black parents so that they can provide financially for their children. Parents in the black community also have a responsibility in the fight against delinquency by teaching appropriate behaviors and values, providing proper role models, and refraining from using violence against their children.

SUMMARY

Preventing delinquency is more desirable than trying to rehabilitate delinquents. Several attempts have been made to devise delinquency prevention programs, both on the individual and on the societal level. However, not only has delinquency increased over the years, but also the delinquents appear to be younger and more violent than before. The focus should shift from treatment and punishment to prevention. If the root causes of delinquency are not addressed, society will be fighting a losing battle in the long run.

Particular attention must be given to black youths. If the problems that plague young blacks are not dealt with seriously, then these youths may continue to be overrepresented in the juvenile justice system. Black delinquents are victimizers, but they are also victims of this society.

11

Black Youths, and the Future of Juvenile Justice

The juvenile justice system evolved as an attempt to deal with neglected and delinquent children within an informal, nonadversarial setting. Juvenile courts were empowered to intervene in cases in which youngsters were involved in violations of criminal statutes. However, the procedural informality of the juvenile court procedures denied juveniles their constitutional rights. Thus, as a result of a series of legal challenges, the U.S. Supreme Court extended certain procedural rights to juveniles. Yet after almost a century since the juvenile justice system was initiated by the child savers movement, some debate has arisen as to the success or failure of the system. It appears that the juvenile justice system has met some of its original goals to some extent. It is more humane, less punitive, and less stigmatizing than the criminal justice system. The system is far from being successful, however.

The juvenile justice system's long-standing mission is to correct youthful offenders so that they do not return to the system or continue on to an adult criminal career. Many treatment techniques have been tried in order to accomplish rehabilitation; these include therapy, counseling, guided group interaction, and intensified individual, group, and family counseling programs. Although some of these strategies do work in some situations with some offenders, the overall results have not been sufficient to lower recidivism rates. Juvenile courts and juvenile institutions appear to have failed to effectively prevent delinquents from further involvement in lawbreaking. One difficulty faced by juvenile justice is trying to rehabilitate youths some of whom were never socialized to accept society's norms and values.

Deficiencies in the juvenile justice system have led to reforms over the years. In the 1970s several reforms of the juvenile justice system--the so-called Four Ds of juvenile justice--were effected: diversion, decriminalization, deinstitutionalization, and due process.

Diversion involved attempts to minimize the juvenile's contact with the juvenile justice system, thereby avoiding the negative effects of being adjudicated a delinquent. To achieve this goal, several programs were instituted in police departments, schools, and the community. One national evaluation of diversion programs reported mixed results. It found that diversion programs reduced neither the stigma nor the incidence of delinquent acts. However, the results also indicated that diversion programs were less coercive, less controlling, and more helpful than the juvenile justice agencies (Finckenauer, 1984).

Decriminalization limited the range of behaviors for which juveniles can be held liable by the juvenile justice system. It involved the removal of status offenses and some minor delinquent acts from the jurisdiction of the juvenile justice system. The argument for decriminalization was that legal intervention into the lives of juveniles results in a labeling process. Consequently, a self-fulfilling prophecy results, with those labeled delinquent acting like delinquents. By the late 1970s, several states had separated status offenders from juvenile offenders.

Deinstitutionalization attempted to divert as many delinquents as possible into community-based programs and away from institutions. Although alternatives to institutionalization have been devised, including small, specialized, community-based residential facilities, boot camps, ranches, forestry camps and farms, delinquency remains high. These programs appear to achieve results comparable to those of training schools, but it is not quite clear whether these alternatives are markedly more successful than training schools. However, most of these programs are less expensive than institutionalization, which is a strong argument for their continued use.

Abuses in the juvenile justice system prompted expansion of due process rights. Starting with the 1966 *Kent* decision, the United States Supreme Court extended basic legal rights to juveniles in an attempt to restrict the power derived from the doctrine of *parens patriae*.

Today, the juvenile justice system is very much a legal system, yet it has not been successful in fulfilling its goal of rehabilitation. The juvenile justice system is faced with the issue of what to do with violent and hard-core juveniles. Although many of them are dangerous, the system displays extreme caution when dealing with such offenders because they are protected by several due process rights. Very often, these hard-core juveniles are prosecuted as adults in criminal court, and, if convicted and placed in a juvenile institution, they become leaders in inmate subculture. If placed in an adult correctional facility, they are prey for adult inmates (Bartollas & Miller, 1994). In either institution, there is no rehabilitation. Thus, so once these "criminals" are released, they are likely to break the law and return to the system.

Large-scale delinquency prevention programs directed at environmental changes have been instituted, but these prevention strategies seem to be inefficient since the youths are not being deterred from delinquency.

Presently, the juvenile justice system is under attack from all quarters. Few support keeping the juvenile justice system as it has been. Some want to increase the number of youths transferred to the adult court, while others advocate the merging of the juvenile justice system with the adult justice system

(Bartollas & Miller, 1994). However, the general national mood is a "get tough" attitude, and legislatures, both state and federal, have taken a crime control approach to deal with juvenile delinquency. This attitude is producing a rise in the population of juvenile correctional institutions and a loss of support for community-based corrections and diversionary programs. Determinate and mandatory sentencing for juveniles has been established in several states. More than ever, juvenile offenders are being transferred to the adult courts (Bartollas & Miller, 1994). As the public's fear of juvenile and adult crime intensifies, the juvenile justice system is likely to become more punitive instead of rehabilitative.

One of the most contentious issues for the juvenile justice system is the overrepresentation of blacks in the system. The two major explanations for this disparity are discrimination in the processing of black youths and the actual involvement of black youths in serious and violent crimes. No matter what explanation is accepted, it is clear that society has to initiate reforms in the juvenile justice system and provide delinquency reduction programs for black youths.

REFORMING THE SYSTEM

A review of the data and research in the preceding chapters indicates that black youths are overrepresented at every stage of the juvenile justice system. Research has shown that black youths are disproportionately arrested, adjudicated as delinquents, transferred to adult court, and incarcerated than any other group of youths. The official national data show that black youths accounted for 27% of all juvenile arrests in 1992; 58% were petitioned to juvenile court in 1991 and of these 57% were adjudicated delinquent. They constituted 32% of all juveniles in private facilities in 1991 (Maguire & Pastore, 1994). This pattern is reflected in states including New York, New Jersey, Delaware, and California.

The data also reveal that black youths are arrested more often than any other group; they are transferred to adult court more often than any other group; they receive longer sentences than other youths; and they more often are sentenced to death than any other racial or ethnic group. A major question has been whether or not discriminatory treatment of black youths plays a role in their high arrest, conviction, and incarceration rates. Research supports the notion that discrimination has a direct impact on decisions at several points in the juvenile justice process. According to Bishop and Frazier (1988), African-American youths are more likely to be recommended for formal processing, referred to court, adjudicated delinquents, and given harsher dispositions than their white counterparts.

The juvenile justice system is in need of reform. Whether or not racial discrimination in the system is intentional, this issue needs to be addressed. Juvenile justice personnel should be trained to be more sensitive to the needs of black youths in the juvenile justice system. To be effective, juvenile justice personnel should understand their clientele, which has become more and more culturally diverse. Through cross-cultural knowledge, sensitivity, and understanding, professionals can demonstrate greater competence and professionalism in their jobs. Mandatory cultural and sensitivity training should be provided to personnel in the juvenile justice system. The states should make funds available for such training, and the training should be ongoing, making use of workshops, seminars, and lectures. This training should sensitize police officers, judges, intake officers, and others to the cultural and racial background of black youth.

States also need to increase the employment of minority personnel in the juvenile justice system. Black police officers are underrepresented in many major cities such as New York and Los Angeles. Professionalism in the system includes the hiring of minority officers to represent their communities. There should, therefore, be a comprehensive policy of recruiting blacks for positions throughout the juvenile justice system.

DELINQUENCY REDUCTION

As noted earlier, the 1994 crime bill will increase the number of police officers on the street. Police presence on the streets may deter people from committing delinquent acts, but it cannot prevent delinquency, since a large proportion of illegal behavior goes undetected by the police. Similarly, the elimination of discrimination in the juvenile justice system will not seriously reduce the delinquency rate. Both are reactive mechanisms, but preventive measures are needed. The basic causes of delinquency need to be addressed. Society as a whole is criminogenic, and factors such as poverty, lack of economic opportunities, racism, broken homes, and deteriorating environments have all been identified as contributors to crime and delinquency among blacks. The policy implication is straightforward: expand the social and economic opportunities for blacks, and crime and delinquency among this particular group will decrease.

Black youths in the urban areas of America have lived through some painful experiences: a history of discrimination, high unemployment, low status, and rejection by the society. Many black youths do not have a stake in conformity because they are shut out of the mainstream. Many of these youths have reacted to these painful experiences with resentment, self-destruction, anger, and rage--all predisposing factors of delinquency.

There is a feeling of hopelessness among many black youths. Many view the future with pessimism and are resigned to a future of unemployment, violence, and even an early death. This feeling of hopelessness has also contributed to high rates of drug and alcohol use, gang involvement, teenage pregnancies, and crime and delinquency. The feeling of hopelessness has resulted in violence as young blacks kill or maim one another. This is the black youths' most destructive response to pain and hopelessness.

Black youths' involvement in violence is well known. They are paraded daily in front of television cameras for the world to see; they appear in juvenile courts on a frequent basis; and they inhabit detention centers and institutions for long periods of time.

While one-sixth of all Americans under the age of 18 are black, in the past several years nearly 50% of all juveniles arrested for homicides have been black (Ewing, 1990). Many of these murderers are getting not only more violent but also younger. For example, recently, Robert Sandifer, an 11 year-old African-American boy, in an attempt to impress his gang members, engaged in a drive-by shooting that accidentally killed an innocent 14 year-old black girl. This shooting resulted in national media attention, and it is alleged that, in an attempt to prevent this young murderer from confessing, his fellow gang members viciously killed him and dumped his body by a bridge. Later, two brothers, 16 and 14 years old, were charged with his murder (*Jet*, 1994).

Gangs represent a real tragedy for the black community. They control many of the inner-city communities and have spread to several small towns throughout the nation. In cities such as New York, Boston, Detroit, Chicago, Washington, D.C. and Los Angeles, gangs have been causing havoc with their killings of rival gang members, as well as many innocent individuals in drive-by shootings.

American society must take positive steps to reduce the problems of black youths. While the complete elimination of delinquency is unrealistic, the forces that contribute to such behavior could be lessened. Structural changes are needed to reduce the pain and hopelessness experienced by black youths.

Janet Reno (1993), the present Attorney General, has suggested that if society wants to change all the delinquent children, it has to start early. Reno has also reported that when she was the prosecutor of Dade County, Florida, she realized that crime, drugs, delinquency and dropouts, youth gangs, and teen pregnancy were symptoms of a deeper social problem. For the last thirty and forty years, she said, Americans have forgotten and neglected children. She has recommended that society give these youths an opportunity to belong, to contribute, to feel competent, and to be involved. She has also pleaded for society to save these youths early without labeling them, to support their parents, to provide them with relevant marketable skills, and to develop meaningful programs in the community. She expressed similar sentiments in her address to the participants of the American Society of Criminology at its annual conference in Miami, in Florida, 1994. The Attorney General should be commended for her insight but her words need to be translated into action. More needs to be done to help black youths.

Early intervention is necessary for black youths who are at risk before they get caught up in the mechanisms of the juvenile justice system. Future policies dealing with delinquency, especially violence among black youths, should focus on prevention rather than on control. Delinquency among black youths is a societal problem and should be viewed as such. Governmental policies should be directed at easing the pain and hopelessness of black youths and providing them with nourishing environments that will bring hope and optimism. This would necessitate that the states address the needs of black families and the deficits in the educational system, and also improve the conditions in black communities.

The problem of delinquency among black youth has been linked to the instability of the black family. Many of these families are headed by females and so experience hardships because they have only one income. In addition, many of the children are born to young mothers. According to Reverend Jesse Jackson, black families consist of a generation of 15-year-old mothers, 28-year-old grandmothers, and 50-year-old great grandmothers--three generations of children without fathers or jobs (LaVelle, 1994). To add to their problems, some of these children live in families where neglect, emotional abuse, physical abuse, and sexual abuse are regular occurrences. Marian Wright Edelman, president of the Children's Defense Fund, has noted that many children are victims of violence in the home. Dr. Alwin Poussaint, a black psychiatrist at Harvard Medical School, remarks that many of those children who commit violence at age 13 were damaged in the first years of their lives by parents who did not know how to raise children (LaVelle, 1994). Joseph and Green (1994) found that 95% of the delinquents in their study came from households headed by females.

Black families "at risk" should be the targets of social policy to prevent delinquency. Society must intervene early in the life of the black child. All black families must have access to programs capable of providing direction, emotional support, and concern in solving their problems. Programs that are comprehensive, intensive, and holistic in their approach are needed.

Joblessness pervades the inner cities, as young black males lack economic opportunities. The black population in the inner city has been described as "the truly disadvantaged" (Wilson, 1987) and is enmeshed in a "culture of poverty" (Lewis, 1966). Many of the unemployed black youths are actually unemployable, for they have very little education and few marketable skills. The rapidly expanding black underclass is one of the most serious social problems facing this nation, and this underclass is made up of the poorest of the poor, who are trapped at the bottom of the social structure. The high rate of children born out-of-wedlock helps perpetuate the welfare and poverty cycle into another generation. The black underclass's high unemployment rate has made it possible for illegal alternative modes of economic success, such as the selling of drugs, theft, and robbery, to flourish. Comprehensive job training is vital for black youths, and jobs must be created in these neighborhoods. The government should provide subsidies to businesses to train and hire more black youths.

Inner-city schools are in a state of decay; they are poorly staffed, housed in antiquated buildings, drug infested and racially and ethnically segregated. Furthermore, schools that are white middle-class institutions offer little positive experience for many black children. Many of these schools offer a curriculum that is meaningless to blacks; an intelligence test that is culturally and socially biased; teaching staff that is predominantly white; teaching styles that are inappropriate; and a tracking system that is discriminatory. Consequently, the dropout rate and disruptive behavior in school have increased.

Inner-city schools have also become very violent. Gangs battle for territory in the schools, and innocent youths are beaten and killed on school premises. The violence is so extensive that some schools have taken precautions against violence. For example, back-to-school fashions for some New York schools include school blazers or other jackets fitted with bullet-resistant pads (*Rocky Mountain News*, 1990). In Oakland, California, students have been taught how to move away from windows and to crouch under their desks to avoid bullets fired into the classroom. In Baltimore, students wear identification tags, and in Philadelphia, the schools have installed electronically locked doors (*Education Week*, 1988).

Daniels (1994) argues that the school systems are targeting black boys for failure and are stripping them of their self-confidence which they never regain. According to Daniels, at a very early age, boys are labeled "trouble makers" or "discipline problems." Such a labeling process severely hinders, and even derails, their chances of academic success in schools. Fundamental changes in the structure of the present educational system are needed if black youths are to experience academic success in the school. These changes entail modification of the curriculum, employment of more black teachers, elimination of tracking systems and intelligence tests, and introduction of appropriate teaching styles. While governor of New York, Mario Cuomo, signed a bill that mandates school to teach about slavery, the Holocaust, and other human rights injustices (*Jet*, 1994a). However, mere modifications in the structure and organization of schools are inadequate. A total social reconstruction of the educational system is needed if schools are to become positive environments for black youths.

Thousands of black youths reside in pathologically diseased neighborhoods infested with extreme poverty and high unemployment. These communities are ravaged by dilapidated and inadequate housing, high rates of diseases, scarcity of food, unwanted pregnancies, and a lack of community political and social organization. These neighborhoods are frequently battlegrounds for drugs, territory, and scarce resources. Brace (1967) wrote that the inner city was filled with a new and dangerous element, whose lives are characterized by alcoholism, unemployment, family disruption, and crime. He also stated that the young men there seemed to be amoral, with no respect for law and order. Brace was referring to European immigrants, but his words can also be appropriately used to describe the plight of young blacks in urban areas. Community-oriented delinquency programs, which attempt to improve conditions in the community and strengthen social relationships, need to be increased in black neighborhoods. Improving one's immediate environment will undoubtedly improve one's personal image and hopes for the future.

THE RESPONSIBILITY OF THE BLACK COMMUNITY

The black community has a responsibility to assist in the reduction of delinquency among black youths. The black community is central to the socialization of black youths through formal and informal networks that help to shape their behavior.

Members of black communities need to get more involved in institutions, such as the schools and local politics, that affect their children's lives. A constant complaint is that few black families get involved in community organizations, especially parent-teacher organizations. When parents do not participate in such organizations, they are unable to have any impact on policies and legislations.

Many black youths need guidance. The black community should provide positive mentors and role models for these youths to emulate. It is imperative that successful blacks work with these youths, so that they can aspire to legitimate careers other than drug dealing and murder.

More cooperation and cohesion are needed in the black communities. Many of the communities are fragmented with conflicts between light-skinned and dark-skinned blacks, educated and uneducated, and male and female blacks. Problems also exist between different groups of blacks, such as those from the Caribbean and Africa. This kind of fragmentation weakens the black community, helps to reinforce negative stereotypes, and negatively affects black youths. The black community needs to strengthen its identity, improve bonds among its members, and unite as a racial group.

Blacks need to create businesses in inner-city neighborhoods. Many of the existing businesses in these neighborhoods are owned not by blacks, but by other races, who often do not reside in those neighborhoods. Wealthy blacks should invest in the black community and in black youth, who are the future generation. Many people, however, appear to have given up on the present generation of black youths. But the black community cannot afford to give up on its youth. Some attempt should be made to redeem these youths if blacks are to continue to make a significant contribution to this society.

Some black organizations have been actively working with the youths. For example, Operation PUSH has a four-prong program that focuses on marching, mentoring, manning the streets, and meeting. The vice president, Jesse Jackson, Jr., recently asked parents to get involved with their children and urged black men in the community to become role models and mentors (*Jet*, 1994b).

To curb the violence in the black community, several organizations have been established all over the country. These include Mothers of Murdered Offspring (MOMO) in Charlotte, North Carolina; Motivating African-American Youth for Success (MAAS) in Oakland, California; Teens on Targets in Oakland and Seattle, Washington; Parents of Murdered Children in Cincinnati, Ohio; Victims Outreach in Dallas, Texas; and Save Our Sons and Daughters in Detroit, Michigan. In addition, community leaders and lawmakers have been attending conferences dealing with gang violence, conflict resolution, curfews, and stricter sentences for juveniles (*Jet*, 1994b).

One effort made by the black community is in the area of education. Private boarding schools flourished during the 1960s but became rare after integration. Because of the problems of crime, violence, drugs, and the high failure rate of black children in the public schools, black private schools are becoming popular again. The Institute of Education in Washington, D.C., estimates that there are more than 300 black private schools (*Jet*, 1994c). Moreover, with the breakdown of the value system in the society, some African-American leaders are operating Christian-oriented schools (Shipp, 1994).

In September 1994, sixteen black colleges and universities were awarded a total of $4.25 million by the federal government to prevent violence among black men. College officials hope that the funding will be for three years. Each school will establish a "family life center" on campus to assess the needs of minority communities and to implement prevention programs in those communities. Students will be actively involved in the fight against violence as they work with the communities (Price & Cowles, 1994).

The Nation of Islam, a controversial black religious group, has promoted economic self-sufficiency. In the Robert Taylor Homes, Chicago's most notorious public-housing project, the Nation has been successful in reducing fighting between the gangs. Its *The Final Call*, the country's largest black newspaper, claims to have a readership of 600,000. At the end of February 1995, Nation opened a new restaurant and bakery complex, called Salaam, in the heart of Chicago's depressed South Side. The Nation also plans to build a 2,000-seat theater and parking complex. It is also pushing ahead its plans to develop farmland in Michigan and Georgia to grow organic vegetables and to purchase trucks to distribute the produce (*The Economist*, 1995).

The above projects indicate initiatives by some members of the black community, but more needs to be done. The black community must be willing to fight for the lives of its youths. Every black child who becomes involved in the juvenile justice system weakens the black community, for the strength of any race lies in its youths. The black community, which is losing its youths in large numbers on a daily basis, has a responsibility to reverse this trend. Ignoring the problems of its youth will have grave consequences for the black community.

SUMMARY

In general, the juvenile justice system has undergone a series of changes over the years. Initially, juveniles were treated as adults, but after much criticism and activism by community groups, a separate system was established for juveniles. A policy of rehabilitation was followed by an emphasis on due process and then the crime control approach. At the present time, the public apparently wants more and more juveniles to be treated as adults.

Today the juvenile justice system is in a state of uncertainty. Both its philosophy and its practice have been questioned. Some favor a more punitive system, while others call for the merging of the juvenile justice system into the criminal justice system. What will happen in the future is difficult to predict, but the present problems in the juvenile justice system threaten its very existence.

As the end of twentieth century approaches, American society needs to address the plight of black youth in the juvenile justice system. If the present epidemic of black youth delinquency is allowed to go unchecked, the situation will deteriorate and the society will lose generations of its members.

References

Abner, A. (1994, September). Gangsta girls. *Essence*, p. 66.

Abrahamsen, D. (1960). *The psychology of crime*. New York: Columbia University Press.

_____. (1944). *Crime and human mind*. New York: Columbia University Press.

Aday, D. P., Jr. (1986). Court structure, defense attorney use, and juvenile court decisions, *Sociological Quarterly*, 27, 107-119.

Agnew, R. (1983). Physical punishment and delinquency: A research note. *Youth and Society*, 15, 225-236.

Aguirre, A., & Baker, D. V. (1990). Empirical research on racial discrimination in the imposition of the death penalty. *Criminal Justice Abstracts*, 22, 147-148.

Akers, R. (1985). *Deviant behavior: Social learning approach* (3rd Ed.). Belmont, Calif.: Wadsworth.

Alder, F., Mueller, G. O., & Laufer, W. (1991). *Criminology*. New York: McGraw-Hill.

Allen, L., & Tausig, M. (1979). Theoretical interpretations of social class and racial differences in legal decision-making for juveniles. *Sociological Quarterly*, 20, 197-207.

Allen, P. (1993). The Gould-Wysinger Awards: A tradition of excellence. *Juvenile Justice*, 1, 24, 27.

Allinson, R., & Potter, J. (1983). Is New York's tough juvenile law a charade? *Corrections*, 9, 40-45.

American Public Welfare Association. (1986). *One child in four*. New York: American Public Welfare Association.

Anderson, D. B., & Schoen, D. F. (1985, Summer). Diversion programs: Effects of stigmatization on juvenile/status offenders. *Juvenile and Family Court Journal*, 36, 13-25.

Anderson, P. R., & Newman, D. J. (1993). *Introduction to criminal justice*. New York: McGraw-Hill.

Andrew, D. A., Zinger, I., Hoge, R. D., Bonta, J., Gendreau, P., & Cullen, F. T.

(1990). Does correctional treatment work? A clinically relevant and psychologically informed meta-analysis. *Criminology*, 28, 369-404.

Anglin, M., & Speckart, G. (1988). Narcotics use and crime: A multisample, multi-method analysis. *Criminology*, 26, 197-233.

Arnold, W. R. (1971, September). Race and ethnicity relative to other factors in juvenile court dispositions. *American Journal of Sociology*, 77, 211-227.

Austin, J., & Krisberg, B. (1981). Wider, stronger, and different nets: The dialectics of criminal justice reform. *Journal of Research in Crime and Delinquency*, 18, 165-196.

Austin, J., Dimas J., & Steinhart, D. (1992). *The over-representation of minority youth in the California Juvenile Justice System: Report summary*. San Francisco: National Council on Crime and Delinquency.

Austin, R. (1983). The Colonial model, subcultural theory and intragroup violence. *Journal of Criminal Justice*, 11, 93-104.

Austin, R. L. (1978). Race, father absence and female delinquency, *Criminology*, 15, 487-504.

Bachman, J. G., Johnson, L. D., & Patrick P. M. (1988). *Monitoring the future: Questionnaire responses from the nation high school seniors*. Ann Arbor: University of Michigan, Institute of Social Research.

_____. (1991). *Monitoring the future 1990*. Ann Arbor: University of Michigan, Institute of Social Research.

Bailey, W. C. & Peterson, R. D. (1981). Legal vs. extralegal determinants of juvenile court dispositions. *Juvenile and Family Court Journal*, 32, 41-45.

Bailey, W. (1990). Murder, capital punishment, and television: Execution publicity and homicide rates. *American Sociological Review*, 55, 628-633.

_____. (1980). A multivariate cross-sectional analysis of the deterrent effect of the death penalty. *Sociology and Social Research*, 64, 183-207.

Bailey, W., & Peterson, R. (1989). Murder, capital punishment: A monthly time-series analysis of execution publicity. *American Sociological Review*, 54, 722-743.

Baldus, D. C., Pulaski, C., & Woodworth, G. (1983). Comparative review of death sentences: An empirical review of Georgia experience. *Journal of Criminal Law and Criminology*, 74, 661-753.

Baldwin, J. (1961). *Nobody knows my name: More notes of a native son*. New York: Dial Press.

Ball, R., Huff, R., & Lilly, R. (1988). *House arrest and correctional policy: Doing time at home*. Newbury Park, Calif.: Sage Publications.

Bandura, A. (1973). *Aggression: A social learning theory*. Englewood Cliffs, N.J.: Prentice-Hall.

Banfield, E. (1974). *The unheavenly city, Revisited*. Boston: Little, Brown.

Bartollas, C., Miller, S. J. & Dinitz, S. (1975). The informal code in juvenile institutions: Guidelines for the strong. *Journal of Southern Criminal Justice*, 1, 33-52.

Bartollas, C., & Miller, S. J. (1994). *Juvenile justice in America*. Englewood Cliffs, N.J.: Regents/Prentice-Hall.

Bartollas, C., Miller, S. J., & Dinitz, S. (1976). *Juvenile victimization: The institutional paradox*. New York: Halstead Press.

_____. (1965). The informal code in a juvenile institution: Guidelines for the strong. *Journal of Southern Criminal Justice*, 1, 33-52.

Bartollas, C., & Sieverdes, C. M. (1981). The victimized white in juvenile correctional system. *Crime and Delinquency*, 27, 534-543.

Barton, W., & Butts, J. (1990). Viable options: Intensive supervision programs for juvenile delinquents. *Crime and Delinquency*, 36, 238-246.

Baucom, D. H., Besch, P. K., & Callahan, S. (1985). Relationship between testosterone concentration, sex role identity and personality among females. *Journal of Personality and Social Psychology*, 48, 1218-1225.

Bayley, D. H., & Mendelsohn, H. (1969). *Minorities and the police*. New York: Free Press.

Becker, H. (1963). *Outsiders: Studies in sociology of deviance*. Glencoe, Ill.: Free Press.

Bell, D., & Lang, K. (1985). The intake dispositions of juvenile offenders. *Journal of Research in Crime and Delinquency*, 22, 309-328.

Belson, W. A. (1978). *Television violence and adolescent boys*. Farnborough: Saxon House.

Billingsly, A. (1987). Black families in a changing society. In J. Dewart (ed.), *National urban league: State of black America 1987*, (pp. 97-111). New York: National Urban League.

Bishop, D., & Frazier, C. (1988). The influence of race in juvenile justice processing *Journal of Research in Crime and Delinquency*, 25, 242-263.

Bishop, D., Frazier, Charles E., & Henretta, J. C. (1989). Prosecutorial waiver: Case study of a questionable reform. *Crime and Delinquency*, 35, 179-201.

Black, C. L. (1984). *Capital punishment: The inevitability of caprice and mistake*. New Haven, Conn.: Yale University Press.

Black, D. J. (1970). The production of crime rates. *American Sociological Review*, 35, 733-748.

Black, D. J., & Reiss, A. J. (1970). Police control of juvenile delinquents. *American Sociological Review*, 35, 63-77.

Blackmore, J., Brown, M. & Krisberg, B. (1988). *Juvenile justice reform--The bellweather states*. Ann Arbor, Mich.: Center for Study of Youth Policy, University of Michigan.

Blau, P., & Blau, J. (1982). The cost of inequality: metropolitan structure and violent crime. *American Sociological Review*, 147, 114-129.

Blauner, R. (1972). *Racial oppression in America*. New York: Harper & Row.

_____. (1969). Internal colonialism and ghetto revolt *Social Problems*, 16, 393-408.

Block, C. R., & Block, R. (1993). *Street gangs in Chicago*. Washington, D.C.: U.S. Department of Justice, National Institute of Justice.

Bloomberg, T. (1984). *Juvenile court and community corrections*. Lanham, Md.: University Press of America.

Blumstein, A. (1982). On the racial disproportionality of the United States prison population. *Journal of Criminal Law and Criminology*, 73, 1259-1281.

Boggs, S. L. (1965). Urban crime patterns. *American Sociological Review*, 30, 899-908.

Bohm, R. (1991). Race and death penalty in United States. In M. J. Lynch & E. Britt Patterson (eds.), *Race and Criminal Justice* (pp. 71-85). Albany, N.Y.: Harrow & Heston, Publishers.

Bortner, M. A. (1986). Traditional rhetoric, organizational realities: Remand of juveniles to adult court *Crime and Delinquency*, 32, 153-73.

Bortner, M. A., Schneider, A. L., Hermann, R., Miller, L. C., & Cech-Soucy, M. (1990). *Black adolescents and juvenile justice: Background report to Arizona black Town Hall*. Tempe, Ariz.: University of Arizona.

Bortner, M. A., & Reed, W. L. (1985). The preeminence of process: An example of refocused justice research. *Social Science Quarterly*, 66, 413-425.

Bowers, W. J. (1984). *Legal homicide: Death as punishment in America, 1864-1982*. Boston: Northeastern University Press.

Bowker, L. H. (1977). *Prison subculture*. Lexington, Mass.: D. C. Heath.

Boydstun, J. H. (1975). *San Diego field interrogation: Final report*. Washington, D.C.: The Police Foundation.

Boykin, A. W. (1978). Psychological/behavioral verve in academic/task performance: Pretheoretical considerations. *Journal of Negro Education*, 47, 343-354.

Brace, C. L. (1967). *The dangerous classes of New York*. New York: Patterson Smith.

Brady, P. C., Bray, J., & Zeeb, L. (1986). Behavior problems of clinic children: Relation to parental marital status, age, and sex of child. *American Journal of Orthopsychiatry*, 56, 399-412.

Breed v. Jones, 421 U.S. 519 (1975).

Briar, S., & Piliavin, I. (1965). Delinquency situational inducements and commitment to conformity, *Social Problems*, 13, 35-45.

Britts, J., & Sickmund, M. (1991). *Update on statistics: Offenders in juvenile court, 1989*. Washington, D.C.: Department of Justice.

Brook, K. (1993). Police violence is excessive. In M. D. Biskup (ed.), *Criminal justice: Opposing viewpoints* (pp. 173-179). San Diego, Calif.: Greenhaven Press.

Brown, C. (1988, May 22). *St. Paul Pioneer Press Dispatch*.

Brown, S. E. (1984). Social class, child maltreatment, and delinquent behavior. *Criminology*, 22, 259-278.

Brown, W. K., Miller, T., Jenkins, R. L., & Rhodes, W. K. (1989). The fallacy of radical nonintervention. *International Journal of Offender Therapy and Comparative Criminology*, 33, 177-182.

Brown, W. K., Rhodes, W. A., Miller, T., & Jenkins, R. L. (1990). The negative effects of racial discrimination on minority youth in juvenile justice system. *International Journal of Offender Therapy and Comparative Criminology*, 34, No. 2, 87-93.

Brown v. Mississippi, 297 U.S. 278 (1936).

Burns, T., Chasnoff, I., & Scholl, J. (1986). Prenatal drug exposure: Effects on neonatal and infant growth. *Neurobehavioral Toxicology and Teratology*, 8, 351-387.

Burt, K. (1987). Prosecution of street gangs. Presentation to National College of District Attorneys cited in S. Cox & J. Conrad. *Juvenile justice, A guide to practice and theory* Dubuque, Iowa: Wm. C. Brown Publishers.

California Office of the Attorney General. (1981). *Report on youth gang violence in California*. Washington, D.C.: National Institute of Justice.

Canter, R. J. (1982a). Sex differences in self-report delinquency. *Criminology*, 20, 149-67.

_____. (1982b). Family correlates of male and female delinquency. *Criminology*, 20, 149-67.

Carmichael, S., & Hamilton, C. V. (1967). *Black power*. New York: Oxford University Press

Carson, R. C., Butcher, J. N., & Coleman, J. C. (1988). *Abnormal psychology and modern life*. Boston: Scott, Foresman.

Carter, D., Sapp, Allen A., & Stephens, D. W. (1989). *The state of police education: Policy directions for 21st century*. Washington, D.C.: Police Executive Research Forum.

Centers for Disease Control. (1986a). *Report of the Secretary's Task Force on Black and Minority Health, Vol. 1*. Washington, D.C: U.S. Department of Health and Human Services.

_____. (1986b). Premature mortality in United States. *Morbidity and Mortality Weekly Report*, 35, 15-115.

_____. (1990). Homicide among young black males. *Morbidity and Mortality Weekly Report*. Washington, D.C: U.S. Department of Health and Human Services.

_____. (1991). Weapon carrying among high school Students, United States 1990. *Morbidity and Mortality Weekly Report*. Washington, D.C: U.S. Department of Health and Human Services.

Cernknovich, S. A. (1979). A comparative analysis of male and female delinquency. *Sociological Quarterly*, 20, 131-145.

_____. (1978). Value orientations and delinquent involvement. *Criminology*, 15, 443-458.

Cernkovich, S., & Giordano, P. C. (1979). Delinquency, opportunity and gender. *Journal of Criminal law and Criminology*, 70, 145-151.

_____. (1987). Family relations and delinquency. *Criminology*, 25, 295-321.

Cernkovich, S., Giordano, P., & Pugh, M. (1985). Chronic offenders: The missing cases in self-report delinquency research. *Journal of Criminal Law and Criminology*, 76, 705-732.

_____. (1979). Delinquency, opportunity and gender. *Journal of Criminal Law and Criminology*, 70, 145-51.

Chambers, O. R. (1983). *The juvenile offender: A parole profile*. Albany: Evaluation and Planning Unit, New York State Division of Parole.

Chambliss, W. (1988). *Exploring criminology*. New York: Macmillan.

_____. (1966). Sociological analysis of law of vagrancy. *Social Problems*, 12, 67-77.

Chambliss, W. J., & Nagasawa, R. H. (1969). On the validity of official statistics: A comparative study of white, black and Japanese high school boys. *Journal of Research in Crime and Delinquency*, 6, 71-77.

Champion, D. J. (1992). *The juvenile justice system: Delinquency, processing, and the law.* New York: Macmillan.

_____. (1989). Teenage felons and waiver hearings: Some recent trends, 1980-1988. *Crime and Delinquency*, 35, 577-585.

Chesney-Lind, M., & Shelden, R. G. (1992). *Girls, delinquency, and juvenile justice.* Pacific Grove, Calif.: Brooks/Cole Publishing Co.

Chevigngy, P. (1969). *Police power.* New York: Pantheon Books.

Children Defense Fund. (1992). *The state of America's children 1991.* Washington, D.C.: Children's Defense Fund.

Chilton, R. (1987). Twenty years of homicide and robbery in Chicago: The impact of the city's changing racial and age composition. *Journal of Quantitative Criminology*, 3, 195-213.

Chilton, R., & Markle, G. (1972). Family disruption, delinquent conduct and the effects of subclassification. *American Sociological Review*, 37, 93-99.

Christiansen, K. (1977). A preliminary study of criminality among twins. In S. A. Mednick & K. O. Christiansen (eds.), *Biosocial bases of criminal behavior* (pp. 89-108). New York: Gardner Press.

_____. (1968). Threshold of tolerance in various population groups illustrated by results from the Danish criminologic twin study. In A. V. S. de Reuck & R. Porter (eds.), *The mentally abnormal offender* (pp. 107-116). Boston: Little, Brown.

Chronicle of Higher Education Almanac. (1994, September 1). College enrollment by racial and ethnic group: Selected years, p. 15.

_____. (1994, September 1). Average scores on the Scholastic Assessment Test by sex and racial and ethnic group, p. 13.

Clark, J. R. (1994, April). Does community policing add up? *Law Enforcement News*, 20, No. 399, 1, 8.

Clarke, K. (1965). *Dark ghetto.* New York: Harper & Row.

Clarke, S. H., & Koch, G. G. (1980, Winter). Juvenile court: Therapy or crime control, and do lawyers make a difference? *Law and Society Review*, 14, 263-308.

Clear, T., & Cole, G. (1994). *American corrections* (2nd ed.). Pacific Grove, Calif.: Brooks/Cole.

Cleckley, H. (1959). Psychopathic states. In S. Aneti (ed.) *American handbook of psychiatry.* New York: Basic Books.

Cloward, R., & Ohlin, L. E. (1960). *Delinquency and opportunity: A theory of delinquency gang.* New York: Free Press.

Cohen, A. (1955). *Delinquent boys.* Glencoe, Ill.: Free Press.

Cohen, J., Fields, K., Lettre, M., Stafford, R., & Walker, C. (1973). Implementation of the JUSSIM Model in a criminal justice planning agency. *Journal of Research in Crime and Delinquency*, 10, 117-131.

Cohen, L. E. (1975). *Delinquency dispositions: An empirical analysis of processing decisions in three juvenile courts.* Washington, D.C.: U.S. Government Printing Office.

Cohen, L. E., & Kluegel, J. R. (1978). Determinants of juvenile court dispositions: Ascriptive and achieved factors in two metropolitan courts. *American Sociological Review*, 43, 162-176.

Cohen, S. (1979). Community control - A new utopia. *New Society*, 15, 609-611.

Cole, G. (1992). *The American system of criminal justice* (6th ed.). Pacific Grove, Calif.: Brooks/Cole.

Coleman, J., Campbell, E., Hobson, C. F., McPartland, J., Mood, A., Weinfeld, F. D., & York, R. L. (1966). *Equality of Educational Opportunity*. Washington, D.C.: U.S. Government Printing Press.

Comer, J. P. (1985). Black violence and public policy. In L. Curtis (ed.), *American violence and public policy* (pp. 63-86). New Haven, Conn.: Yale University Press.

Conger, R. D. (1980). The child as victim: An emerging issue of child abuse. *Journal of Crime and Justice*, 3, 35-60.

_____. (1976). Social control and social learning models of delinquent behavior: A synthesis. *Criminology*, 14, 17-40.

Conklin, J. E. (1989). *Criminology* (3rd ed.). New York: Macmillan.

Cortes, J., & Gatti, F. (1972). *Delinquency and crime*. New York: Pinnacle Press.

Council of Juvenile and Family Court Judges. (1990). Minority youth in the juvenile justice system: A judicial response. *Juvenile and Family Journal*, 41, No. 3A, 1-71.

Cowie, J., Cowie, V., & Slater, E. (1968). *Delinquency in girls*. London: Heinemann.

Cox, S., & Conrad, J. (1991). *Juvenile justice, A guide to theory and practice*. Dubuque, Iowa: Wm. C. Brown.

Craft, M. (1978). The current state of XYY and XXY syndromes: A review of treatment implications. *International Journal of Law and Psychiatry*, 1.

Crime Control Digest. (1989, February 27).

Cronin, R. C., Bourque, B. B., Mell, J. M., Gragg, F. E., & McGrady, L. A. (1988). *Evaluation of the habitual serious and violent juvenile offender program: Executive summary*. Washington, D.C.: U.S. Department of Justice.

Cullen, F. T. (1984). *Rethinking crime and deviance theory: The emergence of a structuring tradition*. Totowa, N.J.: Rowman & Allanheld.

Curran, D. (1983). Judicial discretion and defendant's sex. *Criminology*, 21, 41-58.

Currie, E. (1985). *Confronting crime*. New York: Random House.

Curtis, L. (1975). *Violence, race and culture*. Lexington, Mass.: D. C. Heath.

Dalton, K. (1971). *The premenstrual syndrome*. Springfield, Ill.: Charles C. Thomas.

Daniels, L. A. (1994, May). Targeting black boys for failure. *Emerge*, 5, No. 7, 58-61.

Dannefer, D., & Schutt, R. (1982). Race and juvenile justice processing in court and police agencies. *American Journal of Sociology*, 87, 113-132.

Datesman, S. K., & Scarpitti, F. R. (1975). Female delinquency and broken homes. *Criminology*, 13, 33-35.

Datesman, S. K., Scarpitti, F. R., & Stephenson, R. (1975). Female delinquency: An application of self and opportunity theories. *Journal of Research in Crime and Delinquency*, 12, 107-123.

Davis, S. M. (1986). *Rights of juveniles: The Juvenile Justice System* (2nd ed.). New York: Clark Boardman Co.

Davis v. Mississippi, 394 U.S. 721 (1969).

Death Row U.S.A. (1991, August). NAACP Legal Defense and Education Fund.

Department of Health and Human Services. (1985). *Report of the Secretary's Task Force on Black and Minority Health. Vol. I.* Washington, D.C.: Department of Health and Human Services.

Dinitz, S. (1978). Nothing fails like a little success. *Criminology*, 16, 225-238.

Division of Policy and Planning Office of Policy Analysis and Planning. (1991). *Offenders in New Jersey correctional institutions on December 31, 1990 by selected characteristics.* Trenton: New Jersey Department of Corrections.

Dority, B. (1991, July/August). Police Powers Expanded as Abuses Excalate. *The Humanist*, pp. 35-36.

Dorsey, R. (1991). *Blacks in New Jersey: Crime, drugs, justice and African Americans.* Newark, N.J.: New Jersey Public Policy Research Institute.

Dreeban, R., & Garmora, A. (1986). Race, instruction and learning. *American Sociological Review*, 51, 660-669.

Drowns, R. W., & Hess, K. M. (1995). Juvenile Justice. St. Paul, Minn.: West Publishing Company.

Duke, D. L., & Duke, R. M. (1978). The prediction of delinquency in girls. *Journal of Research and Development in Education*, 11, 18-33.

Durkheim, E. (1933). *The division of labor in society.* Glencoe, Ill.: Free Press.

Duster, T. (1987). Crime, youth unemployment, and the black underclass. *Crime and Delinquency*, 33, 300-316.

Duxbury, E. (1973). *Evaluation of Youth Service Bureau.* Sacramento, Calif.: California Youth Authority.

Eaton, J., & Polk, K. (1961). *Measuring delinquency.* Pittsburgh: University of Pittsburgh Press.

The Economist (1995, April 1). The bow ties of Allah, 335, p. 22.

Eddings v. Oklahoma, 455 U.S. 104 (1982).

Edelman, M. W. (1988). Growing up black in America. In J. H. Skolnick & E. Currie (eds.), *Crisis in American institutions* (pp. 143-162). Glenview, Ill.: Scott, Foresman.

Eder, D. (1981). Ability grouping as a self-fulfilling prophecy: A micro-analysis of teacher-student interaction. *Sociology of Education*, 54, 151-162.

Education Week (1988, June). School being forced to cope with growing impact of violence.

Ehrlich, I. (1975). The deterrent effect of capital punishment: A question of life and death. *American* Economic Review, 65, 69-79.

Eigen, S. (1981). The determinants and impacts of jurisdictional transfer in Philadelphia. In J. Hall et al, (eds.), *Major issues in juvenile information and training: Readings in public policy.* Columbus, Ohio: Academy for Contemporary Problems.

Eisenberg, T., et al. (1973). *Police-Community action.* New York: Praeger.

Elliot, D. S., Ageton, S. A., & Canter, R. J. (1980). Reconciling race and class differences in self-reported and official estimates of delinquency. *American Sociological Review*, 45, 95-110.

Elliot, D. S., Ageton, S. S., Huizinga, D. H., Knowles, B. A., & Canter, R. J. (1983). *The prevalence and incidence of delinquent behavior 1976-1980: National Youth Survey, Report No. 26,* Boulder, Col.: Behavioral Research Institute.

Elliot, D. S., Huizinga, D., & Ageton, S. S. (1985). *Explaining delinquency and drug use*. Beverly Hills, Calif.: Sage.

Elliot, D. S., & Voss, H. (1974). *Delinquency and dropout*. Lexington, Mass.: D. C. Heath.

Ellis, L. (1982). Genetics and criminal behavior. *Criminology*, 20, 43-66.

Empey, L. T. (1982). *American delinquency*. Homewood, Ill.: Dorsey.

Empey, L. T., & Erickson, M. (1972). *The Provo Experiment: Evaluating community control of delinquency*. Lexington, Mass.: Lexington Books.

Empey, L. T., & Lubeck, S. G. (1971). *Explaining delinquency*. Lexington, Mass.: D. C. Heath.

_____. (1971). *The Silverlake Experiment: Testing delinquency theory and community intervention*. Chicago: Aldine.

Epps, E. G. (1967). Socioeconomic status, race, level of aspirations and juvenile delinquency. *Phylon*, 28, 16-27.

Epps, P., & Bernard, R. W. (1952). Physique and temperament of women delinquents compared with women undergraduates. *British Journal of Medical Psychology*, 25, 249-255.

Erickson, M., & Empey, L. T. (1963). Court records undetected delinquency and decision making. *Journal of Criminal Law, Criminology and Police Science*, 54, 456-469.

Ewing, C. P. (1990). *Kids who kill*. Lexington, Mass.: Lexington Books.

Eysenck, H. J. (1964). *Crime and personality*. Boston: Houghton Mifflin.

_____ & Eysenck, S. B. C. (1976). *Psychoticism as dimension of personality*. London: Hodder and Stroughton.

Fagan, J., Forst, M., & Vivona, S. T. (1987). Racial determinants of judicial transfer decisions: Prosecuting violent youth in criminal court. *Crime and Delinquency*, 33, 359-386.

Fagan, J., Piper, E., & Cheng, Y. (1987). Contributions of victimization to delinquency in inner cities. *Journal of Criminal Law and Criminology*, 78, 586-613.

Fagan, J., Slaughter, E., & Hartstone, E. (1987, April). Blind justice?: The impact of race on the juvenile justice process. *Crime and Delinquency*, 33, 224-258.

Fanon, F. (1965). *The wretched of the earth*. New York: Grove Press.

Fare v. Michael, 442 U.S. 707 (1979).

Fareta, G. (1981). A profile of aggression from adolescence to adulthood: An 18-year followup of psychiatrically disturbed and violent adolescents. *American Journal of Orthopsychiatry*, 51, 439-453.

Farley, R. (1980). Homicide trends in the United States. *Demography*, 17, 177-788.

Farrington, D. P. (1982). Longitudinal analyses of criminal violence. In M. E. Wolfgang & N. A. Weiner (eds.), *Criminal violence* (pp. 289-348). Beverly Hills, Calif.: Sage.

_____. (1986). Age and crime. In M. Tonry and N. Morris (eds.), *Crime and justice, An annual review*, Vol. 7 (pp. 185-250). Chicago: University of Chicago Press.

_____. (1988). Psychobiological factors in the explanation and reduction of delinquency. *Today's Delinquent*, 7, 37-51.

Federal Bureau of Investigation. (1981). *Uniform crime reports*. Washington, D.C.: U.S. Government Printing Office.

————. (1990). *Uniform crime reports*. Washington, D.C.: U.S. Government Printing Office:

————. (1991). *Uniform crime reports*. Washington, D.C.: U.S. Government Printing Office.

————. (1992). *Crime in the United States*. Washington, D.C.: U.S. Government Printing Office.

————. (1993). *Crime in the United States*. Washington, D.C.: U.S. Government Printing Office.

Feldman, P. (1977). *Criminal behavior: A psychological analysis*. New York: John Wiley.

Fenwick, C. R. (1982). Juvenile court intake decision making: The importance of family affiliation. *Journal of Criminal Justice*, 10, 443-453.

Ferdinand, T. N., & Luchterhand, E. G. (1970). Inner-city youths, the police, the juvenile court, and justice. *Social Problems*, 17, 510-527.

Ferguson, B. H., Stroddart, H., & Simeon, J. (1986). Double-blind studies of behavioral and cognitive effects of sucrose-aspartame ingestion in normal children. *Nutrition Reviews Supplement*, 44, 144-158.

Figueira-McDonough, J., Barton, B., & Sarri, R. (1981). Normative deviance: Gender similarities in adolescent subcultures. In M. Q. Warren (ed.), *Comparing female and male offenders* (pp. 17-45). Beverly Hills, Calif.: Sage.

Finckenauer, J. O. (1984). *Juvenile delinquency and corrections: The gap between theory and practice*. Orlando, Fla.: Academic Press.

————. (1982). *Scared straight and the panacea phenomenon*. Englewood Cliffs, N.J.: Prentice-Hall.

Findlay, S., & Silberner, J. (1990, January 29). The worsening spread of AIDS crisis. *U.S. News and World Report*, p. 28.

Fisher, W. S. (1985). *Juvenile waivers to adult court: A report to the New Jersey State Legislature*. Trenton, N.J.: Department of Law and Public Safety, Division of Criminal Justice.

Flowers, R. B. (1990). *Minorities and criminality*. New York: Praeger.

Forst, L., Moffitt, T., & McGee, R. (1989). Neuropsychological correlates of psychopathology in an unselected cohort of young adolescents. *Journal of Abnormal Psychology*, 98, 307-313.

Fox, R. (1971). The XYY offender: A modern myth. *Journal of Criminal Law, Criminology and Policy Science*, 62, 59-73.

Fox, V., & Stinchcomb, J. B. (1994). *Introduction to corrections* (4th ed.). Englewood Cliffs, N.J.: Prentice-Hall.

Francis v. Resweber, 329 U.S. 459 (1947).

Frazier, C. E., & Bishop, D. M. (1985). The pretrial detention of juveniles and its impact on case dispositions. *Journal of Criminal Law and Criminology*, 76, 1132-1152.

Frazier, C. E., & Cochran, J. K. (1986). Official intervention, diversion from juvenile justice system, and dynamics of human services work: Effects of a reform goal based on labeling theory. *Crime and Delinquency*, 32, 157-176.

Frazier, C., Richards, P., & Potter, R. (1983). Juvenile diversion and net widening. *Human Organizations*, 42, 115-122.

Freud, S. (1922). *A general introduction to psychoanalysis.* New York: Boni & Liveright.

Friday, P., & Hage, J. (1988). Youth crime in postindustrial societies. *Criminology*, 14, 347-368.

_____. (1976). Patterns of youth crime in industrial society: An integrative perspective. *Criminology*, 16, 347-368.

Friedlander, K. (1947). *The psychoanalytic approach to juvenile delinquency.* London: Kegan Paul, Trench & Trubner.

Friedrich, R. (1980). Police use of Force: Individuals, situations, and organizations. *Annals of the American Academy of Political and Social Science*, 452, 82-97.

_____. (1979). Racial prejudice and police treatment of blacks. In R. Baker & F. A. Myer (eds.), *Evaluating alternative law enforcement policies* (pp. 149-167). Lexington, Mass.: Lexington Books.

Frost, T. M., & Clarren, S. N. (1984, September). Police entry-level curriculum: A thirty-year perspective. *Journal of Police Science and Administration*, 12, 251-259.

Furman v. Georgia, 408 U.S. 238 (1972).

Fyfe, J. J. (1978). Reducing the use of deadly force: The New York experience. In U.S. Department of Justice, *Police use of force.* Washington, D.C.: U.S. Government Printing Office.

_____. (1981a). Race and extreme police-citizen violence. In R. L. McNeely & C. E. Pope (eds.), *Race, crime and criminal justice* (pp. 89-108). Beverly Hills, Calif.: Sage.

_____. (1981b). Who shoots? A look at officer race and police shooting. *Journal of Police Science and Administration*, 9, 367-382.

_____. (1982). Blind justice: Police shootings in Memphis. *Journal of Criminal Law and Criminology*, 73, 707-722.

_____. (1988). The Metro-Dade Police/Citizen Violence Reduction Project. Unpublished Report, The Police Foundation.

_____. (1989). Police/citizen violence reduction project. *FBI Law Enforcement Bulletin*, 58, 18-23.

Gangi, R., & Murphy, J. (1990). *Imprisoned generation: Young men under the criminal justice custody in New York State.* New York: Correctional Association of New York.

Garrett, C. J. (1985). Effects of residential treatment on adjudicated delinquents: A meta-analysis. *Journal of Research in Crime and Delinquency*, 4, 287-308.

Gates, D. (1991). Playboy Interview: Daryl Gates. *Playboy*, p. 60.

Gaustad, J. (1991). Schools respond to gangs and violence. *Oregon School Study Council Bulletin*, 34, 1-53.

Geller, W., & Scott, M. S. (1992). *Deadly force: What we know.* Washington, D.C.: Police Executive Research Foundation.

Gelles, R. J., & Cornell, C. P. (1985). *Intimate violence in families.* Beverly Hills, Calif.: Sage.

Georges-Abeyie, D. (1989, Summer). Review of William Wilbanks: The myth of a racist criminal justice system. *The Critical Criminologist*, 1, 5-6.

Gershman, C. (1980, October 5). A matter of class. *New York Times*, 24; 92-96; 98-99; 102-105; 109.

Gibbons, D. (1976). *Delinquent behavior* (2nd ed.). Englewood Cliffs, N.J.: Prentice-Hall.

Gibbons, D., & Blake, G. (1976). Evaluating the impact of juvenile diversion programs. *Crime and Delinquency*, 22, 411-420.

Gibbons, D., & Krohn, M. D. (1991). *Delinquent behavior* (5th ed.). Englewood Cliffs, N.J.: Prentice-Hall.

Gibbs-Taylor, J. (1988a). Young black males in America: Endangered, embittered and embattled. In J. Gibbs-Taylor (ed.), *Young black and male in America: An endangered species* (pp. 1-36). Dover, Mass.: Auburn House.

_____. (1988b). The new morbidity: Homicide, suicide, accidents, and life-threatening behaviors. In J. Gibbs-Taylor (ed.), *Young black and male in America: An endangered species* (pp. 258-293). Dover, Mass.: Auburn House.

Ginsburg, B., & Carter, B. (1987). *Premenstrual syndrome: Ethical and legal implications in biochemical perspective*. New York: Plenum.

Giordano, P.S., Cernkovich, S., & Pugh, M. (1986). Friendships and delinquency. *American Journal of Sociology*, 91, 1170-1202.

Glasgow, D. (1981). *The black underclass*. New York: Vintage Book.

_____. (1980). *The black underclass: Poverty, unemployment and entrapment of ghetto youth*. Chicago: University of Chicago Press.

Glueck, S., & Glueck, E. (1956). *Physique and delinquency*. New York: Harper & Row.

_____. (1950). *Unravelling juvenile delinquency*. Cambridge, Mass.: Harvard University Press.

Gold, M. (1963). *Status forces in delinquent boys*. Ann Arbor: Institute of Social Research, University of Michigan.

_____. (1966). Undetected Delinquent Behavior. *Journal of Social Research in Crime and Delinquency*, 3, 27-46.

_____. (1970). *Delinquent behavior in America*. Belmont, Calif.: Brooks/Cole.

_____. (1978). School experiences, self esteem, and delinquent behavior: A theory of alternative schools. *Crime and Delinquency*, 24, 294-295.

Gold, M., & Reimer, D. (1975). Changing patterns of delinquent behavior among Americans 13 to 16 years old, 1967-1972. *Crime and Delinquent Literature*, 7, 483-517.

Goldkamp, J. (1976). Minorities as victims of police shootings: Interpretations of racial disproportionality and police use of deadly force. *Justice System Journal*, 2, 169-183.

Goldman, N. (1963). *The differential selection of juvenile offenders for court appearance*. New York: National Council on Crime and Delinquency.

Goldstein, A. P. (1991). *Delinquent gangs: A psychological perspective*. Champaign, Ill.: Research Press.

Gordon, R. (1976). Prevalence: The rare datum in delinquency measurement and its implications for the theory of delinquency. In M. W. Klein (ed.), *The juvenile justice system* (pp. 201-284). Beverly Hills, Calif.: Sage Publications.

Gottfredson, D. (1986). An empirical test of school-based environmental and individual interventions to reduce the risk of delinquent behavior. *Criminology*, 24, 705-731.

Gottfredson, D. C., & Barton, W. (1993). Deinstitutionalization of juvenile offenders. *Criminology*, 31, 591-608.

Gottfredson, G. D. (1987). Peer group interventions to reduce the risk of delinquent behavior: A selective review and a new evaluation. *Criminology*, 25, 671-714.

Gottfredson, M., & Hirschi, T. (1983). Age and the explanation of crime. *American Journal of Sociology*, 89, 552-843.

Gould, L. C. (1969). Who defines delinquency: A comparison of self-reported and officially reported indices of delinquency for three racial groups. *Social Problems*, 16, 325-336.

Gove, W. (1985). The effect of age and gender on deviant behavior: A biopsycho-social perspective. In A. S. Rossi (ed.), *Gender and the life course* (pp. 115-144). New York: Aldine.

Gove, W., & Crutchfield, R. (1982). The family and juvenile delinquency. *Sociological Quarterly*, 23, 301-319.

Governor's Juvenile Justice and Delinquency Prevention Advisory Committee. (1990). *The disproportionate incarceration of black and Hispanic youth in New Jersey*. Trenton, N.J.: State Law Enforcement Planning Agency.

Gray, G. (1986). Diet, crime and delinquency: A critique. *Nutrition Reviews Supplements*, 44, 89-94.

Gray-Ray, P., and Ray, M. C. (1990). Juvenile delinquency in the black community. *Youth and Society*, 22, 67-84.

Greenberg, D. (1985). Age, crime and social explanations. *American Journal of Sociology*, 91, 1-21.

Greenfeld, L. A., & Stephan, J. J. (1993). *Capital punishment 1992*. Washington, D.C.: U.S. Department of Justice, Bureau of Justice Statistics.

Greenwood, P., & Turner, S. (1987). *The Vision Quest Program: An evaluation*. Santa Monica, Calif.: Rand Corp.

Gregg v. Georgia, 428 U.S. 153 (1976).

Grier, W., & Cobbs, P. (1968). *Black rage*. New York: Basic Book.

Griswold, D. (1978). Police discrimination: An elusive question. *Journal of Police Science and Administration*, 6, 65-66.

Groves, E. W., & Rossi, P. H. (1971). Police perceptions of a hostile ghetto: Realism or projection? In H. H. Hanh (ed.), *Police in urban society* (pp. 175-191). Beverly Hills, Calif.: Sage Publications.

Guttentag, M., & Ross, M. (1972). Movement responses in simple concept learning. *American Journal of Orthopsychiatry*, 42, 657-665.

Hagan, J., Gillis, A. R., & Simpson, J. (1987). Class in the household: A power-control theory of common delinquent behavior. *American Journal of Sociology*, 92, 788-816.

_____. (1985). The class structure of gender and delinquency: Toward a power-control theory of common delinquent behavior. *American Journal of Sociology*, 90, 1151-1178.

Hairston, G. E. (1981). Black crime and the New York State Juvenile Offender Law: A consideration of the effects on lowering age of criminal responsibility. In J. Hall et al. (eds.), *Major issues in juvenile information and training: Readings in public policy*. Columbus, Ohio: Academy for Contemporary Problems.

Haley v. Ohio, 332 U.S. 596 (1948).

Halleck, S. (1977). *Psychiatry and dilemma of crime*. Berkeley: University of California Press.

Hamparian, D. M., Estep, L. K., Muntean, S. M., Priestino, R. R., Swisher, R. G., Wallace, P. L., & White, J. L. (1982). *Major issues in juvenile justice information and training, youth in juvenile court: Between two worlds*. Washington, D. C.: U. S. Department of Justice.

Hamparian, D. M., Schuster, R., Dinitz, S., & Conrad, J. (1978). *The violent few: A study of dangerous juvenile delinquents*. Lexington, Mass.: D. C. Heath.

Hampton, R. (1992). *Unfinished business: Racial and ethnic issues facing law enforcement II*. NOBLE and PERF sponsored conference, Reno Nevada, September 27-29.

Hansen, J. O. (1988, October 27). A new report on Georgia's juvenile justice system. *Atlantic Journal Constitution*, p. 1.

Hanson, C. (1984). Demographic, individual, and familial relationships correlates of serious and repeated crime among adolescents and their siblings. *Journal of Consulting and Clinical Psychology*, 52, 528-538.

Hargreaves, D. H. (1967). *Social relations in a secondary school*. New York: Humanities Press.

Harlow, C. W. (1985). *Reporting crimes to the police*. Washington, D.C.: U.S. Department of Justice, Bureau of Justice Statistics.

Harvey, W. B. (1986). Homicide among young black adults: Life in the subculture of exasperation. In D. F. Hawkins (ed.), *Homicide among black Americans* (pp. 153-171). Lanham, Md.: University Press of America.

Hays, J. R., & Solway, K. S. (1972). The role of psychological evaluation in certification of juveniles for trial as adults. *Houston Law Review*, 9, 709-715.

Henderickson v. Griggs, 672 F. Supp. 1126 (1987).

Henkoff, R. (1992, August 10). Kids are killing, dying, bleeding. *Fortune*, pp. 62-65, 68-69.

Hepburn, J. R. (1978). Race and the decision to arrest: An analysis of warrants issued. *Journal of Research in Crime and Delinquency*, 15, 54-73.

————. (1975). The role of the audience in deviant behavior and deviant identity. *Sociology and Social Research*, 59, 387-405.

Herbert, E. E. (1993, November). Doing something about children at risk. *National Institute of Justice*, pp. 4-9.

Herrnstein, C. (1978). *Criminal violence, criminal justice*. New York: Random House.

Herrnstein, R., & Murray, C. (1994). *The bell curve: Intelligence and class structure in American life*. New York: Free Press.

Hill, R. (1981). The economic status of black Americans. In *National Urban League: The State of Black America 1981* (pp. 1-59). New York: National Urban League.

Hillard, A. G. (1984). I. Q. testing as the Emperor's Clothes. In C. R. Reynolds & R. T. Brown (eds.), *Perspectives on bias in mental testing* (pp. 139-169). New York: Plenum Press.

Hindelang, M. (1973). Causes of delinquency: A partial replication and extension. *Social Problems*, 20, 471-487.

_____. (1970). Age, sex, and versatility of delinquent involvements. *Social Problems*, 18, 522-535.

Hindelang, M., Hirschi, T., & Weis, J. (1981). *Measuring delinquency*. Beverly Hills, Calif.: Sage Publications.

Hippchen, L. (1981). Some possible biochemical aspects of criminal behavior. *Journal of Behavioral Ecology*, 2, 1-6.

Hirschi, T. (1969). *Causes of delinquency*. Berkeley: University of California Press.

Hirschi, T., & Hindelang, M. (1977). Intelligence and delinquency: A revisionist review. *American Sociological Review*, 42, 572-587.

Hoffer, A. (1976). Children with hearing and behavioral disorders. *Journal of Orthomolecular Psychiatry*, 5, 228-230.

Hohenstein, W. (1969). Factors influencing the police disposition of juvenile offenders. In T. Sellin & M. E. Wolfgang (eds.), *Delinquency: Selected studies* (pp. 138-49). New York: John Wiley.

Holman, J. E., & Quinn, J. F. (1992). *Criminology: Applying theory*. St. Paul, Minn.: West Publishing Co.

Hongeller, S. (1989). *Delinquency in adolescence*. Newbury Park, Calif.: Sage.

Hook, E. B. (1973). Behavioral implications of the human XYY Genotype. *Science*, 5, 139-150.

Horney, J. (1978). Menstrual cycles and criminal responsibility. *Law and Human Behavior*, 2, 25-36.

Horwitz, A., & Wasserman, M. (1980). Some misleading conceptions in sentencing research. *Criminology*, 18, 411-424.

Horwitz, A., & White, H. R. (1987). Gender role orientations and styles of pathology among adolescents. *Journal of Health and Social Behavior*, 28, 158-170.

Hubert Humphrey Institute of Public Affairs. (1986). *The incarceration of minority*. Minneapolis: Humphrey Institute.

Huizinga, D., & Delbert E. (1987). Juvenile delinquency: Prevalence, offender incidence and arrest rates by race. *Crime and Delinquency*, 33, 206-223.

Huttman, E. D. (1981). *Introduction to social policy*. New York: McGraw-Hill.

In re Gault, 387 U.S. 1, 87 S.Ct. 1248 (1967).

In re Winship, 397 U. S. 358, 90 S.Ct. 1068 (1970).

Incardi, J. (1986). *The war on drugs*. Mountainview, Calif.: Mayfield Press.

Inmates of Boys Training School v. Affleck, 346 F.Supp. 1354 (D.R.I. 1972).

Izzo, R., & Ross, R. R. (1990). Meta-analysis of rehabilitation programs for juvenile delinquents: A brief report. *Criminal Justice and Behavior*, 17, 134-142.

Jacobs, P. A., Brunton, M., & Melville, M. M. (1965). Aggressive behavior, mental subnormality and the XYY male. *Nature*, 208, 1351-1352.

Jaffe, P., Wolfe, David, W. S., & Zak, Lydia. (1986). Similarities in behavior and social maladjustment among child victims and witnesses to family violence. *American
Journal of Orthopsychiatry*, 55, 142-146.

Jenkins, B., & Faison, A. (1974). *An analysis of 248 persons killed by New York City
policemen*. New York: Metropolitan Applied Research Center.

Jensen, A. (1979). *Bias in mental testing*. New York: Free Press.

———. (1969). How much can we boost IQ and scholastic achievement? *Harvard
Educational Review*, 39, 1-23.

Jensen, C. F., Stauss, J. H., & Harris, V. W. (1977). Crime, delinquency, and the
American Indian. *Human Organization*, 36, 252-257.

Jensen, C. F. & Wiltfang, G. (1987). Gender adolescent self evaluations. Unpublished
manuscript cited in Jensen and Rojek, *Delinquency and youth crime*. Prospect
Heights, Ill.: Waveland Press.

Jensen, G., & Raymond, E. (1976). Sex differences in delinquency: An examination of
popular sociological explanation. *Criminology*, 13, 427-448

Jensen, G., & Rojek, D. (1992). *Delinquency and youth crime*. Prospect Heights, Ill.:
Waveland Press.

Jet. (1994a, October 10). Private black schools. Chicago: Johnson Publishing.

Jet. (1994b, September 26). Kids killing kids. Chicago: Johnson Publishing.

Jet. (1994c, August 22). Education. Chicago: Johnson Publishing.

Joe, T. (1987). Crime and unemployment and the black urban underclass. *Crime and
Delinquency*, 33, 300-316.

Johnson, J. B., & Secret, P. E. (1990). Race and juvenile court decision making revisited. *Criminal Justice Policy Review*, 4, No.2, 159-187.

Johnson, L. (1991). The death penalty does not discriminate against blacks. In C.
Wekesser (ed.), *The death penalty, opposing viewpoints* (pp. 148-151). San Diego,
Calif.: Greenhaven Press.

Johnson, R. (1979). *Juvenile delinquency and its origins: An integrated theoretical
approach*. New York: Cambridge University Press.

Joint Center for Political Studies. (1988). *Black elected officials: A national roster*.
Washington, D.C.: Joint Center for Political Studies.

Joseph, J. (1992). A comparative study of delinquent behavior. Paper presented at
American Society of Criminology, New Orleans, Louisiana.

———. (1994). Young, black and sentenced to die: Black youths and the death
penalty. Paper presented at the Forty-Sixth Annual Meeting of American Society of
Criminology, Miami, Florida.

———. (1995). Juvenile delinquency among African Americans. *Journal of Black
Studies*, 25, 475-491.

Joseph, J., & Greene, H. T. (1994). Incarcerated black female delinquents. Paper
presented at the Forty-Sixth Annual Meeting of American Society of Criminology,
Miami, Florida.

Juvenile Delinquency Commission. (1993). *Profile '93: A sourcebook of juvenile justice data and trends in New Jersey*. Trenton, N.J.: State of New Jersey Juvenile
Delinquency Commission.

Juvenile Justice Bulletin. (1989). *The juvenile court's response to violent crime*.

Washington, D.C.: U.S. Department of Justice.

————. (1993). *OJJDP Model Programs 1992*. Washington, D.C.: Office of Juvenile Justice and Delinquency Prevention.

Kantrowitz, B., & McCormick, J. (1992). A head start does not last. *Newsweek*, January 27, pp. 44-45.

Kaplan, S. L., & Busner, J. (1992). Note on racial bias in the admission of children and adolescents to state mental health facilities versus correctional facilities in New York. *American Journal of Psychiatry*, 149, 768-772.

Katz, J., & Chambliss, W. J. (1991). Biology and crime. In J. F. Sheley (ed.), *Criminology*, pp. 275-303. Belmont, Calif.: Wadsworth Publishing Co.

Keil, T. J., & Vito, G. F. (1990). Race and the death penalty in Kentucky murder trials: An analysis of post-Gregg period. *Justice Quarterly*, 7, 189-207.

Keiter, R. (1973). Criminal or delinquent: A study of juvenile cases transferred to the juvenile court. *Crime and Delinquency*, 19, 528-538.

Kelley, C. (1977). *Crime in U.S.: Uniform Crime Reports, 1976*. Washington, D.C.: U.S. Government Printing Office.

Kelly, D., & Grove, W. (1981). Teacher's nominations in the perpetuation of academic misfits. *Education*, 101, 246-263.

Kelly, D., & Pink, W. (1973). School containment, youth rebellion and delinquency. *Criminology*, 10, 473-485.

Kent v. United States, 388 U.S. 541 (1966).

Key, V. O. (1949). *Southern politics*. New York: Random House.

Kifner, J. (1990, August 2). Evidence shows youth hands up when Teaneck officer killed him. *New York Times*, pp. A1, B2.

Kilborn, P. T. (1994, July 17). Minorities in blue: A special report. *New York Times*, p. 1.

Klein, B. (1990). *State workplan on the disproportionate representation of minority youth in secure facilities*. Delaware Criminal Justice Council.

Klein, J. F. (1980). Revitalizing restitution: Flogging a horse that may have been killed for a just cause. In M. D. Schwartz, T. R. Clear & L. F. Travis (eds.), *Corrections: An issues approach*, (pp. 280-299). Cincinnati, Ohio: Anderson Publishing Co.

Klein, M. W., Teilmann, K. S., Styles, J. A., Lincoln, S. B., & Labin-Rosenweig, S. (1976). The explosion of police diversion programs: Evaluating the structural dimension of a social fad. In M. W. Klein (ed.), *The juvenile justice system* (pp. 101-119). Beverly Hills, Calif.: Sage Publications.

Kobler, A. (1975). Police homicide in a democracy. *Journal of Social Issues*, 31, 163-184.

Kohlberg, L. (1969). *Stages in development of moral thought and action*. New York: Holt, Rinehart & Winston.

Krassner, M. (1986). Diet and brain function. *Nutrition Reviews*, 44, 12-15.

Krisberg, B., Austin, J., & Steele, P. A. (1989). *Unlocking juvenile corrections: Evaluating the Massachusetts Department of Youth Services*. San Francisco: National Council on Crime and Delinquency.

Krisberg, B., Schwartz, I., Fishman, G., Eisikovits, Z., Guttman, E., & Joe, K.

(1987). The incarceration of minority youth. *Crime and Delinquency*, 33, 173-205.

Krisberg, B., & Austin, J. (1978). *The children of Ishmael*. Palo Alto, Calif.: Mayfield.

Krisberg, B., & DeComo, R. (1993). *Juveniles taken into custody: Fiscal year 1991*. Washington, D.C.: Office of Juvenile Justice and Delinquency Prevention.

Kruez, L. E., & Rose, R. M. (1972). Assessment of aggressive behavior and plasma testosterone in young criminal population. *Psychomatic Medicine*, 34, 321-332.

Lab, S. P. (1988). *Crime prevention*. Cincinnati: Anderson.

Lab, S., & Allen, R. B. (1984). Self-report and official measures: A further examination of the validity issue. *Journal of Criminal Justice*, 12, 445-455.

LaFree, G. (1980). The effect of sexual stratification by race on official reactions to rape. *American Sociological Review*, 45, 842-854.

Landry, B. (1987). *The new black middle class*. Berkeley: University of California Press.

Latessa, E., Travis, L., & Wilson, G. (1984). Juvenile diversion. In S. Decker (ed.), *Juvenile justice policy* (pp. 145-165). Beverly Hills, Calif.: Sage Publications.

Laub, J., & Sampson, R. (1988). Unravelling families and delinquency: A reanalysis of the Gluecks' data. *Criminology*, 26, 355-380.

Laurence, S. E., & West, B. R. (1985). *National evaluation of the New Pride Replication Program: Final report Vol. 1*. Lafayette, Calif.: Pacific Institute for Research and Evaluation.

LaVelle, A. (1994, September 10). Should children be tried as adults? *Essence*, 25, No. 5, 85-88.

Lawder, E., Andrews, R., & Parsons, J. (1974). *Five models of foster family group homes, Report of Child Welfare League of America*. New York: Child Welfare League.

Leiber, M. J. (1992). *Juvenile justice decision making in Iowa: An analysis of the influence of race on case processing in three counties, technical report*. Des Moines, Iowa: Iowa Criminal and Juvenile Justice Planning Agency.

Leiber, R. (1994). A comparison of juvenile court outcomes for Native Americans, African Americans, and Whites. *Justice Quarterly*, 11, 257-279.

Lejins, P. (1967). The field of prevention. In W. Amos & C. Wellford (eds.), *Delinquency prevention: Theory and practice* (pp. 1-21). Englewood Cliffs, N.J.: Prentice-Hall.

Lemert, E. (1951). *Social pathology: A systematic approach to the theory of sociopathic behavior*. New York: McGraw-Hill.

Levin, J., & McDevitt, J. (1993). *Hate Crimes*. New York: Plenum Press.

Levine, J. (1976) The potential for crime overreporting in criminal victimization surveys. *Criminology*, 14, 307-330.

Lewis, O. (1966). The culture of poverty. *Scientific American*, 215, 19-25.

Linden, E., & Hackler, J. (1973). Affective ties and delinquency, *Pacific Sociological Review*, 16, 27-46.

Linden, R., & Filmore, C. (1981). A comparative study of delinquency involvement. *Canadian Review of Sociology and Anthropology*, 18, 343-361.

Liska, A. E. & Tausig, M. (1979). Theoretical interpretations of social class and racial differences in legal decision-making for juveniles. *Sociological Quarterly*, 20, 197-207.

Liska, A. (1973). Delinquency involvement and delinquent peers. *Sociology and Social Research*, 58, 23-36.

Lockett v. Ohio, 438 U.S. 536 (1978).

Loeber, R., & Stouthamer-Loeber, M. (1986). Family factors as correlates and predictors of juvenile conduct, problems and delinquency. In M. Tonry & N. Morris (eds.), *Crime and delinquency: An annual review of research*, 7, (pp. 29-49). Chicago: University of Chicago Press.

Lombroso, C. (1911). *Crime: Its causes and remedies.* (Translated by H. P. Horton/orginally published in 1876.) Boston: Little.

Lombroso, C., & Ferrero, G. (1916). *The female offender*. New York: Appleton.

Loy, P., & Norland, S. (1981). Gender convergence and delinquency. *Sociological Quarterly*, 22, 275-283.

Louisiana ex. rel. Francis v. Resweber, 329 U.S. 459 (1947).

Lundman, R. J., Sykes, R. E., & Clark, J. P. (1978). Police control of juveniles: A replication. *Journal of Research in Crime and Delinquency*, 15, 74-91.

Lynch, M. A. (1978). The prognosis of child abuse. *Journal of Child Psychology and Psychiatry*, 19, 175-180.

Maguire, K., & Flanagan, T.(1993). *Sourcebook of criminal justice statistics 1992.* Washington, D.C.: U.S. Department of Justice, Bureau of Justice Statistics.

Maguire, K., & Pastore, A. L. (1994). *Sourcebook of criminal justice statistics 1993.* Washington, D.C.: U.S. Department of Justice, Bureau of Justice Statistics.

Mann, R. C. (1986). Black women who kill. In D. F. Hawkins (ed.), *Homicides among Black Americans* (pp. 157-186). Lanham, Md.: University Press of America.

_____. (1989). Random thoughts on the ongoing Wilbanks-Mann discourse. *The Critical Criminologist*, 1, 3-4.

Mapp v. Ohio, 367 U.S. 643 (1961).

Marger, M. (1991). *Race and ethnic relations: American and global perspectives.* Belmont, Calif.: Wadsworth.

Marshall, I. H., & Thomas, C. W. (1983). Discretionary decision-making and the juvenile court. *Juvenile and Family Court Journal*, 34, No. 3, 47-59.

Martin, S. E., Sechret, L. B., & Redner, R. (1981). *New directions in the rehabilitation of criminal offenders.* Washington, D.C.: National Academy Press.

Matsueda, R. L. (1982). Testing control and differential association. *American Sociological Review*, 47, 489-504.

Maxson, C. L., & Klein, M. W. (1990). Street gang violence: Twice as great, or half as great. In C. R.. Huff (ed.), *Gangs in America* (pp. 71-100). Newbury Park, Calif.: Sage Publications.

McBay, S. (1992). The condition of African American education: Changes and challenges. In B. J. Tidwell (ed.), *The state of black America 1992* (pp. 141-156). New York: National Urban League.

McCaghy, C. H. (1976). *Deviant behavior: Crime, conflict and interest groups.* New York: Macmillan.

McCarthy, B. R., & Smith, B. L. (1986). The conceptualization of discrimination in the juvenile justice process: The impact of administrative factors and screening decisions on juvenile court dispositions. *Criminology*, 24, 41-64.

McCleskey v. Zandt, No. 89-7662 (1991).

McClesky v. Kemp, 478 U.S. 1019 (1987).

McCord, W., McCord, J., & Zola, I. K. (1959). *Origins of crime*. New York: Columbia University Press.

McGee, R. (1981). *Prisons and politics*. Lexington, Mass.: Lexington Books.

McKeiver v. Pennsylvania, 402 U.S. 528, 91 S.Ct. 1976 (1971).

McPherson, S. J., McDonald, L. E., & Ryer, C. W. (1983). Intensive counseling with families of juvenile offenders. *Juvenile and Family Court Journal*, 34, 27-33.

Meade, A. C. & Marsden, M. E. (1981). An integration of classic theories of delinquency. In A. C. Mead (ed.), *Youth and society: Studies of adolescent deviance*. Chicago: Institute for Juvenile Research.

Mednick, S. A., Gabrielli, W. F., & Hutchings, B. (1984). Genetic influences in criminal convictions: Evidence from adoption cohort. *Science*, 224, 891-894.

Mednick, S., & Volavka, Jan. (1980). Biology and crime. In N. Morris & M. Tonry (eds.), *Crime Justice: An Annual Review of Research*, Vol. 1 (pp. 85-158). Chicago: University of Chicago.

Mednick, S., Volavka, J., Gabrielli, W., & Turan, M. (1981). EEG as a predictor of antisocial behavior. *Criminology*, 19, 219-229.

Mendelsohn, H. (1971). *Minorities and the police: Confrontation in America*. New York: Free Press.

Mercer, J. (1972, September). IQ: The lethal label. *Psychology Today*, pp. 44-47.

Merton, R. (1938). Social structure and anomie. *American Sociological Review*, 3, 712-719.

Miami Herald (1983, March 27), p. 18A.

Milich, R., & Pelham, W. (1986). Effects of sugar ingestion on the classroom and playgroup behavior of attention deficit disordered boys. *Journal of Counseling and Counsulting Psychology*, 54, 714-718.

Miller, P., & Simon, W. (1974). Adolescent sexual behavior: Context and change. *Social Problems*, 22, 58-76.

Miller, W. (1958). Lower class culture as a generating milieu of gang delinquency. *Journal of Social Issues*, 14, 5-19.

Milton, C., Halleck, J. W., Lardner, J., & Albrecht, G. L. (1977). *Police use of deadly force*. Washington, D.C.: The Police Foundation.

Minsky, T. (1984, February 23). The odds on being slain--Worse for young black males, *Boston Globe*, 1, 47.

Miranda v. Arizona, 384 U.S. 436 (1966).

Moffitt, T., Gabrielli, W., Mednick, S., & Schalsinger, F. (1981). Socioeconomic status, IQ and delinquency. *Journal of Abnormal Psychology*, 90, 152-156.

Monahan, J., & Steadman, J. H. (1983). Crime and mental disorder: An epidemiological approach. In M. Tonry & N. Morris (eds.), *Crime and Justice*, 4 (pp. 145-193). Chicago: University of Chicago Press.

Morales v. Thurman, 364 F.Supp. 166 (E.D. Tex. 1973).

Morash, M., & Rucker, L. (1990). A critical look at the idea of boot camp as a correctional reform. *Crime and Delinquency*, 36, 204-205.

Morgan v. Sproat, 432 F. Supp. 1130 (S.D. Miss. 1977).

Morgan, H. (1980). How schools fail black children. *Social Policy*, 10, No. 4, 49-54.

Morris, R. (1964). Female delinquency and relational problems. *Social Forces*, 4, 82-89.

Moses, M. (1993, November). Girls Scouts in prison. *National Institute of Justice Journal Issues*, No. 227, 10-12.

Moynihan, D. (1965). *The Negro family: The case for national action*. Washington, D.C.: U.S. Government Printing Office.

Mullen, J., Chabotar, K. J., & Carrow, D. M. (1985). The *privatization of corrections*. Washington, D.C.: U.S. Department of Justice.

Mulrey, E., & LaRosa, J. (1986). Delinquency cessation and adolescent development: Preliminary data. *American Journal of Orthopsychiatry*, 56, 212-224.

Natalino, K. (1980). *Testing two theories of delinquency among urban black adolescents*. Prepared for Presentation at the 1980 Annual Meeting of North Central Sociological Association, May 1-3, Dayton, Ohio.

National Advisory Commission on Criminal Justice Standards and Goals. (1973). *A national strategy to reduce crime*. Washington, D.C.: U.S. Government Printing Office.

_____. (1966). Undetected Delinquent Behavior. *Journal of Social Research in Crime and Delinquency*, 3, 27-46.

National Center for Health Statistics. (1986). *Health, United States*. Hyattsville, Md.: Public Health Service.

_____. (1989). *Health, United States*. Hyattsville, Md.: Public Health Service.

_____. (1991). *Health, United States, 1990*. Hyattsville, Md.: Public Health Service.

_____. (1992). *Health, United States, 1991*. Hyattsville, Md.: Public Health Service.

National Center for Juvenile Justice. (1993). *National estimates of juvenile court delinquency cases; 1986-1990*. Pittsburgh, Pa.: Office of Juvenile Justice and Delinquency Prevention.

National Council of Juvenile and Family Court Judges. (1990). Minority Youth in the Juvenile Justice System: A Judicial Response. *Juvenile and Family Journal*, 41, No. 3A1-71 (pp. 1-69).

National Council on Crime and Delinquency (1992). *The overrepresentation of minority youth in the California juvenile justice system*. San Francisco: NCCD.

National Education Association. (1982). *Nationwide teacher opinion poll 1981*. Washington, D.C.: National Education Association.

National Institute of Drug Abuse. (1980). *Current trends and issues in drug abuse*. Rockville, Md.: ADAMHA.

National Minority Advisory Council on Criminal Justice. (1982). *Inequality of justice*. Washington, D.C.: U.S. Department of Justice.

National Research Center. (1989). *A common destiny: Blacks and American society*. Washington, D.C.: National Academy Press.

National School Safety Center. (1990). *Gangs in schools: Breaking up is hard to do*. Malibu, Calif.: Perperdine University.

NBC News Special. (1987, July 26). Crime, punishment, and kids.

Needle, J. A., & Stapleton, V. (1983). Police handling of gangs. *Reports of the National Juvenile Justice Assessment Centers*. Washington, D.C.: U.S. Department of Justice.

Nelson v. Heyne, 491F.2d 352 (7th Cir., 1974).

New Jersey v. T.L.O., 105 S. Ct.733 (1985).

Newman, Maria. (1993, January 10). Report details variations in police review boards. New York Times, p. 26.

New York Times (1987, October 19). Crack brings violence to areas of New York, p. 13.

Newsweek, May 11, 1992.

Nye, F. I. (1957). Child adjustment in broken and unhappy homes. *Marriage and Family*, 19, 356-361.

_____. (1958). *Family relationships and delinquent behavior*. New York: John Wiley.

Nye, F. I., Short, J., & Olson, V. (1958). Socioeconomic status and delinquent behavior. *American Sociological Review*, 63, 381-389.

Obgu, J. U. (1982). Social forces as a context of ghetto children school failure. In L. Feagans & D. C. Farran (eds.), *The language of children reared in poverty* (pp. 117-138). New York: Academic Press.

O'Brien, R. (1987). The interracial nature of violent crime: A reexamination. *American Journal of Sociology*, 92, 817-835.

Ohlin, L., Miller, A., & Coates, R. (1976). *Juvenile correctional reform in Massachusetts*. Washington, D.C.: U.S. Government Printing Office.

Olson-Raymer, G. (1983). The role of the federal government in juvenile prevention. *Journal of Criminal Law and Criminology*, 74, 594-595.

Orfield, G. (1984). *The Chicago study of access and choice in higher education*. Chicago: Committee on Public Policy Studies, University of Chicago.

Pace, D. (1993). *Community relations concepts*. Paceville, Calif.: Coperhouse.

Palmer, T. (1992). *The re-emergence of correctional intervention*. Newbury, Calif.: Sage.

Palmer, T., & Lewis, R. V. (1980). *An evaluation of juvenile diversion*. Cambridge, Mass.: Oelgeschlager, Gunn & Hain.

Parent, D. G. (1989). *Shock incarceration: An overview of existing programs*. Washington, D.C.: U.S. Government Printing Office.

Parent, D. G., Leiter, V., Kennedy, S., Livens, L., Wentworth, D., & Wilcox, S. (1994). *Conditions of confinement: Juvenile detention and corrections facilities*. Washington, D.C.: Office of Juvenile Justice and Delinquency Prevention.

Parisi, N. (1982). Exploring female crime patterns. In N. Rafter & E. Stanko (eds.), *Judges, lawyers, victim, thief: Women, gender roles and criminal justice* (pp. 111-130). Boston: Northeastern University Press.

Patterson, G. (1982). *A social learning approach: Coercive family process* 3. Eugene, Ore.: Castalia.

_____. (1980). Mothers: The unacknowledged victims. *Monograph of the Society for Research in Child Development*, Vol. 45. Chicago: University of Chicago Press.

Paul, F. (1987). *Declining access to educational opportunities in Metropolitan Chicago*. Chicago: Metropolitan Opportunity Project, University of Chicago.

Paulsen, M. (1991, March). Securing police compliance. *New York Times*, pp. 396-402.

Pavlov, I. P. (1928). *Lectures on conditioned reflexes*. New York: International Publishers.

Pemberton, D. A., & Benady, D. R. (1973). Consciously rejected children. *British Journal of Psychiatry*, 123, 575-578.

Pena v. New York State Division for Youth, 419 F.Supp. 203 (S.D.N.Y.1976).

Perry, R. (1985). Differential dispositions of black and white juveniles: A critical assessment of methodology. *The Western Journal of Black Studies*, 9, 189-197.

Petersilia, J. (1983). *Racial disparities in the criminal justice system*. Santa Monica, Calif.: The Rand Corporation.

Peterson, R. D. (1988). Youthful offender designations and sentencing in New York Criminal courts. *Social Problems*, 32, 111-130.

Peterson, R., & Bailey, W. (1991). Felony murder and capital punishment: An examination of the deterrence question. *Criminology*, 29, 367-395.

Pfohl, S. (1985). *Images of deviance and social control: A sociological history*. New York: McGraw-Hill.

Philadelphia Police Study Task Force (1987). *Philadelphia and its police: Toward a new partnership*. Philadelphia: The Task Force.

Phillips, D. J. (1980). The deterrent effect of capital punishment: New evidence on an old controversy. *American Journal of Sociology*, 86, 139-148.

Phillips, L. (1994, August 26). Democrats call GOP bluff. *U.S.A. TODAY*, p. 6A.

Phillips, L., & Hasson, J. (1994, August 26). Senate passes Crime Bill. *U.S.A. Today*, p. 1A.

Piaget, J. (1932) *The moral judgement of the child*. London: Kegan Paul.

Pierce, H. B. (1986). Blacks and law enforcement: Toward police brutality reduction. *The Black Scholar*, 17, 49-54.

Piliavin, I., & Briar, S. (1964). Police encounters with Juveniles. *American Journal of Sociology*, 70, 206-214.

Pogrebin, M., Poole, E., & Regoli, R. (1984). Constructing and implementing a model of juvenile justice diversion program. *Youth and Society*, 15, 305-324.

The Police Foundation. (1981). *The Newark foot police experiment*. Washington, D.C.: The Police Foundation.

Polk, K. (1984). Juvenile diversion. *Crime and Delinquency*, 30, 648-659.

Polk, K., & Schafer, W. (1972). *Schools and delinquency*. Englewood Cliffs, N.J.: Prentice-Hall.

Pollack, J. (1978). Early theories of female criminality. In L. Bowker (ed.), *Women, crime and the criminal justice system*. Lexington, Mass.: Lexington Books.

Pollack, O. (1950). *The criminality of women*. Westport, Conn.: Greenwood Press.

Poussaint, A. (1983). Black-on-Black violence: A psychological-political perspective. *Victimology*, 8, 161-169.

President's Commission on Law Enforcement and Administration of Justice. *Field studies, 1V, The police and the community* Vol. 1. Washington, D.C.: U.S. Government Printing Office.

Prettyman, B. (1961). *Death and the Supreme Court*. New York: Harcourt, Brace & World.

Price, T., & Cowles, A. (1994, September 15). Morehouse, Clark share federal grant. *The Atlanta Journal/The Atlanta Constitution*.

Project New Pride. (1985). Washington, D.C.: U.S. Government Printing Office.

Pulkkinen, L. (1982). Self control and continuity from childhood to late adolescence. In P. B. Baltes & O. G. Brim (eds.), *Life span development*, 4. New York: Academic Press.

The Quality of Education for Minorities Project (1990). *Education that works: An action plan for education of minorities*. Cambridge, Mass.: Massachusetts Institute of Technology.

Quay, H.C., & Love, C. T. (1977). The effects of a juvenile diversion program on re-arrests. *Criminal Justice and Behavior*, 4, 377-396.

Quicker, J. C. (1974). The effects of goal discrepancy on delinquency. *Social Problems*, 22, 76-86.

Quinney, R. (1977). *Class, state and crime: On the theory and practice of criminal justice*. New York: David McKay.

Radelet, M. L., & Bedau, H. A. (1988). Fallibility and fanality: Type II errors and capital punishment. In K. C. Haas & J. A. Inciardi (eds.), *Challenging capital punishment: Legal and social science approaches* (pp. 91-112). Newbury Park, Calif.: Sage.

Rankin, J. (1979). School factors and delinquency: Interactions by sex. *Sociology and Social Research*, 64, 420-434.

Rausch, S. P., & Logan, C. H. (1983). Diversion from juvenile court: Panacea or pandora's box. In J. R. Klugel (ed.), *Evaluating juvenile delinquency* (pp. 19-30). Beverly Hills, Calif.: Sage.

Rawlings, S. (1993). *Households and family characteristics*. Washington, D.C.: U.S. Government Printing Office.

Ream, D. (1983). *Serious solutions for serious juvenile crime*. Chicago: Chicago Law Enforcement Study Group.

Reckless, W. (1961). A new theory of delinquency and crime. *Federal Probation*, 25, 42-46.

Reed, W. L. (1984). *Racial differentials in juvenile court decision-making: Final report*. Washington, D.C.: U.S. Department of Justice, National Institute of Juvenile Justice and Delinquency Prevention.

Regoli, R., Wilderman, E., & Pogrebin, M. (1985). Using an alternative evaluation measure for asserting juvenile diversion programs. *Children and Youth Services Review*, 7, 32-38.

Regoli, R. M., & Hewitt, J. D. (1994). *Delinquency in society: A child-centered approach* (2nd ed.). New York: McGraw-Hill.

Reiss, A. J., Jr. (1971). *The police and the public*. New Haven, Conn.: Yale University Press.

_____. (1968, July-August). Police brutality--Answers to key questions. *Transaction*, 5, 10-19.

_____. (1951). Delinquency as the failure of personal and social controls. *American*

Sociological Review, 16, 196-207.

Reno, J. (1993, Summer). The whole approach to crime. *Spectrum*, 66, No. 3, 31-36.

_____. (1995). Keynote Address: 1994 ASC Meeting in Miami, Florida. *Criminologist*, 20, No. 2, pp. 1,4, 8-9.

_____ Reynolds, Rhonda. (1993). School violence: Drugs/gangs. *Black Enterprise*, p. 47. New York: Earl G. Graves Publishing Co.

Rist, M. C. (1990). *The shadow children: Preparing for the arrival of crack babies in school, Research Bulletin.* Bloomington, Ind.: Phi Delta Kappa.

Robbins, L. N., Helzer, J. E., Weissman, M. M, Orvaschel, H., Gruenberg, E., Burke, J. D., & Regier, D. (1984). Lifetime prevalence of specific psychiatric disorders in three sites. *Archives of General Psychiatry*, 41, 949-958.

Robbins, W. (1988, December 4). California gangs staking claims across the United States. *Tribune*, p. 29A.

Robertson, I. (1987). *Sociology* (3rd ed.). New York: Worth.

Robin, G. (1963). Justifiable homicide by police officers. *Journal of Criminal Law, Criminology, and Police Science*, 54, 225-231.

Robinson, S. P. (1987). Taking charge: An approach to making educational problems of blacks comprehensible and manageable. In J. E. Jacob (ed.), *The state of black America* (pp. 31-36). New Brunswick, N.J.: Transaction Books.

Rocky Mountain News (1990, September). Back-to-school fashions include bullet proof jackets.

Rodman, H. (1963). The lower-class value stretch. *Social Forces*, 42, 205-215.

Roebuck, J. B. (1967). *Criminal typology: The legalistic, physical-constitutional hereditary, psychological-psychiatric and sociological approaches.* Springfield, Ill.: Charles C. Thomas.

Rogers, C. (1991, October). Children in gangs. *The UNESCO Courier*, pp. 19-21.

Rojek, D., & Erickson, Maynard. (1981/1982). Reforming the juvenile justice system. *Law and Society Review*, 16, 241-264.

Rojek, D. G. (1982). Juvenile diversion: A study of community cooptation. In D. Rojek & G. F. Jansen (eds.), *Readings in juvenile delinquency* (pp. 316-321). Lexington, Mass.: D.C. Heath.

Rosanthal, R., & Jacobsen, L. (1968). *Pygmalion in the classroom: Teacher expectations and pupils' intellectual development.* New York: Holt, Rinehart & Winston.

Rose, H. (1990). *Race place and risk: Black homicide in urban America.* Albany, N.Y.: State University of New York.

Rosen, L. (1985). Family and delinquency: Structure or function. *Criminology*, 23, 553-573.

Rosen, L., & Neilson, K. (1982). Broken homes. In L. Savitz & N. Johnson (eds.), *Contemporary criminology* (pp. 126-135). New York: John Wiley.

Rosenbaum, J. L. (1989). Family dysfunction and female delinquency. *Crime and Delinquency*, 35, 31-44.

Rossi, P. H., Berk, R. A., & Edison, B. K. (1974). *The roots of urban discontent: Public policy, municipal institutions, and the ghetto.* New York: John Wiley.

Rowe, D. (1986). Genetic and environmental components of antisocial behavior: A study of 265 twin pairs. *Criminology*, 24, 513-532.

_____. (1990). As the twig is bent: The myth of children rearing influences on personality development. *Journal of Counseling and Development*, 68, 606-11.

Rowe, D. & Osgood, D. W. (1984). Heredity and sociological theories of delinquency: A reconsideration. *American Sociological Review*, 49, 526-540.

Rubin, T. (1985). *Behind the black robes: Juvenile court judges and the court*. Beverly Hills, Calif.: Sage Publications.

Rudman, C., Hartstone, E., Fagan, J., and Moore, M. (1986). Violent youth in adult court: Process and punishment. *Crime and Delinquency*, 32, 75-96.

Rudwick, E. M. (1964). *Race riot at East St. Louis*. Carbondale, Ill.: Southern Illinois University Press.

Rudwick, E., & Meier, A. (1969). *Negro retaliatory violence in the twentieth century*. In A. Meier and E. Rudwick (eds.), *The making of black America: Essays in negro life and history, Vol. 2* (pp. 406-417). New York: Atheneum.

Ruester, J. (1989, September). L. A. fights gang crime with unusual weapon. *Law and Order*, pp 41-42.

Rutter, M. & Quinton, D. (1988). Parental psychiatric disorder: Effects on children. *Psychological Medicine*, 14, 853-880.

Salmans, S. (1988, April 10). The tracking controversy. *New York Times Education Supplement*, pp. 56-62.

Sampson, R. J. (1987). Urban black violence: The effects on jobless and family disruption *American Journal of Sociology*, 93, 348-382.

_____. (1985). Structural sources of variation in race-age-specific rates of offending across major U. S. cities. *Criminology*, 23, 647-673.

Sanders, A. (1989, July 10). Bad News for Death row. *Times*, pp. 48-49.

Sarri, R. (1983). Gender issues in juvenile justice. *Crime and Delinquency*, 29, 381-397.

Sarri, R., & Vinter, R. (1975). Juvenile justice and injustice. *Resolution*, 18, 43-51.

Scarr, S., & Weinberg, R. (1976). IQ test performance of black children adopted by white families. *American Psychologist*, 31, 726-739.

Schafer, W. E., Olexa, C., & Polk, K. (1972). Programmed for social class: Tracking in high school. In K. Polk & W. E. Schafer (eds.), *Schools and Delinquency* (pp. 34-54). Englewood Cliffs, N. J.: Prentice-Hall.

Schall v. Martin, 104 S.Ct. 2403 (1984).

Schauss, A. (1980). Diet, crime and delinquency. Berkeley, Calif.: Parker House.

Schauss, A., & Simonsen, C. (1979). A critical analysis of the diets of chronic juvenile offenders, Part 1. *Journal of Orthomolecular Psychiatry*, 8, 222-226.

Schiavi, R., Theilgaard, A., Owen, D., & White, D. (1984). Sex anomalies, and aggressivity. *Archives of General Psychology*, 41, 93-99.

Schmitt, B., & Kempe, C. H. (1975). Neglect and abuse of children. In V. Vaughan & R. McKay (eds.), *Nelson textbook of pediatrics*. Philadelphia: W. B. Saunders.

Schneider, A. L., & Schneider, P. R. (1984). *A justice philosophy for the juvenile court*. Salem, Oreg.: Institute for Policy Analysis.

Schoenberg, R. (1975). A structural model of delinquency. Unpublished doctoral dissertation, University of Washington, Seattle. Cited in R. Johnson, *Juvenile delinquency and its origins: An integrated theoretical approach*, New York: Cambridge

University Press.

Schoenfield, C. G. (1971). A psychoanalytic theory of juvenile delinquency. *Crime and Delinquency*, 19, 469-480.

Schoenthaler, S., & Doraz, W. (1983). Types of offenses which can be reduced in an institutional setting using nutritional intervention. *International Journal of Biosocial Research*, 4, 74-84.

Schutt, R., & Dannefer, D. (1988). Detention decisions in juvenile court cases: JINS, JDs and genders. *Law and Society Review*, 22, 509-520.

Schwartz, I. M. (1989). *(In) justice for juveniles: Rethinking the best interests of the child*. Lexington, Mass.: Lexington Books.

Schwartz, I. M., Fishman, G., Halfield, R. R., Krisberg, B. A., & Eisikovits, Z. (1987). Juvenile detention: The hidden closets revisited. *Justice Quarterly*, 4, 219-235.

Schwartz, I. (1990, April). Correcting juvenile corrections. *The World and 1*, pp. 505-507.

Seagrave, J. O., & Hastad, D. N. (1983). Evaluating structural and control models of delinquency: A replication and extension. *Youth and Society*, 14, 437-456.

Selke, W., & Pepinsky, H. (1982). The politics of police reporting in Indianapolis 1948-78. *Law and Human Behavior*, 6, 327-342.

Sellin, T. (1980). *The penalty of death*. Beverly Hills, Calif.: Sage.

_____. (1938). *Culture, conflict and crime*. New York: Social Science Research Council.

Shade, B. J. (1982). Afro-American cognitive styles: A variable in school success? *Review of Educational Research*, 52, 291-244.

Shah, S., & Roth, L. (1974). Biological and psychophysiological factors. In D. Glaser (ed.), *Handbook of Criminology* (pp. 101-73). Chicago: Rand McNally.

Shannon, L. (1982). *Assessing the relationship of adult criminal careers to juvenile careers: A summary*. Washington, D.C.: U.S. Government Printing Office.

_____. (1963). Types and patterns of delinquency referral in middle-sized city. *British Journal of Criminology*, 3, 24-36.

Shaw, C., & McKay, H. (1942). *Juvenile delinquency and urban areas*. Chicago: University of Chicago Press.

Sheldon, W. (1942). *The varieties of temperament*. New York: Harper Brothers.

Sherman, R. F. (1994, September). Dispute resolution: Providing for positive youth development and the prevention of violence. *National Institute for Dispute Resolution Forum*, No. 25, 8-14.

Shipp, E. R. (1994, May). Filling the gap. *Emerge*, 5, No. 8, 48-52.

Shockley, W. (1967). A "try simplest cases" approach to the heredity-poverty-crime problem. *Proceedings of the National Sciences*, 57, No. 6, 1767-1774.

Shoemaker, D. (1990). *Theories of delinquency: An examination of explanations of delinquent behavior*. New York: Oxford University Press.

Short, J. F. (1990). *Delinquency and society*. Englewood Cliffs, N.J.: Prentice-Hall.

Short, J., & Nye, F. I. (1958). Extent of unrecorded juvenile delinquency: Tentative conclusions. *Journal of Criminal Law, Criminology and Police Science*, 49, 296-302.

Shusta, R., M., Leveine, D. R., Harris, P. R., & Wong, H. (1995). *Multiculturalism law enforcement. strategies for peackeeping in a diverse society.* Englewood Cliffs, N.J.: Prentice-Hall.

Siegel, L. (1992). *Criminology.* St. Paul, Minn.: West Publishing.

Siegel, L. J., & Senna, J. J. (1994). *Juvenile delinquency: Theory, practice and law* (5th ed.). St. Paul, Minn.: West Publishing.

_____. (1993). *Juvenile delinquency: Theory, practice and the law* (4th ed.). St. Paul, Minn.: West Publishing.

Silberman, B., & Yanowitch, M. (1974). *The worker in post-industrial capitalism.* New York: Free Press.

Silberman, C. (1978). *Criminal violence, criminal justice.* New York: Random House.

Simmons, R. (1978). The meaning of the IQ-Delinquency relationship. *American Sociological Review,* 43, 268-270.

Simon, R. L., & Gray, P. A. (1989). Perceived blocked opportunities as an explanation of delinquency among lower-class black males: A research note. *Journal of Research in Crime and Delinquency,* 26, 90-101.

Simons, R. L., Miller, M. G., & Aigner, S. M. (1980). Contemporary theories of deviant and female delinquency. *Journal of Research in Crime and Delinquency,* 17, 42-57.

Singer, S. L. (1985). *Relocating juvenile crime: The shift from juvenile to criminal justice.* Albany, N.Y.: Nelson A. Rockefeller Institute of Government.

Singh, A., Celinski, H., & Jayewardene, C. H. S. (1980). Ecological correlates of crime in Ottawa. *Canadian Journal of Criminology,* 22, 78-85.

Skinner, B. F. (1974). *About behaviorism.* New York: Alfred A. Knopf

Skolnick, J. (1968). *The police and the urban ghetto.* Chicago: American Bar Foundation.

_____. (1967). *Justice without trial.* New York: John Wiley.

Skolnick, J., & Fyfe, J. J. (1993). *Above the law: Police and excessive use of force.* New York: Free Press.

Smart, C. (1976). *Women, crime and criminology.* London, England: Routledge & Kegan Paul.

Smith, C. P., Alexander, T. V., & Roberts, C. F. (1980). *A national assessment of serious juvenile crime and the juvenile justice system (Final report).* Sacramento, Calif.: American Justice Institute.

Smith, D. A., Visher, A. L., & Davidson, L. A. (1984). Equity and discretion justice: The influence of race on police arrest decisions. *Journal of Criminal Law and Criminology,* 75, 234-269.

Smith, D. A., Graham, N., & Adams, B. (1991). Minorities and the police: Attitudinal and behavioral questions. In M. J. Lynch & E. Britt Patterson (eds.), *Race and criminal justice* (pp. 22-35). New York: Harrow & Heston, Publishers.

Smith, D., Visher, Ch., & Davidson, L. A. (1984). Equity and discretionary justice: The influence of race on police discretion. *Journal of Criminal Law and Criminology,* 74, 234-249.

Soler, M., Bell, J., Jaimeson, E., Shauffer, C., Shotton, A., & Warboys, L. (1989). *Representing the child client.* New York: Matthew Bender Co.

Speirs, V. L. (1986). *School safety programs*. Washington, D.C.: National Institute of Justice (NIJ) Reports.

Spergel, I. (1964). *Racketville, Slumtown and Halburg: An exploration study of delinquent subcultures*. Chicago: University of Chicago.

_____. (1990). Youth gangs: Continuity and change. In M. Tonry and N. Morris (eds.), *Crime and justice: A review of research,* Vol. 12 (pp. 171-275). Chicago: University of Chicago Press.

Spergel, I. A., Reamer, F. G., & Lynch, J. P. (1981). Deinstitutionalization of status offenders: Individual outcome and system effects. *Journal of Research in Crime and Delinquency*, 18, 34-46.

Stack, S. (1987). Publicized executions and homicide, 1950-1980. *American Sociological Review*, 52, 532-540.

Stanford v. Kentucky, 429 U.S. 361 (1989).

Staples, R. (1974). Internal colonialism and black violence. *Black World*, 23, 16-34.

_____. (1975). White racism, black crime and American justice: Application of the colonial model to explain race and crime. *Phylon*, 36, 14-22.

_____. (1989). *The urban plantation*. Oakland, Calif.: The Black Scholar Press.

Staples, W. G. (1987). Law and social control in juvenile justice dispositions. *Journal of Research in Crime and Delinquency*, 24, 7-22.

Star-Ledger Wire Services (1995, April 18). Affirmative action dealt court setback. *The Star-Ledger*, pp. 1, 15.

State of New Jersey Commission of Investigation. (1993). *Criminal street gangs*. Trenton: State of New Jersey.

State v. Lovery, 230 A.2d 907 (1967).

State v. Middlebrooks, 840S.W.2d. 317 (1992).

State v. Werner, 242 S.E. 2d 907 (W.Va. 1978).

Steinhart, D. (1988). California legislation ends jailing children--The story of a policy reversal. *Crime and Delinquency*, 34, 169-189.

Stewart, M. A., Deblois, C. S., Meardon, J., & Cummings, C. (1980). Aggressive conduct disorders of children: The clinical picture. *Journal of Nervous Mental Disorder*, 68, 604-610.

Stojkovic, S., & Lovell, R. (1992). *Corrections: An introduction*. Cincinnati, Ohio: Anderson Publishing.

Stover, D. (1986, August). A new breed of youth gang is on the prowl and a bigger threat than ever. *American School Board Journal*, 173, No. 8, 19-24, 35.

Streib, V. (1986). *Testimony on the death penalty for juveniles*. Washington, D.C: U.S. Government Printing Office.

_____. (1987). *Death penalty for juveniles*. Bloomington, Ind.: Indiana University Press.

_____. (1990). Imposing the death penalty on children. In R. Weisheit & Robert Culberton (eds.), *Juvenile delinquency: A justice perspective* (pp. 145-59). Prospect Heights, Ill.: Waveland Press.

_____. (1993). The juvenile death penalty today. Unpublished mimeograph. Cleveland: Cleveland State University.

Sutherland, E. (1939). *Principles of criminology*. New York: J. B. Lippincott.

Swanson, C., Chamelin, N., & Territo, L. (1992). *Criminal Investigation*. New York: McGraw-Hill.

Swinton, D. (1993). The economic status of African Americans during the Reagan-Bush Era: Withered opportunities, limited outcomes, and uncertain outlook. In B. Tidwell (ed.), *The state of black America 1993*, (pp. 135-200). New York: National Urban League.

Synder, H. N. (1990). *Growth in minority detentions attributed to drug law violators*. Washington, D.C.: Office of Juvenile Justice and Delinquency Prevention.

Takagi, P. (1974). A garrison state in a "democratic" society. *Crime and Social Justice*, 5, 34-43.

Tannebaum, F. (1938). *Crime and the community*. Boston: Ginn.

Tatum, B. (1994). The colonial model as a theoretical explanation of crime and delinquency. In A. Sulton (ed.), *African-American perspectives on crime causation, criminal justice administration and crime prevention* (pp. 33-52). Englewood, Colo.: Sulton Books.

Teeters, N. K., & Hedblom, J. H. (1967). *Hang by the neck*. Springfield, Ill.: Charles C. Thomas.

Tennessee v. Garner, 471 U.S. 1 (1985).

Territo, L., Halstead, J., & Bromley, M. (1992). *Crime and justice in America: A human perspective*. St. Paul, Minn.: West Publishing Co.

Terry, R. (1967). Discrimination in the handling of juvenile offenders by social-control agencies. *Journal of Research in Crime and Delinquency*, 4, 218-230.

Theilgaard, A. (1983). Aggression and the XYY personality. *International Journal of Law and Psychiatry*, 6, 413-421.

Thomas, C. W., & Bilchik, S. (1985). Prosecuting juveniles in criminal courts: A legal and empirical analysis. *Journal of Criminal Law and Criminology*, 76, 439-479.

Thompson v. Oklahoma, 102 S. Ct. (1988).

Thornberry, T. P. (1973). Race, socioeconomic status and sentencing in the juvenile justice system. *Journal of Law and Criminology*, 64, 90-98.

Thornberry, T., & Farnsworth, M. (1982). Social correlates of criminal involvement: Further evidence of the relationship between social status and criminal behavior. *American Sociological Review*, 47, 643-656.

Thornberry, T., Farnsworth, M., & Lizotte, A. (n.d). *Peer influence and the initiation to drug use*. Albany, N.Y.: Hindelang Criminal Justice Research Center.

Thrasher, F. M. (1927). *The gang*. Chicago: University of Chicago Press.

Tidwell, B., Kuumba, M., Jones, D., & Watson, B. (1993). Fast facts: African Americans in 1990s. In B. J. Tidwell (ed.), *The state of black America 1993*, (pp. 35-57). New York: Urban League.

Tittle, C. (1983). Social class and criminal behavior: A critique of the theoretical foundation. *Social Forces*, 62, 353-355.

Tittle, C. R., & Curran, Debra A. (1988, September). Contingencies for dispositional disparities in juvenile justice. *Social Forces*, 67, 23-58.

Toby, J. (1957). The differential impact of family disorganization. *American Sociological Review*, 8, 40-46.

_____. (1977). The socialization and control of deviant motivation. In D. Glaser (ed.), *Handbook of criminology*. Chicago: Rand McNally.

_____. (1979). The new criminology is the old sentimentality. *Criminology*, 16, 513-526.

_____. (1983). Crime in schools. In J. Q. Wilson (ed.), *Crime and public policy* (pp. 68-88). San Francisco: Institute for Contemporary Studies.

Tollett, T., & Close, B. C. (1991). The overrepresentation of blacks in Florida's juvenile justice System. In M. J. Lynch & E. B. Patterson (eds.), *Race and criminal justice* (pp. 86-99). Albany, N.Y.: Harrow & Heston.

Torres, J. (1989). Can training reduce police/citizen violence? *The Trainer.*

Tracy, P. (1987). Race and class differences in official and self-reported delinquency. In M. E. Wolfgang, T. Thornberry, & R. Figlio (eds.), *From boy to man, from delinquency to crime* (pp. 87-121). Chicago: University of Chicago Press.

Trasler, G. (1987). Some cautions of a biological approach to crime. In S. Mednick, T. Moffitt, & S. Stack, *The causes of crime, New biological approach* (pp. 7-24). Cambridge: Cambridge University Press.

Turk, A. (1982). *Political criminology: The defiance and defense of authority*. Beverly Hills, Calif.: Sage Publications.

Tuttle, W. (1970). *Race riot: Chicago in the red summer of 1919*. New York: Atheneum.

U. S. and World News Report (1987, May 18). The burgeoning educational underclass, pp. 66-67.

U. S. Bureau of Census. (1992). *Educational attainment in U.S. 1991*. Washington, D.C.: U.S. Government Printing Office.

U. S. Commission of Civil Rights. (1980). *Characters in textbooks*. Washington, D.C.: U.S. Government Printing Office.

U. S. Department of Commerce. (1989). *1980-1989 Statistical abstracts of United States*. Washington, D.C.: U.S. Government Printing Office.

_____. (1991a). *Marital status and living arrangements, Current population reports*, Series P-20, No. 461. Washington, D.C.: U.S. Government Printing Office.

_____. (1991b). *Poverty in United States: 1990*. Washington, D.C.: U.S. Government Printing Office.

_____. (1992a). *Money, income and poverty status in United States 1991*. Washington, D.C.: U.S. Government Printing Office.

_____. (1992b). *The statistical abstracts of United States*. Washington, D.C.: U.S. Government Printing Office.

_____. (1993a). *Money income of household, families, and persons in United States 1992*. Washington, D.C.: U.S. Government Printing Office.

_____. (1993b). *Poverty in United States: 1992*. Washington, D.C.: U.S. Government Printing Office.

U. S. Department of Health and Human Services, National Center for Health Statistics (1992, September 30). Annals summary of births, marriages, divorces, and deaths: United States 1991. *Monthly Vital Statistics Report*, 40, No. 13.

U. S. Department of Justice. (1991). *Criminal victimization 1990*. Washington, D.C.: Bureau of Statistics.

_____. (1992a). *Criminal victimization 1991*. Washington, D.C.: Bureau of Statistics

_____. (1992b). *Teenage victims*. Washington, D.C.: Bureau of Statistics.

_____. (1992c). *Capital punishment 1991. Bulletin NCJ-136946*. Washington, D.C.: U.S. Government Printing Office.

_____. (1993a). *Criminal victimization 1992*. Washington, D.C.: Bureau of Statistics.

_____. (1993b). *Crime and the nation households, 1992*. Washington, D.C.: Bureau of Statistics.

_____. (1993c). Criminal Victimization in the United States, 1992. Washington, D.C.: Bureau of Statistics.

_____. (1993d). *Drugs And facts 1993*. Washington, D.C.: Bureau of Statistics.

_____ (1993e) *Estimates of juvenile court delinquency cases: 1966-1990*. Pittsburgh, Pa.: National Center for Juvenile Justice.

_____. (1993f). *Correctional populations in United States 1991*. Washington, D.C: U.S. Government Printing Office.

U. S. Department of Labor. (1992). *Employment and earnings*. Washington, D.C.: U.S. Government Printing Office.

_____. (1991). *Employment and earnings*. Washington, D.C.: U.S. Government Printing Office.

U.S.A. Today, November 11, 1992.

Vaughn, J. B. (1989). A survey of juvenile electronic monitoring and home confinement programs. *Juvenile and Family Court Journal*, 40, 1-36.

Voight, L., Thornton, W., Barrile, L., & Seaman, J. M. (1994). *Criminology and justice*. New York: McGraw-Hill.

Volavka, J. (1987). Electroencephalogram among criminals. In S. Mednick, T. Moffitt, & S. Stack (eds.), *The causes of crime, new biological approaches* (pp. 137-45). Cambridge: Cambridge University Press.

Vold, G. B. & Bernard, T. J. (1986). *Theoretical criminology* (3rd. ed.). New York: Oxford University Press.

Waddington, P. A., & Braddock, Q. (1991). "Guardians" of "bullies"?: Perceptions of the police amongst adolescent black, white and Asian boys. *Police and Society*, 2, 31-45.

Waitrowski, M., Hansell, S., Massey, C., & Wilson, D. (1982). Curriculum tracking and delinquency. *American Sociological Review*, 47, 151-60.

Walker, S. (1992). *The police in America: An introduction*. New York: McGraw-Hill.

_____. (1989). Employment of black and Hispanic officers, 1983-1988: A follow-up study. *Occasional Paper 89-1*. Omaha: University of Nebraska, Center for Applied Urban Research.

Walker, S., & Bumpus, V. W. (1991). *Civilian Review of the Police: A National survey of 50 Largest Cities, 1991*. Omaha, Nebraska: Department of Criminal Justice, Univeristy of Nebraska.

Washburn, S. L. (1951). Varieties of delinquent youth: An introduction to constitutional psychiatry. *American Anthropologist*, 53, 561-563.

Weaver, G. (1992, September). Law enforcement in culturally diverse society. *FBI Law Enforcement Bulletin*, pp. 1-7.

Weiner, N., & Willie, C. (1971). Decisions by juvenile offenders. *American Journal of Sociology*, 77, 199-210.

_____. (1971). Decisions by juvenile officers. *American Journal of Sociology*, 88, 199-210.

Weis, J. (1976). Liberation and crime: The invention of a new female criminal. *Crime and social control*, 6, 17-27.

Weisheit, R., & Mahan, S. (1988). *Women, crime and criminal justice*. Cincinnati: Anderson.

Werthman, C., & Piliavin, I. (1967). Gang members and the police. In D. J. Bordua (ed.). *The police* (pp. 56-98). New York: John Wiley.

West, D. J. (1982). *Delinquency: It roots, careers and prospects*. Cambridge, Mass.: Harvard University Press.

West, D. J., & Farrington, Davis P. (1977). *The delinquent way of life*. London: Heinemann.

West, W. G. (1975a). Adolescent deviance and the school. *Interchange*, 6, No. 2, 49-55.

_____. (1981). Education, moral reproduction and the state. *Interchange*, 12, No. 2-3, 86-101.

Whitaker, J. M., & Severy, L. J. (1984). Service accountability and recidivism for diverted youth: A client-and-service comparison analysis. *Criminal Justice and Behavior*, 11, 47-74.

White v. Reid, 125 F. Supp. 647 (D.D.C.) 1954.

White, H. R., & LaGrange, R. (1987). An assessment of gender effects in self-report delinquency. *Sociological Focus*, 20, 195-213.

White, J., Moffitt, T., & Silva, P. (1989). A prospective replication of the protective effects of IQ in subjects at high risk for juvenile delinquency. *Journal of Consulting and Clinical Psychology*, 37, 719-724.

Whitehead, J. T., & Lab, S. P. (1989). A meta-analysis of juvenile correctional treatment. *Journal of Research in Crime and Delinquency*, 26, 276-295.

Whitman, D., & Thornton, J. (1986, March 17). A nation apart *U.S. News and World Report*, p. 22.

Wilbanks, W. (1986). Are female felons treated more leniently by the criminal justice system? *Justice Quarterly*, 8, No. 2, 517-530.

_____. (1987). *The myth of the racist criminal justice system*. Monterey, Calif.: Brooks-Cole.

Wilkins v. Missouri, 109S.Ct 2969 (1989).

Williams, D. (1969). Neural factors related to habitual aggression--Consideration of differences between aggressives and others who have committed crimes of violence. *Brain*, 92, 503-520.

Williams, H. (1991). Building against crime: Crime prevention and the African-American community. In *Blacks in New Jersey: Crime, drugs, justice and African-Americans* (pp. 37-52). Newark, N.J.: New Jersey Public Policy Research Institute.

Williams, J. R., & Gold, M. (1972). From delinquent behavior to official delinquency. *Social Problems*, 20, 209-228.

Williams, T. (1989, Summer). Cocaine kids: The underground American dream.

Perspectives Quarterly, 6, No. 2, 21-23.

Wilson, J., & Herrnstein, R. (1985). *Crime and human nature*. New York: Simon & Schuster.

Wilson, J. Q. (1968). The police and the delinquent in two cities. In S. Wheeler (ed.), *Controlling Delinquents* (pp. 9-30). New York: John Wiley.

_____. (1973). *Varieties of police behavior*. New York: Atheneum.

_____. (1990). Drugs and crime. In M. Tonry & J. Q. Wilson (eds.), *Crime and justice: A review of research* Vol. 13. Chicago: University of Chicago.

Wilson, J. W. (1987). *The truly disadvantaged: The inner city, the underclass, and public policy*. Chicago: University of Chicago Press.

_____. (1981). The black community in 1980s: Question of race, class and public policy. *Annals of American Academy of Political and Social Science*, 454, 26-41.

_____. (1980). *The declining significance of race*. Chicago: University of Chicago Press.

Winfree, T. L., Griffiths, Curt, & Sellers, Christine (1989). Social learning theory, drug use, and American Indian youths: A cross-cultural test. *Justice Quarterly*, 6, 393-417.

Witkin, G. (1991, August 19). The men who created crack. *U.S. News and World Report*, pp. 44-53.

Witkin, H. A., Mednick, S. A., Schulsinger, F., Bakkestrom, E., Christiansen, K. O., Goodenough, D. R., Hirschhorn, K., Lundsteen, C., Owen, D. R., Phillip, J., Rubin, D. B., & Stocking, M. (1976). XYY and XXY men: Criminality and aggression. *Science*, 193, 547-555.

Wolfgang, M. E., & Ferracuti, F. (1967). *The subculture of violence: Toward an integrated theory in criminology*. London: Tavistock Publications.

Wolfgang, M., Figlio, R., & Sellin, T. (1972). *Delinquency in a birth cohort*. Chicago: University of Chicago Press.

Woodson, R. (1981). *Youth crime and urban policy: A view from the inner city*. Washington, D.C.: American Enterprise Institute for Public Policy Research.

Yetman, N. (1985). *Majority and minority*. Boston: Allyn and Bacon.

Yochelson, S., & Samenow, S. E. . (1976). *The criminal personality*, Vols. 1 and 2. New York: Jason Aronson.

Young, J. (1988). Radical criminology in Great Britain: The emergence of a competing paradigm. *British Journal of Criminology*, 28, 159-183.

Zayed, Z. A., Lewis, S. A., & Britain, R. P. (1969). An encephalographic and psychiatric study of 32 insane murderers. *British Journal of Psychiatry*, 115, 1115-1124.

Zeisel, H. (1976). The deterrent effect of the death penalty: Facts v. faith. In P. E. Kurland (ed.), *The Supreme Court Review* (pp. 317-343). Chicago: University of Chicago.

Zimring, F. (1981). Kids, groups and crime: Some implications of well-known secrets. *Journal of Criminal Law and Criminology*, 72, 867-885.

Zinsmeister, K. (1990, June). Growing up scared. *The Atlantic*, pp. 49-66.

Index

About the Author

JANICE JOSEPH is an Associate Professor of Criminal Justice at the Richard Stockton College of New Jersey. She holds a B.A. from the University of the West Indies, and a M.A. and Ph.D. from York University in Toronto, Canada.

ISBN 0-275-94909-5

9 780275 949099

90000>

HARDCOVER BAR CODE